LEGITIMATING TELEVISION

Legitimating Television: Media Convergence and Cultural Status explores how and why television is gaining a new level of cultural respectability in the 21st century. Once looked down upon as a "plug-in drug" offering little redeeming social or artistic value, television is now said to be in a creative renaissance, with critics hailing the rise of Quality series such as *Mad Men* and *30 Rock*. Likewise, DVDs and DVRs, web video, HDTV, and mobile devices have shifted the longstanding conception of television as a household appliance toward a new understanding of TV as a sophisticated, high-tech gadget.

Newman and Levine argue that television's growing prestige emerges alongside the convergence of media at technological, industrial, and experiential levels. Television is permitted to rise in respectability once it is connected to more highly valued media and audiences. Legitimation works by denigrating "ordinary" television associated with the past, distancing the television of the present from the feminized and mass audiences assumed to be inherent to the "old" TV. It is no coincidence that the most validated programming and technologies of the convergence era are associated with a more privileged viewership. The legitimation of television articulates the medium with the masculine over the feminine, the elite over the mass, reinforcing cultural hierarchies that have long perpetuated inequalities of gender and class.

Legitimating Television urges readers to move beyond the question of taste—whether TV is "good" or "bad"—and to focus instead on the cultural, political, and economic issues at stake in television's transformation in the digital age.

Michael Z. Newman is Assistant Professor in the Department of Journalism, Advertising, and Media Studies at the University of Wisconsin-Milwaukee and the author of *Indie: An American Film Culture*.

Elana Levine is Associate Professor in the Department of Journalism, Advertising, and Media Studies at the University of Wisconsin-Milwaukee and the author of *Wallowing in Sex: The New Sexual Culture of 1970s American Television* and co-editor of *Undead TV: Essays on Buffy the Vampire Slayer*.

LEGITIMATING TELEVISION

Media Convergence and Cultural Status

*Michael Z. Newman
and Elana Levine*

Routledge
Taylor & Francis Group

NEW YORK AND LONDON

First published 2012
by Routledge
711 Third Avenue, New York, NY 10017

Simultaneously published in the UK
by Routledge
2 Park Square, Milton Park, Abingdon, Oxon OX14 4RN

Routledge is an imprint of the Taylor & Francis Group, an informa business

Library of Congress Cataloging in Publication Data
Newman, Michael Z.
    Legitimating television: media convergence and cultural status/
    by Michael Z. Newman and Elana Levine.
    p. cm.
    Includes bibliographical references.
    1. Television broadcasting—Social aspects. 2. Television—
    Technological innovations. I. Levine, Elana, 1970–. II. Title.
    PN1992.55.N49 2011
    302.23′45—dc22   2011013429

ISBN: 978–0–415–88025–1 (hbk)
ISBN: 978–0–415–88026–8 (pbk)
ISBN: 978–0–203–84764–0 (ebk)

Typeset in Bembo and Stone Sans
by Florence Production Ltd, Stoodleigh, Devon

Printed and bound in the United States of America on acid-free paper
by Walsworth Publishing Company, Marceline MO

For Leo and Noah

CONTENTS

FIGURES

ACKNOWLEDGEMENTS

We are grateful for the advice and assistance of a number of friends and colleagues whose help was essential to our work. Melissa Zimdars was our research assistant. James Carviou, Jane Dye, Derek Granitz, Linda Henzl, Berna Heyman, John Vanderhoef, and Tom Yee provided us with information we could not have found otherwise. Christine Becker, Daniel Chamberlain, Max Dawson, Jonathan Gray, Michele Hilmes, Derek Kompare, Barbara Ley, Alison McCracken, Caryn Murphy, Jason Mittell, and Philip Sewell shared research or resources. Mary Beth Johnson and Marc Tasman gave much-needed advice about working with images. We are especially grateful to Ira Wagman and Ron Becker, who read our work in progress and were generous with their feedback. Thank you!

1

LEGITIMATING TELEVISION

Taste classifies, and it classifies the classifier.
Pierre Bourdieu[1]

In November 2008, the creator of the NBC series *Heroes* tried to explain why his show's Nielsen ratings were falling. Speaking to the challenges of garnering a regular broadcast audience in an age of DVDs, DVRs, downloads, and streaming video, Tim Kring contended that a serialized drama like *Heroes* suffers in the ratings—measured primarily on the basis of live viewership, and thus not including these new distribution outlets—because the kind of viewers it attracts prefers new ways of accessing media content. As he explained, "Now you can watch [TV] when you want, where you want, how you want to watch it, and almost all of those ways are superior to watching it on air. So [watching it] on air is related to the saps and the dipshits who can't figure out how to watch it in a superior way."[2] In Kring's conception, an upscale, sophisticated series like *Heroes* was having trouble succeeding in the ratings because the show and its viewership were a mismatch for television and its typical audience, the "saps" and "dipshits" who tune in each week to follow a narrative, with nothing better to do than to be at home, in front of the set, sitting through the commercials.

Critics, bloggers, and TV fans pounced on Kring, eager to hold up new technologies as the savior rather than the downfall of Quality TV.[3] Yet at least one prominent writer, *TV Week*'s Josef Adalian, endorsed the logic of Kring's remarks, pointing out that, "Since advertisers really only care about those folks who watch commercials within three days of a show's airing, anyone smart or busy or young enough to figure out how to avoid watching a series in real time doesn't really count."[4] Adalian solidified his case by contrasting those programs that are *not* frequently time-shifted with the "cooler, more intricate" shows that he and his readers clearly valued. For Adalian, the polar opposite of a show like *Heroes* was the game show *Deal or No Deal*, and he underscored his analysis by noting that *Deal* was one of the highest rated—and least DVRd—shows of the moment.[5] The popularity of that series, and the "old-fashioned" viewing practices that accompanied it, were the "mass" against which the "class" experiences of DVRs and dramas like *Heroes* were distinguished.

This kerfuffle over Kring's remarks illuminates a key set of tensions marking American television during the contemporary period, as the cultural value of the medium undergoes negotiation and revision. Serialized dramas are heralded as a chief reason that "television is just better" than ever before, even as certain other genres and programs are routinely derided. Showrunners like Kring are well-known public figures, credited as both the creators and destroyers of TV greatness, even as many of the medium's production personnel remain anonymous. And new technologies like the DVR, DVD, web video, and HD are seen to be allowing for new ways of appreciating television, often on the viewer's own terms, even as the "saps" and "dipshits" are still watching "live" TV with commercials.[6] In this era, an emergent set of discourses proposes that television has achieved the status of great art, or at least of respectable culture, disturbing long-standing hierarchies that placed the medium far below literature, theater, and cinema in social, cultural, and technological worth. At the same time, the very discourses that have denigrated and delegitimated the medium for many decades persist.

When *Heroes* debuted in 2006, it was among the most buzzed about of its crop of new network shows. It was presented as exemplary of a new kind of TV storytelling: a large, multicultural cast, intricate stories continuing week to week, episodes labeled as "Chapters" that were parts of longer arcing "Volumes," deliberate connections to the worlds of comic books and feature films.[7] The program capitalized on new experiments in TV storytelling and promotion, embracing transmedia formats such as webisodes and an online comic as a way to extend its story world and engage viewers, in particular the passionate fan audience the series courted by previewing the pilot at the annual Comic-Con convention.[8] The program was also directly tied to the realm of TV scholarship, with *Heroes* producers taking inspiration from Henry Jenkins's *Convergence Culture* for their transmedia efforts and Kring participating in a panel at the 2010 Society for Cinema and Media Studies conference, as well as commenting on a blog post about the show written by TV scholar Jason Mittell.[9]

Hoping to follow in the footsteps of ABC's *Lost*, *Heroes* sought the kind of respectability and cultural cachet other series at the time were finding. But Kring's remarks reveal the ideological implications of television seeking such a rise in status. As his comments exposed, and as the reaction of writers like Adalian reinforced, the cultural legitimation of television is premised upon a rejection and a denigration of "television" as it has long existed, whether in the form of conventional programming (*Deal or No Deal*), low-tech viewing (real time, with commercials), or the elite conception of a mass audience too passive or stupid to watch differently. Cultural legitimation may seem to be an important step forward for those who value, enjoy, and feel invested in television. But it is premised on a set of hierarchies that ultimately reinforce unjust social and cultural positions. In the shape it is taking, the legitimation of television does more harm than good.

Legitimating Television examines these discourses of television's changing cultural value as they are emerging and struggling for dominance. Such discourses seem to be according respect to a medium that has long been denied it, challenging prevailing cultural hierarchies to welcome, progressive ends. But discourses of television's cultural legitimation do not dismantle prevailing structures of status. They perpetuate them by seeking to move television up in the contemporary cultural hierarchy while leaving in place the distinctions of value and respectability that denigrated the medium in the first place. The hierarchies themselves persist, with some genres, instances, technologies, and experiences of television positioned below their legitimated counterparts. Because those distinctions reproduce unequal structures of social position more generally—certainly those of class and gender— we find them inherently troubling. As a result, we both document emergent discourses of legitimation and critique them, seeking to expose and denaturalize their ideological underpinnings, as well as opening lines of inquiry into other ways to consider the medium. We historicize and contextualize the rise of legitimation discourses as they are intensifying in the *convergence era*, the contemporary period of the economic, technological, aesthetic, and experiential merging of media.

Legitimation and the Coming of Convergence

In the mid-twentieth century, television was established as society's most important medium for the communication of information and entertainment. In its first several decades, TV in the United States and around the world meant over-the-air broadcasting received by relatively small, standard-definition, picture-tube sets. In the U.S., the big three networks commanded up to 90 percent of prime time audiences, and viewers watched programs only as they aired. Under these conditions and in the eyes of cultural commentators of all stripes—from the most popular and colloquial to the most erudite and intellectual—television's cultural significance revolved around its status as a commercial medium experienced collectively, mostly in domestic spaces. This led to a number of negative associations based on the perceived class and gender identities of the mass audience. During the network era, television sometimes achieved a degree of respectability from the perspective of elites for its public affairs and educational programs or its evening dramas. On the whole, however, the dominant view of television was as a waste of time at best, and possibly also a source of serious and widespread social problems. Television was seldom considered as an artistic medium, and lay people and scholars alike more often considered its value (or lack of it) in sociological rather than aesthetic terms.

Since CBS, NBC, and ABC began to share their viewers with numerous new channels, fracturing the mass audience into multiple narrow segments, television's reputation has changed for the better. Within the U.S., and in much of the western world, many prime time programs are considered as artworks, and intellectual culture has become hospitable to respectful and admiring discussions of some fictional TV shows. Experiences of television have changed as well. Screens have become wider, larger, flatter, and high-definition. A cluster of digital technologies has built on the potentials of remote controls and video cassettes to give television viewers means of "programming" their own experience. No longer defined by the oligopoly of three national networks whose content is viewed as an essentially live and continuous flow of programming, the U.S. television landscape is marked by a multitude of broadcast, cable, and satellite channels, and by numerous new technologies used to access content. In our convergence era, many media come together and begin to blur into one another. Movies are watched most often on television sets, television shows are frequently screened on personal computers and mobile devices, and all of the electronic media have become digital. Television's cultural status has shifted as one consequence of these developments in media industries and technologies.

The cultural legitimation of television has in some ways been an ongoing project since the emergence of TV broadcasting in the 1940s. As Chapter 2 charts, processes of legitimation intensified following the Quality TV trends of the 1970s and 1980s, when the fragmentation of the audience made for increased opportunities to direct programming at sophisticated, affluent niches. Highbrow publications began to treat upscale television shows in terms once reserved for more established arts. More students studied television from an aesthetic perspective, and more scholars taught and published about television in this same mode of appreciation. Beginning in the late 1990s, a number of developments marked a growing shift in the medium's cultural positioning, making discourses of television's improvement more powerful and pervasive. The convergence era of the twenty-first century has intensified this. The introduction of TV shows on DVD and the TiVo and ReplayTV digital video recorders, along with HDTV and digital sources of content, changed the ways many viewers watched television. Television did not become wholly legitimated upon the debut of *The Sopranos* or the first use of a DVR to pause live TV. Rather, legitimation is an ongoing cultural process that is still incomplete even in its heightened, present state. There are many anticipatory moments of rising legitimacy in the 1970s, 1980s, and 1990s. But in the convergence era this process has come to a head, producing a culture of legitimacy around television that contrasts boldly with the medium's earlier low status even as it continues to rely upon the denigration of some TV.

One of the central strategies employed in discourses of television's legitimation is comparison with already legitimated art forms, such as literature and cinema. Deep immersion in a season of a premium cable drama like *The Sopranos* is thus described by analogy to reading a thick nineteenth-century social realist novel by Balzac, Dickens, or Tolstoy.[10] But the more ubiquitous legitimating strategy is cinematization: certain kinds of television and certain modes of experiencing television content are aligned with movies and the experience of movies. In the convergence era, premium cable dramas are described as megamovies, flat-panel television sets have high-definition widescreen displays modeled on the film screen, and TV on DVD and web-accessed programming make the viewing of movies and television series more equivalent, allowing for television consumption without antenna reception or cable or satellite subscription. It is seldom flattering to liken a movie to a TV show, but TV shows are routinely praised for being cinematic. When a *Newsweek* critic announced in 2007 that "Television is running circles around the movies," this was a provocative, counterintuitive statement given the historical valuation of these two media.[11] Movies have long been elevated culturally above television, especially since the post-war years of art cinema and *auteurism*, and the subsequent establishment of cinema studies as a humanistic field growing out of literary studies. Legitimation works in part by aligning television with that which has already been legitimated and aestheticized.

It also works by distancing more respectable genres of TV and more technologically advanced modes of watching from those forms and viewing practices rooted in the medium's past, and associated with less valued audiences who had previously been seen as central to television's cultural identity—women, children, the elderly, those of lesser class status, people who spend their days at home. Legitimation is deeply invested in discourses of progress and improvement, and it works by elevation of one concept of television at the expense of another. For some kinds of television to be consecrated as art, other kinds must be confirmed in inadequacy. New is elevated over old, active over passive, class over mass, masculine over feminine.

Convergence is a crucial context for legitimation, establishing conditions under which television's status is being renegotiated. Convergence is not merely a technological process, nor need it refer only to digital media. Television's convergence is aesthetic and social as much as it is technological, and cinema is as important for television's convergence as computers. In the context of convergence, movies and television (and, to an extent, video games) become less distinct and more interchangeable. Digital tools such as streaming video and flat-panel HDTV sets bring audiences audiovisual content of many varieties, and investment in historical distinctions between media as art and trash, public and private, serious and frivolous, enduring and ephemeral, are rendered less and less pertinent. Television's convergence with computers likewise extends beyond technology to the aesthetic and the social, offering new modalities of textual experience and new forms of agency in determining how television is programmed. The historical modes of television textuality and experience rooted in the U.S. network era are revealed in their manifold limitations, as the present of media is valorized at the expense of the past. In this way, television is a problem that convergence solves.

The History and Politics of Taste

Television's improvement in status might seem like a welcome development to champions of the medium and more generally to lovers of popular arts and culture. It might appear to come as a long-overdue affirmation of the value of the popular. The historically low position of television has been the product of distinctions between the more legitimated culture of elites and the more denigrated culture of less powerful social groups. Associations between broadcasting and the mass audience in the home have produced suspicion of TV's social effects and contempt for its textual forms. Thus legitimation might appear to mean that the culture of ordinary people has gained the respect it deserves in the face of highbrow snobbery, or that taste cultures are dissolving into a postmodern, "nobrow" scenario in which distinctions between high and low have collapsed.[12] A number of sociologists have argued that, rather than excluding the popular, elites now often have diverse, *omnivorous* tastes, suggesting that one-time hierarchies are disappearing.[13]

But it would be utopian to believe that social divisions as expressed through cultural tastes could melt away within a highly stratified, advanced consumer-capitalist society. Rather than evidence of a decline in cultural hierarchy as such, the turn toward more omnivorous tastes is a way for elites to distinguish themselves in relation to consumers of lower status with narrower taste preferences. Moreover, rather than dividing between high and low cultures, social taste patterns in the contemporary context often follow divisions *within* popular media. Instead of looking at movies *per se* as the culture of the masses, they are categorized in numerous ways, such as Hollywood blockbuster vs. art house or independent film.[14] Rock 'n' roll is no longer the devil's music, but within the world of popular recordings we distinguish between a more corporate and mainstream major label sound and a more authentic and subcultural indie rock.[15] It is not sufficient to note that movies, popular music, and television have gained legitimacy without considering how systems of value operate *within* these media. Distinctions between kinds of television programs—multi-camera versus single-camera sitcoms, daytime soap operas versus prime time serialized dramas—are one way that legitimation functions in contemporary television, as Chapters 4 and 5 explore, respectively.

Distinctions such as these are matters of taste, and taste can be a quite contentious topic, especially as it is so central to constituting individual identity. Judgments of taste might seem purely personal and merely aesthetic, but they are always products of social situations. The deepest function of taste distinction is to reproduce the dominant social structure, to perpetuate unequal divisions by class and other social groupings. Taste, argues Pierre Bourdieu, is a system through which "the social order . . . is inscribed in people's minds."[16] This inscription is generally hidden from our direct perception, naturalized as true value and legitimate hierarchy. Taste denies that it is socially produced; such judgments function as "a system of classificatory schemes which may only very partially become conscious."[17] The work of analyzing patterns of taste judgment and classification is thus to unmask misrecognitions of authentic and autonomous value, bringing to light their political and social functions. Such is the project of this book. We argue that it is a mistake to accept naively that television has grown better over the years, even while such a discourse is intensifying within popular, industrial, and scholarly sites. In contrast, we argue that it is primarily cultural elites (including journalists, popular critics, TV creators and executives, and media scholars) who have intensified the legitimation of television by investing the medium with aesthetic and other prized values, nudging it closer to more established arts and cultural forms and preserving their own privileged status in return.

Bourdieu argues that tastes are markers of classes, reproducing identities by forming common points of reference dependent on knowledge and competence particular to a class formation.[18] Social groups mobilize taste to include and exclude, to identify members and keep boundaries. You are what you like: "taste classifies, and it classifies the classifier."[19] Social identity is produced through differences not only in economic or social circumstances, but in aesthetic preferences. The system of taste judgments works by joining together groups in common prefer-cnccs, but also by rejecting the tastes of groups of differing status. "In matters of taste . . . all determination is negation, and tastes are perhaps first and foremost distastes, disgust provoked by horror or visceral intolerance . . . of the tastes of others."[20] Within the discourse of television's legitimation, we see this powerful negation through the construction of divergent conceptions of television texts, technologies, and audiences, some of which are elevated to a newly respectable status and some of which are associated with the medium's past and its historical lower class and feminine identities. Legitimation produces a bifurcation of the medium into good and bad televisions. The new conception of TV as a good cultural object rejects every characteristic of the pre-convergence-era medium, and new technologies and textualities are seen as progressing beyond and improving upon this past. *Legitimating Television* denaturalizes the logic of this legitimation and by doing so reveals the implications of television's shifting status.

One way of appreciating the dynamics of television's changing valuation is by considering earlier instances of hierarchies revised and reversed. American cultural history offers a number of examples of forms of popular culture rising in legitimacy, and television's change in cultural status in many ways follows an established script. Lawrence W. Levine has shown that what we think of as the fine arts, such as symphonic music, opera, and Shakespeare, were part of the popular culture of nineteenth-century America. Performances of Shakespearean plays and Italian operas were common to rich and poor Americans before social changes around the turn of the twentieth century led to greater distinction between classes and their experiences of dramatic performance. By tracing this history, Levine argues that categories like high and low are not permanent or natural, but undergo negotiation with the emergence of new circumstances. "Because the primary categories of culture have been products of ideologies which were always subject to modifications and transformations, the perimeters of our cultural divisions have been permeable and shifting rather than fixed and immutable."[21] Paul DiMaggio's study of American opera, dance, and theater in the early twentieth century represents a similar historical trajectory of art forms rising to the status of high culture through the separation of audiences by class and the establishment of institutions such as symphony orchestras and art museums functioning outside of the for-profit commercial sector.[22] It might not be possible yet to look at television shows as legitimate culture on the same plane as Mozart or Shakespeare, but at least we may observe their rising status from less to more valued. Perhaps we can consider Quality or cult dramas like *Mad Men* and *Battlestar Galactica* to land somewhere in the middlebrow range, the place, according to Bourdieu, for "major works of minor arts and minor works of major arts."[23] Even the idea of television shows as major works of a minor art is an improvement over earlier constructions of the medium, as well as a contrast against the valuation of as yet unlegitimated programming like reality TV, local news, game shows, soap operas, and daytime talk shows.

In addition to the rise of popular arts in the nineteenth century, the twentieth century offers further examples of new art forms gaining legitimacy. Jazz music and photography came to be accepted as art forms relatively recently in the histories of music and the visual arts. Jazz was burdened by being an African–American style placing more importance on improvisation, rhythm, and virtuosity than traditional European musical values. Photography had to overcome the obstacle of mechanical reproduction seeming less authentic and original than the work done by painters. Their legitimacy was secured by multiple forces, but especially through acceptance within traditional high art spaces such as museums and concert halls, by the formation of critical discourses and institutions to set the terms of their appreciation, and by being taught in universities. In other words, their legitimacy came via alignment with the already established arts and their modes of appreciation. As in Levine's narrative of Shakespeare in America, the trajectory of these forms is from "folk art to fine art," i.e., of elevation from the ordinary culture of the people to the refined sphere of upper class culture.[24] An art world arises around such forms to legitimate them.[25]

An even more proximate comparison case is offered by the movies. Hollywood's origins were in the mass culture of the storefront nickelodeon theaters of the early twentieth century and their largely working-class audiences, which included many women, immigrants, and children. As is often the case with emerging new media, guardians of culture looked on motion pictures as a moral threat. Their stories and characters were seen as a negative influence and the nickelodeon environment was regarded as dangerous, especially to young and female spectators. The movies improved in class status, and became respectable enough to appeal across all of American society, through efforts at attracting middle-class audiences.[26] Movies adopted the forms of bourgeois narrative such as Victorian melodrama and made their theaters into "picture palaces" distinguished by high-style architecture and attentive service.[27] Cinema's rise in legitimacy was especially well served by the institutions of post-war art cinema, such as film festivals, periodicals, and specialty theaters, and by the concomitant development of a learned cinephilia both in and outside of academia. The discourses of authorship that have thrived within cinephile culture beginning with the French *Cahiers du cinéma* group in the 1950s, and soon thereafter in American film criticism as well, provided a means of distinguishing artistic from merely commercial forms of film and authorized a vanguardist aesthetic approach even to Hollywood studio pictures.[28] The importance of authorship for conferring the status of art on the often anonymous and ephemeral objects of popular culture recurs in many examples of legitimation, and has been central to television's rising status through the figure of the "showrunner" writer-producer whose agency is constructed in ways analogous to the film director's, as Chapter 3 explores. Through the identification of author/artist personae, popular art forms become more amenable to intellectualization, a key strategy of cultural legitimation.[29]

Among the lessons from this history of art forms rising in status is the significance of class distinction in legitimating culture, separating higher from lower classes of consumers. One function of legitimation in these historical cases is to manage social change and class mobility, to secure the culture of an elite against the intrusion of undesirable masses, and thus to perpetuate the privilege of the dominant. As Lawrence W. Levine argues, "Popular art is transformed into esoteric or high art at precisely that time when it in fact *becomes* esoteric, that is when it becomes or is rendered inaccessible to the types of people who appreciated it earlier."[30] This is not only a matter of the content of the artwork but also of its literal accessibility. We see this very process in the narrowing of television audiences and the rise of costly premium services, not only the premium cable channels like Showtime and HBO but also digital TV technologies like HDTV, video on demand, DVDs and DVRs, and the numerous other convergence devices that afford internet-dependent or mobile television viewing, as Chapters 6 and 7 explore. Broadband internet service is itself a premium service, a significant monthly expense in addition to the cable or satellite bills many consumers already pay. Such distinctions are visible as well in the burgeoning of both amateur and professional television criticism, which includes fans, journalists, and scholars, a matter we consider throughout, but especially in Chapters 7 and 8. By creating a robust discourse of television analysis, those dedicated to the appreciation of television shows make a new, distinct space for an aestheticized conception of television, in particular the television that is targeted to elite audiences. This functions to divide television viewers by degrees of passion and engagement as well as demographics, and to legitimate those forms of programming that are subjects of admiring, critical appraisal. This discourse of critical reception, both popular and scholarly, is thus one of the multiple sites for the legitimation of television we analyze and denaturalize.

Television follows an established pattern in rising to higher status, but some aspects of TV's legitimation are specific to the history and context of broadcasting. For one, television has long been feminized. In its network-era conception as a mass medium, it fit well with Andreas Huyssen's argument that, in the modern era, mass culture was feminized culture.[31] Feminist media scholars have applied this assertion to the cases of network-age radio and television, citing the simultaneous feminization and devaluation of these media across popular, media industry, and scholarly discourses.[32] Such discourses articulate television not only to the mass and the popular, but also to the domestic and the commercial, such that the denigration of each of these categories has reinforced the denigration of all. These discourses of denigration arose historically across a multitude of sites. For example, the television set was constructed as a feminized and domestic appliance, not unlike the refrigerators and washing machines also being marketed to homemakers in the post-war years of the medium's consumer debut. As Lynn Spigel has documented, discourses of television's introduction in the U.S. of the late 1940s and early 1950s directly addressed the practicalities of the set's placement in the home, as well as its impact on family life. In ads for TV sets and in journalistic coverage of the medium's arrival, television was presented to women as an object for their concern and attention.[33] Lynne Joyrich points us to the implications of this history for the cultural position of television:

> It comes as no surprise that a medium which has been seen as "feminine" is also a medium which is intimately tied to consumerism . . . The "feminization" of the TV viewer thus relates to women's role as primary consumer in our society as much (or more so) as it is derived from the particular dynamics of television spectatorship.[34]

As a result, she contends, "Gender is not simply a potential *subject matter* for television—it is a classificatory strategy, a structuring system, a very significant *matter for subjects* constituted through its terms of enunciation and address."[35] That television has been classified as feminine, and thereby as a less worthy, significant, and serious medium, has been a fact of its history.

With legitimation, however, the association of television with the mass, the commercial, the domestic, and the feminine has begun to shift. The introduction of new television industry strategies to fragment the mass audience, new television technologies promising viewers greater interactivity and mastery, and new modes of textuality and experience function to mark a new identity for TV. This new identity, this cultural elevation, is as much a masculinization as it is a refinement of the medium's class status. The convergence-era validation of television achieves that validation by rejecting the feminized medium that "used to be." Such a discourse of uplift and change embraces a progress narrative that naturalizes classed and gendered hierarchies with its assumption that moving forward means a shift away from the feminized past and toward a more masculinized future. These discourses do not just reverse the gendering of television and thereby solve its problems of status and legitimacy. Rather, they leave in place the role of gender in classifying media. To make television masculinized rather than feminized reinforces an unjust gendered hierarchy, one that has ramifications for social experience far beyond conceptions of television.

Denaturalizing Legitimation

The many problematic implications of these discourses of legitimation may be challenged and thereby denaturalized. But how does one study legitimation in an effort to denaturalize it? Legitimation is a discursive formation made up of a multitude of expressions that echo and reinforce one another and are made powerful in the breadth and frequency of their appearances. We analyze manifestations of legitimation in a broad array of discourses, focusing on representations of television's value and the significance of the transformations it has undergone since the network era. Legitimation is evident in writings in the trade publications of the entertainment industry, in the popular press, and in blogs and other sites of online publishing and discussion where journalists, scholars, and fans alike find a voice. It is also evident in the perspectives and products of the media industries themselves, the statements of creatives and executives, as well as television shows and the promotional texts surrounding them. It can be observed in the forms and functions of television technologies and the representations of these in advertising and other sites in which new media are promoted and made sense of. Legitimation appears as well in traditional academic discourses, in television scholarship complicit in the revaluation of television. Ultimately the power of discourses of legitimation is to shape popular understandings of the medium, and *Legitimating Television* documents these understandings as they emerge in this range of discourses.[36] Discourses of legitimation have come to suffuse discussions of television and cultural value, achieving the status of an inescapable common sense, a "new normal" that is all the more powerful for not being named.

Because this discourse is so increasingly pervasive, capturing it in total is hardly possible. It is wholly present in the U.S. context, and that is the focus of our analysis. But it circulates on a global scale, as well. At least in the western world, the most legitimated of American series are warmly received, airing on terrestrial, cable, and satellite television, as well as leading robust lives on DVD. The global reach of American television is not news, of course, but the convergence-era legitimation of American TV may point to a new implication of that reach: a global circulation of legitimation discourses, whether moving from the U.S. outward or enhancing those discourses within the U.S. by virtue of their international reinforcement. As illustration, note how British television scholar Christine Geraghty laments the seeming exclusive interest of British TV scholars and students in (legitimated) U.S.

programs watched on DVD, rather than domestic fare watched on television proper.[37] This is not a phenomenon exclusive to the British academic world, either, as Geraghty quotes a BBC1 Controller as realizing:

> It does seem there's a lot of snobbery at work when the media industry spends so much time talking and writing about a handful of shows that are largely watched by people like them . . . I wonder whether we are capable of having a debate about popular drama that includes other shows—shows that reach a broader audience and include a wider part of the creative community—or whether the media will remain obsessed with *Mad Men*, *30 Rock*, and *The Wire*.[38]

There is clearly work to be done on the new kind of global dominance of certain U.S. programs that legitimation might perpetuate. Questions of how legitimated programming—and discourses of legitimation more broadly—travel worldwide are outside the scope of this analysis, but are of importance to a fuller understanding of the legitimation of television in the convergence era.

Legitimating Television takes as its focus what we believe to be the primary sites of contemporary discourses of legitimation within the U.S. In the chapters that follow, we examine such discourses as they have intensified over television history, in the stories that are told of a new "Golden Age" of TV programming (Chapter 2), in the rising status of the showrunner-*auteur* (Chapter 3), in the changing valuations of key TV genres such as the sitcom and the primetime drama (Chapters 4 and 5, respectively), in the changing dimensions and qualities of the television image and of television sets themselves (Chapter 6), in the prominence of a host of new technologies that promise new agency for viewers and a new aestheticization of the TV program (Chapter 7), and, finally, in the rise of television studies as an academic field (Chapter 8). We see our project as both history of the present and polemic. The latter might become particularly evident in the final chapter, when we consider the ways that some recent television scholarship perpetuates some of the very discourses of legitimation we critique. In Foucault's terms, this book is a genealogy, tracing the statements and interests that lead to the discursive formation we call legitimation.[39]

As much as we believe our scope to be sufficiently broad and appropriately focused, there are conceivably other sites that might bear investigation. For example, one might consider how reality series are differentiated from one another. How do some achieve a more legitimated status? Or one might ask whether there are discourses of distinction at work in other, seemingly unlegitimated genres, say, daytime soap opera or talk shows. How might legitimation function in relation to children's programming? How do institutions that have long served as sites of distinction—such as the Emmy Awards—participate in the legitimation specific to the convergence era? How will the new technologies of TV distribution and access that are sure to displace those of the present differentiate themselves from what has come before, and how will viewers conceive of their experiences with such technology? How is television's legitimation proceeding in other national contexts? The sites we examine are the beginning of what we hope will be a broader exploration of the power of legitimation as a discourse of television production and reception at both popular and scholarly levels, as well as an impetus to attend to the medium in ways that do not perpetuate these cultural hierarchies.

The legitimation of television we document is an increasingly powerful, emergent discourse, but in many respects it is still being formed. Inherently it depends upon a delegitimated "other" television—that of the past but also that of the contemporary genres, production modes, technologies, and practices that do not receive the stamp of legitimacy. Certainly, some instances of television (such as reality shows like *Jersey Shore* or hype-heavy local TV news) continue to be sites of disparagement, just as some modes of experiencing television (such as live over-the-air viewing, commercials and all) continue to be painted as inferior. Even when instances of television are praised and valued by elites, the specter of "television" as it has long been popularly imagined remains, as the *New York Times* review of the 2006 pilot for *Friday Night Lights* blatantly reveals:

> Lord, is "Friday Night Lights" good. In fact, if the season is anything like the pilot, this new drama about high school football could be great—and not just television great, but great in the way of a poem or painting, great in the way of art with a single obsessive creator who doesn't have to consult with a committee and has months or years to go back and agonize over line breaks and the color red; it could belong in a league with art that doesn't have to pause for commercials, or casually recap the post-commercial action, or sell viewers on the plot and characters in the first five minutes, or hew to a line-item budget, or answer to unions and studios, or avoid four-letter words and nudity.[40]

Alongside the discourse of television's rising respectability, its aestheticization and sophistication, are these reminders of all that has long kept television entertainment from being equal to other arts. Embedded within the discourse of legitimation are often such allusions to the medium's lurking inferiority, even as we hear of the many ways in which TV may be escaping its historical constraints. Legitimation always works by selection and exclusion; TV becomes respectable through the elevation of one concept of the medium at the expense of another.

There is no doubt that convergence-era television is facing significant change. This book documents the *ideas* that accompany and constitute that change, ideas that we identify as signaling an increased legitimacy for a medium long delegitimated, particularly in elite circles, and particularly along aesthetic and technological lines. In what follows we explore these shifts and tensions of discourse, examining their causes and questioning their consequences.

2
ANOTHER GOLDEN AGE?

The idiot box has gained some serious IQ points in the last decade. So let us behold: Television as fulfilling as anything at your local multiplex.

Salon, 2006[1]

In 1969, critic Richard Burgheim surveyed the state of TV reviewing in the United States, finding the enterprise to be an ultimately fruitless task. To him, television was no more than a clunky household appliance, the product of corporate machination, ruled by the plebeian tastes of the masses. It was thus impossible for him to imagine a robust television criticism. "Great criticism springs from a fount of affection for an art or from anguish lest that love be debased . . . How do you love a 19-inch Motorola or a network vice-president?"[2] Forty years later, television criticism is in full flower, seriously practiced by academics, professional journalists, citizen bloggers, passionate fans, and even more casual viewers. According to critic Jaime Weinman, we are in "A Golden Age of Taking TV Seriously."[3] Whether in the pages of the upscale *New York* magazine or in a Facebook status update, television now receives thoughtful consideration by many; indeed, taking television seriously is a given, even among cultural elites. As Alessandra Stanley has written in the pages of the *New York Times*:

> Television used to be dismissed by elitists as the idiot box, a sea of mediocrity that drowns thought and intelligent debate. Now people who ignore its pools and eddies of excellence do so at their own peril. They are missing out on the main topic of conversation at their own table.[4]

The very fact of Stanley's column, along with innumerable other such instances, speaks to the way the contemporary legitimation of television contrasts drastically with the cultural status of the medium in the not-so-distant past. Claims of television's present-day value abound, and are described via a number of admiring terms: today's television is "complex," it is "great art," we are experiencing a "rich television age," the medium's second or third "Golden Age."

The contemporary discourses of legitimation figure convergence-era television as an improvement on the television we knew before. This discourse cites a number of phenomena as causally related to television's improved state: chiefly, the fragmentation of audiences and multiplication of distribution outlets, the technological and aesthetic convergence of film, television, and the internet, and the viewer agency afforded by new technologies. These forces are indisputably central to the production and reception of television in the contemporary context. Yet simply recognizing these forces does not contextualize them adequately, nor does it explain their cultural import. These shifts have not led inevitably to certain kinds of TV programming any more so than they have to discourses of legitimation. Instead, the connection that has been forged between these industrial, technological, and experiential developments and discourses of legitimation builds upon many of the same cultural hierarchies that kept television a *de*legitimated medium for so many years. Hierarchies of class, gender, and social position animate the legitimation of television and make the presentist assumptions of the new Golden Age discourse an assertion of taste and power. To denaturalize such discourse, we turn here to a more historicized conception of discourses of legitimation, delegitimation, and quality across U.S. television history, considering the ways that television has figured as both Quality TV and its polar opposite at various historical moments.

Television as Mass Culture: The Delegitimated Medium

Television has been the chief representative of American mass culture throughout its existence. And mass culture has almost never been seen as a social good. As Patrick Brantlinger has outlined:

> Very little has been written about mass culture, the masses, or the mass media that has not been colored by apocalyptic assumptions . . . the phrase "mass culture" usually needs to be understood as an apocalyptic idea, behind which lies a concern for the preservation of civilization as a whole.[5]

These ideas circulate throughout western culture, but have been especially prominent in the discourses of intellectuals and other elites. From the Frankfurt School theorists' concerns about the linkage between commercialized mass culture and fascism to the more recent arguments of such thinkers as Neil Postman, commercial culture, mass media, and the public's investment in them have been seen as detrimental to children's development, to critical inquiry, to artistic expression, and to the very health of democracy.

Concerns about the impact of mass culture upon individuals and upon the larger public have often placed television at their center. As Brantlinger writes:

> From its commercial beginnings in the late 1940s, television has been accused more often—and from more ideological perspectives—of causing cultural and political decadence than has any earlier communications medium. Whatever it broadcasts is apt to be interpreted as antithetical to high culture.[6]

Mass culture—with television as its prime instance—is regularly articulated to the most vulnerable and manipulable members of the society, those deemed least capable of criticism and most devoid of taste. Indeed, television's mass audience has been compared to herds of cattle being prodded into giving their attention to television's programs and commercials.[7] As Lynne Joyrich reflects:

> The typical viewer is imagined as passive, lazy, vulgar, or stupid—a bored housewife or lethargic child. Behind many critiques of the medium as exploitative, sensational, trivial, and inane lies an unacknowledged disdain for an audience that is deemed infantile and feminine.[8]

This infantilization and feminization is applied not only to the actual children and women to whom it most obviously refers, but also to the elderly, the disabled, the unemployed and under-employed, all those that do not fit the model of sophisticated taste and robust productivity expected of contemporary western cultural and social privilege. The class makeup of television's audience is rarely explicitly discussed, but it is a present absence, lurking beneath the surface of low culture metaphors to describe television such as "three-ring circus" and "glaring, blaring midway," and implicit in comparison of television's irredeemable features with those of authentic arts.[9] Television's legitimation arises in negotiation with the medium's traditionally low reputation and its association with these under-valued publics.

Discourses of television's delegitimation circulate widely, both in American television's network era and in the convergence era, and come from a range of spheres, including the academy, primary and secondary education, politics, medicine, science, and high culture. In many respects, the disparagement of television has been a cultural commonplace of the late twentieth and even the early twenty-first century. For example, casual dismissals of television as "chewing gum for the eyes," or the "one-eyed babysitter," make TV out to be an easy but unedifying and juvenile way of passing leisure time. Names like the "boob tube" and "idiot box" suggest that watching makes people stupid or, more charitably, that TV naturally appeals to viewers of lesser faculties. Tellingly, the substitution of television for religion in its condemnation as "the opiate of the masses" bespeaks at once television's cultural centrality, its ideological narcotizing function as an escape from reality, and its appeal to lower classes rather than to elites. References to television as a "vast wasteland," echoing FCC Chairman Newton Minnow's famous remark, have long been familiar to the point of cliché. Ernie Kovacs quipped that "television is a medium, so called because it is neither rare nor well done," which captured its cultural status quite aptly, at least during the network era.

Beyond such colloquial portrayals, intellectuals have been especially caustic in their appraisal of television, which they often conceive of as a threat to learned culture, especially in its substitution of visual for verbal appeals and its promotion of entertainment as the surest means toward commercial success. These attributes supposedly make televisual discourse and intellectual discourse into natural enemies. For instance, David Foster Wallace argued that TV has made American society passive and cynical.[10] Mark Crispin Miller wrote that television culture trivializes criticism, "the one action that could still counteract TV," a medium he claimed is characterized by a "vast badness."[11] George W.S. Trow denounced television baldly in a widely admired *New Yorker* essay: "No good has come of it."[12]

Television's effects have often been assumed to be especially harmful to children. Television is blamed for causing obesity, inattentiveness and hyperactivity, and violent and aggressive behavior, and it has often been suspected of compromising academic achievement.[13] In *The Plug-In Drug,* an anti-television tirade from 1977 focusing especially on effects on children, Marie Winn observed that young people need to learn self-direction and communication, but TV viewing is passive and inculcates dependency. She refers to television viewing as a form of addiction, likens heavy viewers to zombies, and blames TV for blotting out the real world. Such rhetoric is not a remnant of the past. To this day, a widely observed "Turnoff Week" promoted in schools and public libraries every September and April and endorsed by prominent medical and educational associations attests to an ongoing, widely held disdain for television as a threat to the welfare of children and families.[14]

Television has been figured as a cause of social isolation and civic disengagement across its history, as well. This perspective figures television as breeding an ignorant and apathetic body politic who prefers TV entertainment over all other modes of discourse. In *The Image*, published in 1961, Daniel Boorstin blamed electronic visual media in general but television in particular for substituting inauthentic for authentic experience, causing us to misrecognize the inauthentic as authentic, and for creating a world in which "vivid image came to overshadow pale reality."[15] In 1978, Jerry Mander argued that television causes "utter confusion as to what is real and what is not."[16] Neil Postman's work continued in this tradition, beginning in 1985 and continuing through a 2005 update. Postman accused television of damaging public discourse through its emphasis on spectacular showbiz at the expense of informed and reasoned discussions of public affairs. Television imposes on society a "vast triviality" of images which have transformed the public's ways of thinking from the coherent, serious and rational mode of the "Age of Typography" to a shriveled, absurd, fragmented, and altogether dangerous mode of the "Age of Television," in which everything must be reduced to entertainment.[17] In his influential sociological study from 2000, *Bowling Alone*, Robert Putnam blamed television for declining social capital and civic participation in post-war America, isolating citizens and damaging political culture.[18] Across television history, the medium has often been understood as a waste of people's time. More perniciously, it has been understood as a danger to democracy, public health, and moral order. This message comes from a multitude of authors and scholars, but it is a perspective with vast reach within the popular imagination. It is the logic underwriting the bumper stickers and punk rock anthems imploring, "Kill your television."

Ironically, one of the most notable champions of the mass characteristics of electronic new media, Marshall McLuhan, has been a key influence on the denigration of television in the popular imagination. Much of the anti-television literature and popular discourse is explicitly McLuhanist in its concern not so much with specific genres or programs on television (though it is certainly concerned with these things in many instances) as with television itself as a feature of the media environment. As McLuhan told *Playboy* magazine in 1969, "Effective study of the media deals not only with the content of the media but with the media themselves and the total cultural environment within which the media function." The medium is the message to television's most negative critics, and the medium's effects are seen to be pervasive and devastating. Television is figured in such discussions as a cultural pollutant, analogous to a catastrophic ecological hazard: "It is still possible to turn off the television set. It is no longer possible to turn off the television environment."[19] Thus the anti-television critic sees television as one thing rather than as a diverse array of discourses, and generalizes freely about "the very nature of the television experience."[20] This ecological approach has gone so far as to liken the medium to carcinogenic agents such as tobacco, X-rays, and nuclear power plants.[21]

It is against the overwhelming force of this cultural positioning that discourses of legitimation have struggled to redefine television. In the typical instances of the convergence era, they do so by rearticulating many of these same negative ideals—of television as an at best useless and at worst dangerous medium—as they work to distinguish the legitimated television forms of the present from the delegitimated medium of the past, as well as from forms of contemporary delegitimated TV. Convergence-era discourses of legitimation make particular programs, styles, technologies, or practices the exceptions to the rule of television as a whole. While such exceptions get figured as displacing the television of the past, they can only achieve their stature by lending credence to the long history of the TV-as-corrupter-of-all-that-is-good theme. The television of today achieves legitimation by accepting the delegitimating discourses as true of television overall, but untrue of the contemporary television that the speaker highlights and values.

Past Instances of Legitimation: Struggles for Validation

The convergence era is not the only period of legitimation in the history of American television. Throughout the life of the medium, a range of parties—among them the broadcast industry, program creators, and journalistic and scholarly critics—have sought to validate the medium and its output. The convergence-era legitimation of television seeks to distinguish the present from these past efforts, even while it repeats many of the same discourses. In so doing, this discourse even further reinforces its ahistorical tendencies, insisting upon a fundamental break, rather than a passage of continuities and discontinuities, between the present and the past.

The effort to legitimize American broadcasting predates television; indeed, struggles for cultural validation and respect saturate the history of U.S. network radio. As Michele Hilmes has explored, the very origins of NBC as a radio broadcaster were rooted in claims of cultural legitimation. As she writes, "NBC announced its arrival in November 1926 by promising 'quality' in broadcasting . . . Radio's official social role would be one of uplift, of cultural improvement."[22] The early days of radio broadcasting were rife with instances of this uplift effort—and with challenges to it by more populist content. Shawn Vancour details the tensions around the place of classical music in network radio, pointing out that programming such as New York Symphony composer Walter Damrosch's *Music Appreciation Hour* (NBC) "promised to reach across social and geographical divides and effect an unprecedented transformation of popular taste."[23] Yet the musical elites with an investment in classical forms inevitably found fault with radio's handling, fearing that radio adaptation altered the meaning of classical music and encouraged only superficial aesthetic appreciation as it exposed classical works to popular taste. Cultural elites thus struggled to make sense of radio's cultural role, positioning the new medium as "at once the greatest boon and greatest threat to music appreciation that the country had ever known."[24] Similar battles surrounded early radio figures such as Samuel "Roxy" Rothafel, host of station WEAF's *Roxy and His Gang*. As a theater manager, Roxy was known for his efforts to bring high culture to the masses, marrying classical music, films, and gracious customer service, moving culture "away from the hands of the elite and the wealthy and making it available to all."[25] Bringing this sensibility to radio proved more contentious, however. Indeed, in 1925, the WEAF executives worried that Roxy's folksy, sentimental, populist style "exceeded the bounds of respectable, professional speech" and threatened the station's image as a site for business advertising.[26] In other words, they feared that Roxy's wide appeal delegitimated their efforts to be a resource for serious businesspeople. In WEAF's attempts to contain Roxy, as well as in the anxieties over radio's handling of classical music, the U.S. radio networks strove for cultural respectability, a position more hoped for and hyped than ever securely attained.

Broadcast network radio was eventually as well known for its perpetuation of the low and the crass as it was for its more elite strivings. While advertisers and their ad agencies were initially reluctant to sully the culturally beneficent world of radio with overt sales pitches, the practice of advertiser sponsorship (rather than direct selling) soon became seen as a way to use the new medium without abusing its uplifting potential.[27] The ad world also believed some kinds of programs and times of day to be more appropriate for hard sells than others. For example, understanding ad pitches as a special kind of assistance for listeners led advertisers to embrace daytime radio as a site for their sales messages. Because daytime programming was addressed at women audiences, advertisers could see themselves as helping the homemaker care for her home and family, as well as her own appearance, and they thereby justified using harder sales tactics there than in evening programs.[28] The easy fit between daytime radio and women helped ad agencies reconcile the new medium with their long-standing conception of consumers as a feminized mass beset with poor taste.[29]

The combination of bald ad appeals and feminized content soon brought derision and scorn to daytime radio. Cultural commentators of many stripes— upper-middle-class women's club members, intellectuals, social scientists—joined together to criticize the populism and pandering of daytime radio and especially the serial dramas that dominated it.[30] This sort of criticism would give daytime broadcasting a disreputable air for years to come and, more generally, would serve as the shameful identity against which efforts at legitimation would be pitched. Daytime radio—in particular the serial dramas that soon dominated it—eventually gave all of network radio the taint of feminized commercialism, an association that would carry over to television. Perhaps as a result, TV never carried the discursive potential to be a site of cultural elevation that radio did in its early years.

Still, American television of the 1950s did witness its own struggles over cultural legitimacy. As William Boddy points out, television did not weather a debate over commercialism as did radio—the advertiser-supported logic of the network radio business was assumed to carry over to TV.[31] The kinds of debates that did surround early television centered more on what kinds of programming would best suit the new medium, as well as how the new medium might be taken up by audiences. In these respects, the efforts at legitimating early television concentrated primarily on aesthetic and experiential concerns. The journalistic critics that debated the essential nature of television in the medium's early years focused on differentiating TV from motion pictures. These writers zeroed in on what they saw as television's most unique trait, "the electronic medium's capacity to convey a simultaneous distant performance visually."[32] The power of the live television performance was seen not only as an artistic and technological achievement but also a profound experience for the viewer, who could be both in his home and in the on-screen world simultaneously, experiencing an immediacy that allowed for an understanding of "authenticity, depth, and truth."[33] This belief in television's humanist essence led to a privileging of one early TV genre, the dramatic anthology series, in which an "artist-playwright" penned a freestanding, original teleplay each week.[34] This kind of programming, and the concomitant belief in liveness as television's inherent best, led journalist critics to give this period the label of Golden Age.

The Golden Age designation gave early television the kind of cultural status more frequently reserved for the Broadway stage or the work of literature. Indeed, the privileging of the "artist-playwright" in critical and industrial discourse articulated the live TV dramas to these other media. In addition, while the era overall has been given the Golden Age moniker, in the 1950s, much as in the present, it was really only certain kinds of programming that were so elevated culturally. During the same years, both filmed programming and other kinds of live programming—including daytime's serial dramas and prime time sitcoms and variety shows—also filled the broadcast airwaves. As Levine has written:

> The high praise that distinguished primetime's anthology dramas in the 1950s masked the fact that other kinds of television programming, programming more often derided than celebrated, were also broadcast live . . . Thus it was not the liveness of particular genres that earned them the distinction of being labeled art, but rather a host of gendered and classed cultural associations that allowed some liveness to be heralded while other instances were ignored or even disparaged.[35]

In this respect, American television's first Golden Age was as dependent on cultural hierarchies and exclusions as is the effort at legitimation in the convergence era.

While the 1950s Golden Age would end with the demise of the anthology drama, other periods in U.S. television history have also seen efforts to improve the status and reputation of the medium by emphasizing its most edifying capabilities. In the early 1960s, for example, the broadcast networks sought such an improvement in response to a climate of criticism that peaked with Minnow's "vast wasteland" disparagement. As Michael Curtin details, Minnow and the networks focused on public affairs programming, in particular the network-produced documentary, as a corrective for the medium's perceived failings. According to Curtin, "The documentary was characterized as the key genre for transcending the superficial and commercial aspects of the medium. Produced by network news professionals, it promised to educate and uplift the audience."[36] The early 1960s documentary boom worked as a short-term public relations fix but it did little to change large-scale cultural attitudes toward the medium, in part because the documentaries virtually disappeared after a few years and because their overall viewership was quite low. As in other struggles for legitimation, in this case elites attempted to legitimate the medium by highlighting those qualities that fit their own tastes and interests. But the broader TV audience was not necessarily seeking the kind of uplift that such efforts emphasized.

Other programming of the 1960s also attempted repairs of television's culturally low reputation, more typically as a commercially motivated means of appealing to the youth audience that was then abandoning TV than as a public service or a grab at elite status. Aniko Bodroghkozy has explored the programming that spoke to and about the mounting youth counterculture of the late 1960s. In these instances of striving for cultural relevance, television grappled with various social issues, sometimes in the potentially radical space of the comedy-variety show (e.g., *The Smothers Brothers Comedy Hour*), and sometimes in the more contained realm of the episodic drama (e.g., *The Mod Squad, The Young Lawyers, The Bold Ones*).[37] These efforts had varying degrees of success in attracting viewers and critical praise, and they did not cohere into any kind of notable shift in cultural status for the medium. In other words, they did not elicit the outpouring of critical praise and academic attention that programming seeking to target young, socially aware viewers would in the 1970s, perhaps because the 1960s fare did not occasion the same comparisons to the more legitimated worlds of theater and literature as would their 1970s successors.[38]

The discourses of legitimation surrounding programming of the early 1970s clearly foreshadow more recent legitimating discourses. In addition, then, as now, the programming that occasioned such validation resulted from the strategic business practices of the television industry. In the early 1970s, number one ranked CBS canceled its slate of sitcoms appealing to rural and older viewers and replaced them with a trifecta of "relevant" sitcoms meant to appeal to a 'Quality' audience of younger, more urban, more socially liberal viewers. The popularity of *The Mary Tyler Moore Show, All in the Family*, and *M*A*S*H* certainly improved the cultural status of CBS and network TV overall, but the turn to these shows was primarily calculated as a means of improving the bottom line.[39] As Jane Feuer has explained:

> The crucial change that began to occur around 1970 was a de-emphasis on [overall ratings] numbers and a greater emphasis on "demographics", i.e. directing television shows toward specific audience groups . . . [leading to a] mania for young adult demographics in the form of a "relevance" drive on all three networks, featuring "now" programmes.[40]

The fact that these programs—and the audiences they were designed to attract—were described as Quality helped to obscure the economic rationale for their existence. The Quality label for both people and programs privileged those audiences with the actual and cultural capital to appreciate the "literate" and socially conscientious appeals of these series.[41] As newspaper critic Gary Deeb wrote in 1979, "the first half of the 1970s truly was a 'golden age' for television," one of "wit and style, and . . . a gentle gospel of brotherhood, civility, and social responsibility."[42] As his comments intimate, these programs helped U.S. television of the 1970s achieve a kind of cultural legitimacy more like that ascribed to the 1950s Golden Age than had any other programs in the intervening years.

The culturally legitimated TV of the 1970s was especially notable for the way in which it was distinguished from the rest of the television schedule. Much of

1970s U.S. prime time was filled with mass-appeal programs that used sexual titillation, explicit violence, and conventional plotting to appeal to the wide viewership long valued by advertisers.[43] That this sort of programming was routinely attacked and criticized, charged with perpetuating all manner of social ills, illustrates how dependent television's cultural elevation is upon a disparaged other. In fact, MTM president Grant Tinker described the "anti-MTM" programming as "witless . . . candy for the mind . . . tight leotards and short skirts," while TV critics juxtaposed the MTM shows to the "pratfalls, adolescent ignorance, and cheesecake" that came to dominate in the later 1970s.[44] As such juxtapositions make clear, in this era both the economic rationale and the cultural hierarchies upon which the legitimation of television is based came into relief. From this point on, the discourses of Quality and legitimation that animate the present period became a permanent part of the medium's discursive landscape.

The Golden Age Returns: Quality TV in the 1980s

The convergence-era legitimation of television has deep roots in the Quality TV of the 1970s and the programming that carries on its tradition in the 1980s. A major figure across both decades is MTM Enterprises, the independent production company that created *The Mary Tyler Moore Show* for CBS, and continued to produce Quality series into the 1980s. In fact, in the late 1970s, one critic labeled MTM "the Great White Hope of intelligent television."[45] Alongside producer Norman Lear's Tandem Productions, MTM spun off new hits from its initial successes, as well as spinning off creative talent who would train on one MTM show then head up their own, new show soon thereafter.[46] By the early 1980s, MTM and a number of the company's creative graduates had rebounded from the influx of mass appeal programming, including *Three's Company*, *The Love Boat*, and *The Dukes of Hazzard*, which had seemed to replace Quality fare in the late 1970s. Critics and industry folk alike deemed programs such as *Hill Street Blues* and *St. Elsewhere* a return to form for MTM, albeit in dramatic rather than comedic genres.

As a result, when Grant Tinker left MTM to take over the presidency of NBC in 1981, he was widely seen as pursuing "his MTM strategy of transforming 'quality' into profits," which helped the demographically oriented turn begun in the 1970s become industry wisdom.[47] As journalist Michael Pollan explained in 1983, Tinker's NBC was rejecting the conventional logic of the TV business by accepting a lower rating and share in exchange for more impressive rankings amongst highly valued demographics. In the 1982–1983 season, NBC's share of 18- to 49-year-old viewers had increased 12 percent over the previous season, while the other networks' share of the same group had dropped. And NBC's programs were also quite successful in urban markets, increasing profits at the network's owned and operated stations in those locales. The fact that *Hill Street Blues* (Figure 2.1) and another MTM-influenced NBC hit, *Cheers*, did better in

FIGURE 2.1 The cast of *Hill Street Blues*, the epitome of Quality TV in the 1980s

homes that subscribed to cable than they did in non-cable households was also a key marker, for it suggested that the Quality brand would be a bulwark against the coming incursion of the multi-channel cable universe.[48] *Hill Street Blues* and the other programs that flourished on the Tinker-era NBC schedule thus crucially cemented the economic logic behind Quality fare, a logic that would only intensify in its relevance in the convergence era.

The praise that accompanied *Hill Street* was crucial to its ability to maintain this Quality status. Even in its first season, critics distinguished the show as something different from—and more valuable than—most TV. As Tom Shales wrote in the *Washington Post*, "Is there room on television for a program that is truly in a league by itself?"[49] Pollan's 1983 assessment was quite astute about the economics of the program's existence, yet it also participated in the very legitimation that secured the show's capital. Praising the program's style above all else, Pollan declared that it "demands a new way of watching television," and is "brilliant" in its blending of the feminized and masculinized genres of the soap opera and the cop show.[50] Other takes on the show were at least as effusive, although—like much of the praise of today's culturally elevated TV—they often neglected to address the industry logic that made the show's Quality as much a calculated business decision as an artistic triumph. For example, in 1985, novelist Joyce Carol Oates took to the pages of *TV Guide* to declare the series "one of the few television programs watched by a fair percentage of [her] Princeton colleagues" because it was "as intellectually and emotionally provocative as a good book," a judgment she demonstrated with analysis of the program's themes, plotting, and characterizations.[51] With *Hill Street Blues* and some other, major programs of the 1980s, then, discourses of legitimation began to circulate more and more widely.

It was during this decade, as well, that the mounting competition to broadcast TV from the rapidly growing cable industry encouraged all kinds of alterations in the network business, from changes in ownership to techniques of audience measurement. Many of these developments furthered the movements toward niche audience targeting and programming with demographically specific appeals. For example, as Philip Sewell has analyzed, the networks experimented with a new, hybrid genre, the "dramedy," in the late 1980s as a way to continue to draw the 'Quality' audience while still generating easily syndicated, half-hour (rather than hour-long, dramatic, and more serialized) episodes. These programs initially achieved their intended purposes, but controversy over their fit within the Quality TV category limited their long-term impact.[52] Meanwhile, the Nielsen ratings system introduced the Peoplemeter, a new audience measurement device that distinguished between the demographically distinct viewers in a single Nielsen household, providing quantitative support for the industry's pursuit of narrower audience segments. Across this period, advertisers, producers, broadcast networks, and the new cable channels all struggled to remake the TV business into one that still sought out popularity and cultural buzz but that valued reaching specific audience segments through targeted programs. This was a system that would continue to benefit from the discourses of legitimation swirling around select instances of television.

Twin Peaks and the New TV of the 1990s

With the 1990s, the popular discourse of television's cultural elevation continued. A particularly prominent instance surrounded the appearance of *Twin Peaks* on the ABC schedule. Created by *Hill Street Blues* alum Mark Frost (in the MTM tradition of spinning off "grads" to new series) and feature filmmaker David Lynch, *Twin Peaks* was hailed as something completely new, something downright revelatory in its capacity to "restore one's faith in television."[53] Hailed as "the series that [would] change TV," *Twin Peaks* received an enormous amount of attention upon the airing of its pilot episode in April 1990.[54] Central to the hype around the series was the involvement of the "*auteur*" Lynch, a filmmaker known for his bizarrely erotic and violent features, in the conservative and corporate-managed world of network television. Critics understood *Twin Peaks* to be the antithesis of much TV; the *Village Voice* entitled its piece on the series "*Cheers* It Ain't," even while press coverage—and Frost and Lynch themselves—noted the series' ties to soap opera and to recent Quality dramas such as *Hill Street*.[55] As one critic wrote, "It is more than TV usually attempts, far more than TV usually succeeds at."[56] As one indicator of its difference from most TV, much coverage of the pilot casually noted the less-than-usual time devoted to commercial breaks in the ABC airing.[57] In these respects, *Twin Peaks* fit with the standard logic of the cultural legitimation of television, in that it was distinguished, first and foremost, from TV itself, and especially from its commercial aspects.

The discourses of validation surrounding *Twin Peaks* both kept with and diverged from the discourses of television's legitimation that had circulated previously. While the discourse on the series trafficked in the kinds of hierarchies that had long circulated in American culture, it also regularly acknowledged the economic logic behind the program's existence, suggesting that with legitimation comes a closer look at how and why a program comes to exist. In this way, even a more contextualized take on a series is a sign of its high cultural status, a signal that it is worth understanding in such depth. For example, *Entertainment Weekly* included a feature story alongside its admiring coverage entitled "Why TV had to make *Peaks*," that explicitly detailed the broadcast networks' declining viewership. As Mark Harris wrote, "The 1980s saw the end of network domination as pay cable, basic cable, VCRs, and independent stations led an assault on CBS, NBC, and ABC." The magazine identified *Peaks* as an attempt to draw viewers back to a "Big 3" network by doing something different.[58] Some coverage additionally linked the program to other, recent attempts to reach the Quality demographic. For example, *USA Today* quoted ABC's head of research and marketing, who made a comparison to the "yuppie-friendly *thirtysomething*," explaining, "We've come to understand shows can be much more narrow in appeal but still be successful."[59] As with some of the coverage of *Hill Street Blues*, then, some of the discourse around *Twin Peaks* did acknowledge that the program's existence was indebted, in part, to a particular industrial context in which TV networks would seek to satisfy the sophisticated tastes of upscale viewers.

The critical wonder over *Twin Peaks* also contained the occasional dose of moderation. This was especially so in the program's second season, when its ratings fell and many began to see it as an artistic failure. But there were some intimations of its limitations at the very beginning, as well. Amy Taubin contrasted the program with Lynch's feature film *Blue Velvet*, which also starred *Peaks'* leading man, Kyle MacLachlan. She found *Peaks* wanting in both its visual majesty and its erotic daring. She concluded that *Peaks'* "decadence [was] all compressed into the mid-range," and that, "As movies go, the *Twin Peaks* pilot seems like an exploitation picture made by an extremely creative and resourceful director."[60] She offers praise, to be sure, but it is faint in comparison to that which she—and the culture more generally—would bestow upon cinema.

At the same time, the discourses of legitimation around *Twin Peaks* also offered something new, a sense of television's possibility that would be amplified in the discourse of the convergence era. One strand is the hint that television as a whole may be changing—improving, even—with *Twin Peaks* as a harbinger. In the past, this discourse had been associated with a particular production company—such as MTM—but more typically was linked to a single program, such as *Hill Street Blues*. Some of the discourse around *Twin Peaks* suggested that its radical departure from the TV norm might have signaled a more significant shift in the medium as a whole. This notion was imparted in some of the explanations for why ABC chose to air *Peaks*, as when *Entertainment Weekly* speculated that "It could foretell a decade in which network television programmers will have to face many more excursions into the unknown," a possibility that could "only be taken as good news" for TV viewers.[61] This sentiment was also expressed when *Peaks* was covered amidst other new developments, such as the rise of the new Fox network's brand of brash comedy. In 1990, the *Village Voice* devoted a multi-article section to "Rad TV," including pieces on *Twin Peaks*, Fox, and MTV, and wondering "How can it be that TV—so recently reviled as the boob tube—is suddenly hip? . . . That prime time is the def alternative to sex and drugs and rock n' roll?"[62] These sort of sweeping claims about the medium as a whole would start to become increasingly common.

A less visible strand of discourse on *Twin Peaks* also portended a shift in television's cultural legitimation. This is the centrality of time-shifting (through VCRs) and the internet (through Usenet groups) to the intense fandom that developed around the series. As the 1990s turned into the convergence era, technological developments would become increasingly significant to television's changing status. Once television was less distinguishable from other media—cinema, internet, and digital forms more generally—it could more readily share, or even supplant, the cultural status of those media. This articulation begins with

Twin Peaks fandom, well before digitization, convergence, and internet culture had a wide reach. Nonetheless, the *Twin Peaks* fans that gathered on the alt.tv.twinpeaks Usenet group believed that technological developments were central to the experience of the series. As one remarked, "Can you imagine *Twin Peaks* coming out before VCRs or without the net? It would have been Hell!" These fans used their VCRs "as an analytic tool," poring over details of each episode to suss out the puzzle the program offered.[63] As Henry Jenkins points out, the Usenet fans admired the series for these very qualities, praising "its complexity, its density, its technical precision and virtuosity, its consistency and yet its ability to continually pose problems for interpretation."[64] This cultural elevation depended upon a concomitant degradation of television as a whole, against which *Twin Peaks* could serve as a remarkable exception. As one fan claimed, "*TP* is not a passive work, like all too much of television . . . it is an active process of participation."[65] That the audience activity fans saw as demanded by the series intersected with the technological developments accompanying their viewing reveals the ways that new technologies, select television programs, and viewers' conceptions of themselves as exceptional combine in discourses of television's legitimation.

This kind of fan investment also signaled television's shifting cultural status in that it signaled the start of an intensified era of cult TV and the fandom associated with it. Cult series and passionate fandoms have long existed within western popular culture, and around American television series more specifically. Certainly, the fandom associated with *Star Trek*, beginning in the 1960s, could be identified as cult, as could a number of series and fandoms between the 1960s and 1980s.[66] But the combination of new technologies and increasing cultural legitimation would further expand and enable the designation of series and audience investment in them as cult. While *Twin Peaks* thus offered one step in this direction, the debut of *The X-Files* in 1993 presented an even greater embrace of the cult form; one scholar identifies the series as the beginnings of the "quality/cult" phenomenon.[67] As Sara Gwenllian-Jones and Roberta Pearson have written,

> *The X-Files'* release in 1993 coincided with the rapid expansion of the Internet . . . allowing it to take advantage of the possibilities the Internet presented for word-of-mouth promotion, connectivity between subcultures, and, above all, the rapid expansion of active fandom affected by the accessibility and attractiveness of on-line fan cultures.[68]

The cult TV industry serves the interests of cult fans by flattering their sense of their own distinction from the masses. As Matt Hills has described, cult TV is "a form of 'anti-mainstream' distinction, where cult status is about finding quality in unexpected places and revaluing otherwise devalued/popular texts."[69] In this respect, cult status helps to legitimate the television that achieves this designation.

Conveniently enough, it also serves the interests of the television industry by promoting additional consumerism in the form of DVDs, episode guides, action figures, comic books, and other ancillary paraphernalia that avid fans covet.[70] With the growth of cult television, then, we see an increase in television's legitimation but also the ways that this legitimation serves capitalist interests.

As telling as the uptick in cult fandoms may be as an indicator of television's changing status, cult practices are by definition socially marginal. That the "cult blockbuster" would enter cultural circulation in the 2000s, if not before—as the case of ABC's *Lost* indicates—speaks to the intensifying reach of legitimating discourses over time.[71] When the textual traits and reception practices associated with cult forms gain use in more "mainstream" contexts, the cultural distinction claimed by the marginality of cult also translates. Legitimation allows a particular text to be both "cult" and "blockbuster" at the same time, the idea being that the text is of such exceptional quality that a larger audience than the fringe cult must necessarily appreciate it. That such a belief still manages to flatter the tastes of the "cult blockbuster" viewer demonstrates the ways that distinction remains a central motivator behind the cult label, even when it is applied to a relatively popular text.

The prominence of cult status was just one of multiple paths to legitimation beginning in the 1990s. At this time, elite cultural voices also began to articulate select instances of television to more elevated cultural forms. An especially prominent such indicator came from the *New York Times* in 1995, heralding "The Triumph of the Prime Time Novel." Here, Charles McGrath, editor of the *Times Book Review*, acknowledged the *Times'* reader's cultural milieu of television denial—the widely proclaimed notion that one does not watch TV. McGrath proceeded to use his piece as a means of persuasion, aiming to convince the TV-averse to give the medium a try. It would be well worth their while, McGrath promised, declaring that "TV is actually enjoying a sort of golden age—it has become a medium you can consistently rely on not just for distraction but for enlightenment."[72] While he quickly distinguishes between kinds of TV, dismissing talk shows, sitcoms, prime time soaps, even PBS programs in favor of the networks' weekly dramatic series, he makes claims about "television" itself and thus participates in a discursive shift that legitimates particular kinds of television in the name of the medium as a whole. Much as did the journalist critics of the 1950s Golden Age, McGrath celebrates the centrality of the writer to television and uses his praise for TV writing to favorably compare the medium to literature, film, and the stage. By coining the phrase "the prime-time novel," McGrath helps set in motion a common discourse of the convergence era—the articulation of (certain kinds of) television to another, more conventionally respected medium. In such discourse, television is legitimated when it no longer resembles television; instances of television achieve prominence when they take on the traits of a more culturally validated form.

Cable and the Legitimation of Original Programming

With discourses such as McGrath's circulating by the mid-1990s, the television industry increasingly sought to capitalize upon the growing legitimation of the medium. In particular, this became a promotional tactic of cable channels.[73] Seeking to differentiate themselves from the broadcast networks and to attract the advertisers and/or audiences associated with Quality, cable outlets projected images of themselves as different from, even better than, the TV we have long known. In 1993, basic cable channel Bravo reran *Twin Peaks*, promoting it with the line, "TV too good for TV"[74] (Figure 2.2).

A few years later premium cable channel HBO would adopt a similar slogan. "It's not TV. It's HBO" quickly came to be associated most of all with the channel's original programming (rather than airings of theatrically released films), and is a tag line HBO has continued to use for more than 10 years. As numerous scholars have discussed, even while this slogan has primarily promoted HBO's original series and made-for-TV movies, it has allowed the channel to present itself as distinct from "television" and its historically low cultural reputation. Of course, when the slogan came into use in the mid-1990s, American television was already undergoing a process of legitimation, what with McGrath's article, the ever-increasing audience and programming segmentation encouraged by cable, and the designation of a number of broadcast series as Quality. As a result, as Horace Newcomb points out, "HBO's slogan [has been], in effect, dependent on a set of assumptions about the medium that no longer hold, a retro activation —and implicit denigration—of older general meanings and attitudes." Yet HBO has had success with the slogan because, despite the many shifts toward legitimation, "those older meanings, attitudes, and assumptions [about television] are still quite prevalent."[75] As with all efforts at legitimation, the distinction upon which HBO has built its contemporary reputation depends upon a reinvigoration of the long-standing *de*legitimation of television, indicating the ways that the convergence-era elevation of the medium nonetheless supports anti-television discourses as holding fundamental truths.

As with many instances of convergence-era legitimation, HBO's reliance upon anti-television discourse is economically motivated, although it has more broadly cultural effects, as well. As Avi Santo has detailed:

> Pay cable must appear to offer something that subscribers cannot get either on free TV (the networks) or for the price of basic cable, and which viewers believe is superior to those cheaper alternatives. Thus, HBO must continuously promote discourses of "quality" and "exclusivity" as central to the subscription experience. These discourses aim to brand not only HBO, but its audience as well. In this manner, pay cable sells cultural capital to its subscribers, who are elevated above the riffraff that merely consume television.[76]

FIGURE 2.2 Bravo promotes its reruns of *Twin Peaks* in 1993 with the slogan
"TV Too Good for TV"

HBO must, by necessity, sell itself as a unique product, adding value to one's television experience—the value it most typically claims to add is Quality and the cultural status that designation carries.

The cultural status HBO promises is one associated with high and legitimated arts. Janet McCabe and Kim Akass point out the articulation between HBO's original programming and the "traditional art forms" of theater, international art cinema, and literature, largely through the way the channel presents itself as "a haven for creative integrity."[77] This self-presentation is carefully managed and promoted. Christopher Anderson directs our attention to the massive production, marketing, and promotions budgets behind HBO shows, which function as part of a powerful public relations machine. HBO's efforts result in an overwhelming amount of (usually fawning) press coverage of its programming. As Anderson notes:

> The *New York Times* alone has devoted so many column inches to *The Sopranos* that it sometimes reads like a virtual house organ for HBO. In the echo chamber of cultural production, HBO then feeds the press coverage of its programs back through the public relations machinery, so that people begin to speak about the positive press coverage.[78]

Thus the economics of the HBO system, part of the Time Warner media empire, shape the cultural standing of the channel and its programming.

No HBO series has more centrally carried the flag of the channel's anti-television, high culture distinction than *The Sopranos*. Creator David Chase repeatedly noted that the program simply could not have existed on network television, arguing that "the details, the complexity, the different pacing" were only possible on HBO.[79] HBO executives regularly made similar claims, as did both popular and academic critics. Vincent Canby, writing in the *New York Times*, not only called the program "Dickensian" but labeled it a "megamovie," a form apart from television and more akin to literature or cinema.[80] The paper even published a book-length version of its writings on the series.[81] *Newsweek* described the program (along with HBO's *Oz*) as, on the whole, "smarter, edgier, better written and better acted" than broadcast TV.[82] That *The Sopranos* was an overt refashioning of cinema's exalted *Godfather*—a comparison the characters themselves regularly made—further assisted its positioning as television so artistic, so cinematic, as to earn the status of "not TV" (Figure 2.3).

While *The Sopranos* has been at the forefront of the articulation between HBO and an anti-TV kind of Quality television, the discourses of legitimation that surrounded the program have since attached themselves not only to HBO's fare more generally, but also to many other television instances. Seeking to draw the cultural plaudits heaped upon the premium channel, the broadcast networks and basic cable channels have increasingly appropriated the HBO brand, positioning their own programming as similarly "complex" and "cinematic." As the president of basic cable's FX declared in 2002, "We don't feel that the HBOs and

FIGURE 2.3 HBO's promotion for *The Sopranos* deliberately references the gangster genre, the typeface of the title recalling cinema's *Godfather* trilogy

Showtimes have a monopoly on compelling, quality adult programming."[83] Original programming on basic cable channels has been most closely identified with HBO's premium cable, "not TV" status, and is often juxtaposed with broadcast fare as a strategy of distinction and legitimation. The debut of FX's *The Shield* in 2002 is particularly significant in this regard, in that it was the first of the basic cable originals to be likened to HBO hits like *The Sopranos* and distinguished from broadcast programs in industrial and critical discourse. *TV Guide* critic Matt Roush explicitly connected the series to *The Sopranos* and the HBO tradition: "It's a breakthrough in commercially supported television—it really looks like pay cable. It's the closest show yet to come in the wake of *The Sopranos* to really put out there a vision."[84] Meanwhile, FX's entertainment president Kevin Reilly distinguished the series from broadcast offerings: "Love it or hate it, you won't mistake it for something on ABC."[85] *The Shield* thus helped initiate a key transition in convergence-era television, one that allowed legitimated programming to come not just from the exclusive world of premium cable, but also to exist in advertiser-supported spaces.

Since this shift, many more basic cable series have been associated with legitimated premium programs while also being distinguished from broadcast TV. In the popular and industrial discourses that label *The Shield*, *Nip/Tuck*, *Damages*,

Battlestar Galactica, *Mad Men*, *Breaking Bad*, and other original basic cable series as art, there is a persistent effort to explain such programs' difference from broadcast TV, despite the fact that such series are also advertiser-supported. In order for such shows to achieve legitimated status, they are necessarily contrasted with a low other; because the lack of advertisers is not an explanatory option here, as it is with premium cable, new distinctions get drawn. Thus, National Public Radio interviews Shawn Ryan, creator of *The Shield* and *Terriers*, about the difference between broadcast and cable. Ryan and NPR's Linda Holmes detail three main points of contrast: cable's anti-hero leads versus broadcast's more likeable protagonists, cable's serialized narratives versus broadcast's episodic procedurals, and cable's fewer episodes per season.[86] Such distinctions make sweeping claims about the outputs of the two distribution entities, making it seem as if cable offers no likeable protagonists and no episodic storytelling, while suggesting that serialized narratives are not part of the broadcast landscape. Writing in the *Los Angeles Times*, Neal Gabler explains the difference as one of worldview and moral complexity, in which broadcast TV remains mired in the optimism of American life in the mid-twentieth century while cable faces the grim reality of the present:

> [Cable has] a cosmology for a different America in a different television age than the '50s, '60s and '70s, when things seemed so much simpler. It speaks to our doubts and our debits, to our anxieties and apprehensions. It tells us that we are not necessarily good and that neither is our world. It tells us that not everything can be made right in the end. It is a journey into the American heart of darkness.[87]

More than just an obtusely nostalgic view of American history, this stance serves the interests of legitimation through its presentism and its universalizing effort to characterize all of broadcast and all of cable in one of two ways. When Gabler claims of cable drama, "It's not television. It's life," the television he values escapes all of the medium's problematic cultural associations—as does he as its viewer.[88] In the convergence era, elevating the television one likes—or the television one creates—elevates one's own tastes and choices, distinguishing oneself from the other of the mass broadcast audience.

Legitimating Broadcast Television in the Convergence Era

Despite these persistent efforts to differentiate cable and broadcast, in select instances, broadcast television has also been granted the status of legitimation. That broadcast series can fall under this umbrella is a key discourse of the convergence era. In conceptualizing television more broadly, such discourses *appear* to encompass the medium as a whole, despite the large swaths of programming actually discounted in such claims. Thus a blog post declaring the present the

"3rd Golden Age of Television" uses ABC's *Lost* as well as AMC's *Mad Men* as its chief examples.[89] *New York* magazine's Emily Nussbaum can name-check broadcasts *Buffy the Vampire Slayer*, *The West Wing*, *The Office*, and *30 Rock*, as well as many cable series, to declare the 2000s "most centrally and importantly the first decade when television became recognizable as art, great art."[90] And *New York Times* columnist Stanley points out that "I am not ashamed to say I try never to miss *Mad Men* [AMC] and *Curb Your Enthusiasm* [HBO] and *30 Rock* and also *House* [Fox] and *Sleeper Cell* [Showtime]."[91] The intensification of television's legitimation in the convergence era is most notable in the inclusion of broadcast series in such lists.

This is not to say that the convergence-era discourses of television's "Golden Age" embrace all of TV. Legitimation is ever based in distinction and so there are innumerable others against which the glorified television is contrasted—sometimes explicitly and sometimes without direct mention. Nussbaum argues that the 2000s "produced the best and worst shows in history," the latter identified in particular as reality shows.[92] More often, however, the "television" against which the Golden Age is juxtaposed remains *unnamed* in that it is the television *not* talked about in the popular and trade presses (not to mention in television scholarship), or at least not through the serious, critical lenses brought to bear upon legitimated content. Thus there is little talk of soap opera amidst the praise of cable's serialized dramas; little mention of "mass appeal" multi-camera sitcoms (except to note their baffling popularity or to disparage them and their audience) amidst analyses of contemporary comedic art.

This becomes especially clear when the ignored, non-legitimated programming becomes especially visible. For example, the appearance of more multi-camera sitcoms with laugh tracks at the start of the 2010–2011 TV season inspired one columnist to work overtime to elevate single-camera comedies and disparage the multi-cams. He peppered his analysis of the renewed network investment in multi-camera shows with hierarchizing judgments: these series are cutting "the heart and creativity out of comedy," while the single-camera programs are "art," they are instances of "the medium [television] was meant to be."[93] Likewise, when feature film actor James Franco played a continuing character on the daytime soap opera *General Hospital* at various points between 2009 and 2011, the extensive, puzzled press coverage both revisited the long-standing disparagement of soap opera and sought out an explanation for Franco's actions through reference to more legitimated forms. As one website commented on the news, Franco's *GH* appearance was "a total desecration of the time [he] spent on *Freaks and Geeks*."[94] Not only does the remark call a soap opera role a "desecration," it juxtaposes soap opera with a legitimated, Quality, cult series. In this construction, a daytime soap represents a massive drop in status for Franco, even from his earlier television role. While Franco himself has been respectful in his direct remarks about his *General Hospital* experience, his explanation of the job as an experiment in performance art has helped to legitimate his work. Once the press and blogosphere were able to quote Franco and his performance artist colleague, Carter, on this motivation, the disbelief that marked the initial coverage dissipated.[95] Soap opera could be placed back in its low, easy-to-dismiss position and Franco could continue to be seen as an unpredictable, quirky, yet thoughtful and serious artist. In ruptures such as these, the distinctions that underlie convergence-era legitimation get exposed. Today, "television" may be art, but only as long as certain kinds of television are excluded from the designation.

Costs of Legitimation

Across American television history, different interests within and outside the television industry have sought to validate the medium. Most often, it has been specific programs, producers, or channels that have achieved legitimated status. But the convergence era has seen an intensification of such efforts. This intensification has resulted in television as a whole being marked as artistically legitimate, even while that designation depends upon certain kinds of television being excluded from the discussion. The convergence-era intensification of such discourses is also marked by their ubiquity. On a near-daily basis, and in reference to a wide range of programming, television is figured as art, as better than ever before, as experiencing another "Golden Age."

It is not that this intensification of legitimation discourses is inherently problematic. It is arguably a gesture of inclusion and a welcome expansion of what counts as art for television to gain entrance to such status. However, discourses of legitimation are premised upon cultural hierarchies and hierarchies of all kinds require the denigration of some to justify the elevation of others. In the case of television, it is not other media that suffer this denigration. Rather, it is certain kinds of television that are denigrated, dismissed, or ignored. It is difficult to make the case that the dismissals of reality competitions, or multi-camera sitcoms, or episodic procedurals, or daytime soap operas in and of themselves are politically troubling. But television genres and forms of programming carry with them characteristics and assumptions that reach beyond the world of TV. Both the legitimated and the non-legitimated television carry classed and gendered associations, as well, potentially, of associations on the basis of age, race, region, or other markers of difference. Thus, the multi-camera sitcom is articulated to a mass audience of non-discriminating viewers, people who do not have the cultural capital—not to mention the actual capital—to "appreciate" the purportedly superior appeals of the single-camera comedy.

The daytime soap opera is doubly and perhaps even triply denigrated. Its daytime scheduling associates it with the feminine, the underclass, and the aged— all social identities that may not have "anything better to do" during the normative hours of productivity. Add to this the feminized nature of soap content and the assumption that more "sophisticated" forms of serialized narrative are available in prime time and the dismissal and denigration of daytime soap opera perpetuate hierarchies of taste and power that have long served dominant interests.

When the discourses of television's legitimation differentiate the television of the present from that of the past, assuming a naturalized form of progress over time, they not only ignore the ways in which television has always been embroiled in struggles for legitimacy, but also they separate the "not TV" of the convergence era from the feminized mass culture of earlier periods. In insisting on the qualitative difference of convergence-era, niche-targeted television from the broadly cast television of the network age, such discourse implicitly characterizes the television of the present in terms that associate it with the more powerful sides of a number of unequal cultural binaries. Convergence-era television is masculinized, it is of a higher and more elite class, it is sophisticated and adult (rather than simplistic and juvenile), but still youthfully hip and cool. In such discourse, convergence-era television is just *better* than the television that came before. That such a characterization flatters and elevates the speaker's own taste and position to the detriment of others is inconsequential, for that is the power of legitimation.

3

THE SHOWRUNNER AS *AUTEUR*

I'm responsible for everything in every frame of every show.
Joss Whedon[1]

Television shows, like any cultural artifacts, are products of human agency. In this sense, they are authored by the people who create them, whether these authors are understood to function as autonomous individuals or as a team of collaborators working together. But some shows are more often identified with their authors in discourses of production, promotion, and reception, and in particular with singular author-creators whose work is seen as a form of individual expression. In the era of convergence, this figure has often been known as a showrunner, and he (or sometimes she) is to aestheticized television as the director is to legitimated forms of cinema. The showrunner is potentially an *auteur*: an artist of unique vision whose experiences and personality are expressed through storytelling craft, and whose presence in cultural discourses functions to produce authority for the forms with which he is identified. The rise to prominence of television *auteurs* and of authorship discourses surrounding them functions to distinguish certain kinds of television from others, and, as in cinema, to promote *auteur* productions as culturally legitimate. In aesthetic cultures from music and painting to theater and cinema, it is exceedingly rare to find art without authorship discourses, and the legitimation of newer art forms like cinema is often accomplished through the identification of artworks with artists who create them. As Shyon Baumann argues, cinema's rising legitimation during the 1960s was accomplished through the celebration of autonomous film artists, which functioned to justify an intellectual interest in what had previously been regarded more often as a mass medium than an art form. This, he argues, conforms to Bourdieu's argument that a "'charisma' ideology" underwrites judgments of artistic value.[2]

"Showrunner" is not an official moniker; one never sees the word in television credits and there is no showrunners guild. The term's genesis may be obscure, but it rarely if ever appears in trade papers or the popular press before the mid-1990s, and is seldom used even then. Studies of television authorship from the early and mid-1990s such as *Prime Time, Prime Movers*, first published in 1992, and *Televisuality*, published in 1995, never mention it. The first appearance in the *New York Times* was in 1995, in an article about the production of *ER*.[3] A 2004 *Washington Post* column introduced the term and explained its connotations, which suggests that around this time its use was gaining wider currency.[4] By the middle of the 2000s the term was in wide use, and the WGA strike of 2007–2008 functioned to publicize and promote the role of these television creators who were among the most articulate on the picket lines.[5] Since then the rise of "social media" and self-publishing online sites such as discussion boards, blogs, and Twitter have given TV writer-producers new avenues through which to establish reputations and make themselves available to viewers, publicizing themselves and their programs and increasing their visibility and recognition.[6]

The showrunner is essentially the head of a television production, and programs in many genres, including talk and variety, are led by producers known as showrunners. *Variety*'s "Slanguage Dictionary" defines the role as "executive producer of a television series," although many programs have multiple producers of varying description (executive, supervising, co-producer, etc.), most of whom are not the showrunner.[7] Only in certain forms of television production do we observe the elevation of showrunner to the status of *auteur*. The widening use of "showrunner" to mean television artist has arisen as a strategy of legitimation for certain kinds of programming, calling attention to the artistic status of comedies and dramas promoted and consumed as *authored* television texts.

In scripted narrative genres, the showrunner is a "hyphenate" writer-producer. To be considered a television *auteur*, it is usually necessary for the showrunner to also be a show's original creator, like Aaron Sorkin of *The West Wing*. Thus the same individual is often responsible for a show's conception and its ongoing execution, though shows do change showrunners, often replacing creators with new writer-producers as *The West Wing* did beginning with its fifth season. For decades, producers like Sorkin have most often emerged from writing backgrounds, but while those of earlier eras might have conceived of pilot episodes and overseen script development, the convergence-era showrunner is active in both writing and non-writing production tasks on an ongoing basis, integrating two distinctly different sets of skills and concerns. The role combines corporate management—sometimes the showrunner is called the CEO of a TV show—and creative initiative.[8] In addition to being the storyteller-in-chief, the showrunner has many management responsibilities, including staffing the show with writers, negotiating with network executives, and budgeting. Showrunners, reported a *Los Angeles Times* correspondent in 2007, are "a curious hybrid of starry-eyed artists and tough-as-nails operational managers."[9] A television *auteur* must be seen at once as an effective boss and an inspired genius, and in its ideal form he claims total authority, simplifying the collaborative nature of industrial media production by isolating a singular artist to whom all others in the network of cooperation stand subservient. Matt Nix, showrunner of *Burn Notice*, observes: "People look to showrunners and say, that guy *is* that show."[10]

On one level, then, the primacy of the showrunner as the figure responsible for the aesthetic integrity of the television text, especially of scripted comedies and dramas, has become a convention of television production. It's hard to imagine a show like *Mad Men* coming into existence without a central intelligence overseeing production and storytelling, and indeed its *auteur* Matthew Weiner is reported to assert his agency in myriad aspects of production, from writing and casting to set design and costuming.[11] But the function of the showrunner-*auteur* exceeds the necessities of unifying television creation under the leadership of an effective manager when considering the circulation of authorship discourses both within the creative community of television production and, more importantly, in promotional, critical, fannish, and ordinary reception contexts. We can consider the rise of this role as a practice leading to the creation of certain kinds of legitimated television texts, but also as a term in the reception of those kinds of television. We must distinguish, then, between the centrality of the showrunner-*auteur* as: (1) a production practice; and (2) a term in the discourse of television's legitimation, promoting the author-function of the showrunner as a guarantee of value. Especially since *Twin Peaks* appeared as a model of a kind of small screen art cinema, Quality TV has been quite routinely distinguished by what Derek Kompare calls its "conspicuous authorship."[12] New media such as DVD commentary features (Figure 3.1) and web promotions have helped to make the showrunner into a public role akin to novelist or film director, offering interpretive guidance and production background and answering questions about plot developments.

In many instances, this promotes the notion of individual authorship within the cultures of both television production and consumption: networks and studios see the showrunner as the individual ultimately responsible for a production, and encourage viewers to do the same. The identification of more aesthetically distinguished programs with the artists credited with imagining and producing them validates some kinds of television, making these instances fit within traditional conceptions of art and distancing them from the reputation of TV rooted in the past and in less valued technologies, audiences, and genres.

The Emergence of the Showrunner

The rise of the showrunner-*auteur* is the product of a cluster of interrelated causes. On the production side, the showrunner-*auteur* arises along with the move toward

FIGURE 3.1 Audiences are encouraged to see showrunners as the source of true meaning. Carleton Cuse and Damon Lindelof explain *Lost*'s final season in a special feature from the season 6 DVD box set

greater serialization of prime time scripted series television, which necessitates the active management of long-format stories. One historical conception of the showrunner is of a supervisor who oversees production and fixes problems without necessarily being involved in crafting the story beat by beat. Many of TV history's most notable producers, including Norman Lear and Aaron Spelling, would fit this description. A newer, more *auteurist* notion of the showrunner's role substitutes hands-on narrative creation for this supervisory role, making one individual more responsible for the storytelling than would be the case on shows where different writers might have more autonomy over the crafting of their episodes. This is facilitated by the move from freelance labor to staffs of writers working as a team under the showrunner's management, with entire seasons and series plotted out by a collaborating group tasked with realizing the coherent vision of the *auteur*. When prime time shows were more often episodic and labor was more freelance, individual scribes scripted stand-alone episodes more autonomously than is today's norm, and episodes might be shot in any order.[13] With staffed writing, the process can be more collaborative and ongoing. This shift coincides with the broadcast networks' pursuit of narrow, upscale demographics as in NBC's strategy with *Hill Street Blues* and other Quality dramas in the 1980s, which helped to establish the writer-producer in a position of visible creative control (such as Steven Bochco) as a mark of cultural legitimacy.[14]

Shifting labor practices happen gradually over many seasons of television production. David Wild's (1999) book *The Showrunners* about the making of prime time television comedies and dramas for the 1998–1999 season, including *Friends* and *Beverly Hills 90210,* generally avoids the *auteurism* of later TV authorship discourses, and avoids as well focusing on unique and solitary artists, preferring instead to consider the collaborative nature of television authorship in instances such as the Bright–Kauffman–Crane partnership in producing *Friends* and the Kohan–Mutchnick partnership in making *Will & Grace.*[15] A decade after its publication, the standard discussions of television authorship in popular press and fan sites as well as within the television industry had grown considerably more *auteurist*, emphasizing visionary individuals at the expense of the collaborating team. We can regard this change as both a cause and a symptom of legitimation.

The showrunner-*auteur* functions as a commercial strategy of product differentiation and as a marker of quality.[16] While Romantic notions of authorship are actually rather hard to find in the discourses of network promotion, even in connection with such notably assertive authors as Aaron Sorkin and David E. Kelley, the identity of such figures often finds a place in marketing and promotion. As a guarantee of product distinction, the showrunner-*auteur* is a branding strategy for upscale television as it contrasts the authored series against an undifferentiated mass. By the fall of 1990, when "David Lynch's *Twin Peaks*" was launching its second season and "innovative" television was supposedly the industry's new production trend, certain kinds of television were being promoted by authorial signature.[17] For instance, ABC touted a new series that season as "Steven Bochco's *Cop Rock*" and introduced its premiere episode with the tagline "Tonight Steven Bochco creator of 'Hill Street Blues' and 'L.A. Law' breaks all the rules . . ."[18] (Figure 3.2).

In the convergence era, authorship functions as branding to attract a desirable upscale audience to programming constructed as authentically artistic.[19] The rise to prominence of original premium cable series, especially those on HBO, has further pushed the promotion of authorial autonomy as a marker of quality and distinction. A central strategy of the post-*Sopranos* HBO series, applicable as well to some basic cable fare like *Mad Men,* has been to center shows around authors as brands (Alan Ball's *True Blood,* David Milch's *John From Cincinnati,* David Simon's *Treme*), and to distinguish original cable series from network fare on the basis of this authorial autonomy. Whether working in broadcast or cable, celebrated television creators like Joss Whedon and Matt Weiner hit the interview circuit to promote their new series or seasons, functioning as the television equivalent of a novelist or cineaste. *Lost* showrunners host clip shows and participate in many promotional activities, from podcasts to Comic-Con panels.[20] By contrast, programming of lesser cultural value, such as reality TV competitions, is rarely understood in public forums through such discourses of authorship, and the showrunners of talk and reality programs are much less likely to appear in such sites.

On the reception side, the showrunner-*auteur* as part of an aestheticizing reading strategy is a product of the cult mode of television engagement. This mode has been critical to the success of influential serialized *auteur* shows such as *Twin Peaks,*

FIGURE 3.2 Steven Bochco's reputation is used to promote *Cop Rock* in *TV Guide* upon its September 1990 debut

The X-Files, Buffy the Vampire Slayer, and *Battlestar Galactica,* all of which are understood to have strong authorial voices. This follows the influence of *Star Trek,* the ur-cult-TV text. Henry Jenkins writes of *Star Trek* fans distinguishing the program from most other shows on television on the basis of Gene Roddenberry's personal vision and integrity.[21] In recent years, as formerly cult modes of consumption have gone mainstream, fan practices of obsessive interpretation and exegesis have increasingly surrounded the figure of the worshipped showrunner. The aesthetic disposition of the Quality television audience, whether influenced by a cult mode of engagement or by expectations about aesthetic experience familiar from other media, depends on the identification of authority in an individual and on judgments of artistic integrity on the basis of this authority, as with *Star Trek* and Roddenberry. As Matt Hills argues, cult TV reception often functions to "recuperate trusted *auteur* figures" through textual engagement.[22] In analyzing Usenet discussions of *Twin Peaks* in 1990, Jenkins writes that fans of the show

> consistently appealed to knowledge ... about Lynch as author as the primary basis for their speculations about likely plot developments. Lynch's authorial identity emerged in the net discourse as both that of a wizard programmer who has tapped into the network of previously circulating cultural materials and jerryrigged them into a more sophisticated narrative system and that of a trickster who consistently anticipates and undermines audience expectations.[23]

The obsessive interpretive work of cult TV fans tends to read narratives in relation to (sometimes against) perceived or stated authorial intentions, and positions showrunner commentary as authoritative. Joss Whedon's centrality to discussions of *Buffy, Angel, Firefly,* and *Dollhouse* is indicated by the name of the main fansite for this material, Whedonesque, and by the levels of excitement generated by his occasional appearance as a commenter there. These appearances promise insights about the creative process, art/commerce negotiation, and authorial intentions otherwise inaccessible to fans, and help to promote the idea of the showrunner-*auteur* as a star in his own right. Fan fictions that reimagine or challenge representations are often positioned in relation to authorial meanings, as in the case of *X-Files* "shipper" fans representing a romantic relationship between Mulder and Scully in defiance of Chris Carter's well-known preference to maintain the characters' platonic relations.[24] Even in instances of interpretive negotiation over meaning, the presence of the television author as a figure in this negotiation indicates his salience. Of course cult modes of television consumption position the cult text as a product of quality and distinction, a fact recognizable to the cult formation but not the rest of the viewing public. According to Jenkins, underlying fans' appreciation of *Twin Peaks* "was a profound skepticism about American popular culture and a contempt for most of television."[25] The migration of cult practices such as authorial recognition-cum-worship beyond the narrow communities that originally defined them spreads aesthetic conceptions of television to more viewers, encouraging them to recognize and mobilize tropes of authorship.

Tropes of Authorship

The rise of conspicuous showrunner-*auteurs* inserts into television discourse a number of tropes of authorship familiar from older, already legitimated and aestheticized cultural forms. These operate on levels of both production and reception, which feed back into one another as creative practices and interpretive approaches influence one another. In relation to Quality TV, discourses of television authorship adopt the same strategies already in place for the appreciation of literary, musical, and visual arts. In particular, one proximate cultural form, the cinema, offers models for television authorship to follow, and configuring authorship specifically as a form of quasi-cinematic *auteurism* is an especially effective strategy for legitimating television, as both Hollywood movies and television have historically faced similar commercial/industrial constraints and similar challenges of being perceived as lowbrow mass entertainment rather than serious culture.

The author as guarantee of art

According to still-influential Romantic notions of art as expressive communication, there can be no artworks without artists, and thus works without artists do not count as instances of art. This *auteurist* trope was well articulated by Andrew Sarris in asserting that American cinema could be recognized as an art form as opposed to mere commercial entertainment if its directors were recognized as authors. Sarris proclaims, "The auteur critic is obsessed with the wholeness of art and the artist."[26] This trope protects the artistic productions in a debased commercial medium like television or film from association with run-of-the-mill trash: of course most TV is not conspicuously authored, but artistic TV must be, and this is precisely what allows it to be labeled as different and better. Writing about the Quality television of the 1980s, John Thornton Caldwell asserts that upscale fare was counter-programmed against more ordinary TV on the basis of its "boutique intentionality," giving shows the sense of having been crafted with a "personal touch" in contrast to the more assembly-line fashion of the usual programming.[27] Ordinary television was more likely anonymous, while boutique television—shows like *thirtysomething*, which Caldwell reads as an allegory of writer-producers Edward Zwick and Marshall Herskovitz's creative struggles—was preoccupied with performing and promoting its authors' identities. In the era of convergence the figure of the television *auteur* has achieved new degrees of prominence.

Numerous interviews have given David Chase the opportunity at once to promote his own *auteur* identity and, on that basis, his show *The Sopranos*, while at the same time disparaging television and expressing his contempt for the medium as a whole and his preference to be working in feature films.[28] In 2004, Chase told the *New York Times'* TV critic Virginia Heffernan that "television is at the base of a lot of our problems" because "it trivializes everything." "The function of an hour drama" on network TV, Chase said, "is to reassure the American people that it's O.K. to go out and buy stuff."[29] In 2007, Chase told Peter Biskind, writing for *Vanity Fair,* "I hate television." Among the reasons given: "Network dramas have not been personal." He expressed his admiration for Lynch's *Twin Peaks,* comparing it to masterworks of painting and foreign cinema. In making *The Sopranos,* Chase claimed, he "didn't want it to be a TV show." Rather, he wanted "to make a little movie every week."[30] These statements clearly argue for the superiority of *The Sopranos* in relation to ordinary television on a cluster of interrelated bases: the integrity of Chase's authorship and the show's essentially expressive character, and the very fact of coherent authorship and "vision" as a mark of distinction, as well as the distance between HBO's authored serials and the more anonymous and commercialized products of the broadcast networks. The show's own official paratexts make this same appeal. For instance, the first season DVD box set of *The Sopranos* includes a special feature interview of David Chase set in the Soprano family kitchen conducted by Peter Bogdanovich, the film director and *auteurist* film critic (Figure 3.3).

FIGURE 3.3 Film director Peter Bogdanovich interviews showrunner David Chase on set in the Sopranos' family kitchen. The interview was included with the first season DVD box set, furthering Chase's status as *auteur*

Bogdanovich treats Chase as the lone author of the series, querying him about his personal experiences, his influences, his creative process, and the show's thematic terrain. Chase asserts his role in shaping every episode—choosing music, writing and rewriting, editing—and Bogdanovich observes that this must give the series its "uniform quality," springing from "one person's vision." Much of the discussion includes references to films and film directors, drawing connections between *The Sopranos* and films such as *The Public Enemy* and *Rules of the Game* and *auteurs* from Welles to Buñuel to Scorsese. Very little of the discussion concerns TV history or the influences of television on Chase, who, as always, professes disdain for the medium and a long-standing ambition of making films. The implication is that the feature film is not only understood to be aesthetically superior to lowly television, but also a more likely medium for individual expression. It was no coincidence, then, that the film curator of the Museum of Modern Art chose *The Sopranos* to be the first television series ever to be exhibited there in 2001.[31]

Similarly, the publicity surrounding the launch of *Studio 60 on the Sunset Strip* in the fall of 2006 positioned Aaron Sorkin as a singular and authoritative voice, marking the show as the product of his unique artistic vision and positioning it discursively as Sorkin's critical statement on contemporary mainstream network television. A *New York Times* column anticipating the show—under the headline "TV's Auteur Portrays TV"—opined that "the main reason viewers seem eager to see the new drama is that Aaron Sorkin wrote it."[32] The setting of the show behind the scenes at a network sketch comedy series (a fictionalized *Saturday Night Live*), offered many opportunities for skewering the overly safe and commercialized—and thus morally and culturally compromised—nature of broadcast television production. The pilot episode, in a sequence much circulated online in a preview of the series, begins with the show-within-a-show in a Howard Beale moment, with the producer, played by Judd Hirsch, lambasting the conditions of contemporary television production and regulation in a spontaneous outburst sure to lead to his firing (Figure 3.4).

It would be hard not to read this rant as Sorkin voicing his own strong opinion of the medium he aims to rise above, and depicting his fictionalized show as potentially daring and artistic if only dedicated, passionate creators find the opportunities to achieve their ambitions. His statements to the press would seem to confirm the scribe's disdain for much of ordinary TV, and reproduce his own *auteur* identity as a critic and artist capable of rising above the ordinary, potentially harmful TV fare. He told an audience of television critics at the 2006 Summer TV Press Tour, "Television is a terribly influential part of this country, and when things that are very mean-spirited and voyeuristic go on TV, I think it's bad crack in the schoolyard."[33]

Emily Nussbaum's decade-ending wrap-up article in *New York* magazine in late 2009, "When TV Became Art," is essentially one long *auteurist* celebration, identifying the supposedly newly artistic television with showrunner-*auteurs* including Chase and Sorkin as well as Joss Whedon, Alan Ball, David Simon,

FIGURE 3.4 Showrunner Wes Mendell, stand-in for *Studio 60 on the Sunset Strip* creator Aaron Sorkin, expresses his outrage at the creative constraints of the network television business

David Milch, J.J. Abrams, Matthew Weiner, and Ron Moore, and contrasting the "life-changing and transformative and lasting" work of these artists with the other main trend of the decade, reality TV. It was the work of the showrunner-*auteurs* that made television "something you could not merely enjoy and then discard but brood over and analyze, that could challenge and elevate, not just entertain."[34] By addressing "you," the writer makes her reader an accomplice in distinguishing between the aesthetic and degraded forms of television, making the value of artistic TV seem universal rather than the product of a commercial strategy for appealing to the taste preferences of certain segments of the audience. The consolidation of this kind of conventional wisdom about television's newfound legitimated status makes the art–artist nexus essential to the project of establishing television as a respectable cultural form, borrowing the same terms of understanding artistic culture from the already established media of literature, cinema, music, and visual arts.

The auteur's work as product of personal experience

In contrast to the impersonal conception of industrial culture production, *auteurism* poses the possibility that the individuals who create culture are crafting expressions of their own concerns within the constraints of a commercial medium. This trope is often manifested through the identification of autobiographical elements in television storytelling. It helps us understand television authors' creative functions when we learn that their own lives become fodder for storytelling. For instance,

David E. Kelley came to *L.A. Law* and his other legal dramas from a career as an attorney, and Ronald D. Moore served on a U.S. Naval frigate before his work on *Star Trek* (*Next Generation* and *Deep Space Nine*) and *Battlestar Galactica*, shows with military settings (Figure 3.5).

The filtering of experience through fictionalized narrative situations can be traced back to origins in the personal lives of television creators, and the connections between experience and expression further guarantee the artistry of individualized production and downplay the collaborative nature of industrial media-making. Sometimes this autobiographical storytelling is self-evident, but it always depends on the audience's extra-textual knowledge about the television author for its legitimating effects.

David Simon's work in creating *The Wire* has origins in an earlier series he worked on, the NBC police drama *Homicide: Life on the Street*. Simon was a *Baltimore Sun* reporter whose book about the Baltimore homicide division was the source of the series. Thus the representation of police and criminal gangs springs from this earlier work as a reporter and a participant in making a show about Baltimore cops. In *The Wire* season five, when one storyline is set in the newsroom of a Baltimore daily paper, the audience is invited to see the representation of media work as Simon's thin fictionalizing of his own experiences as a reporter. Avid *Wire* watchers were already familiar with Simon's penchant

FIGURE 3.5 Ronald D. Moore with Edward James Olmos (as Adm. Bill Adama) on the set of *Battlestar Galactica*

Source: Photofest © Sci-Fi Channel

for writing characters who were either based closely on real Baltimore personages, or who were actually played by them. These behind-the-scenes details are often pointed out in the show's DVD commentaries, which frequently focus on the numerous correspondences between fictional and real-life persons.

Studio 60 was covered in the popular press not just as the new Aaron Sorkin show, but also as Sorkin's effort to represent his own creative struggles as a television maker. Many reports noted that Sarah Paulson's character Harriet, the Christian ex-flame of Matthew Perry's character, was based on Kristin Chenowith, with whom Sorkin had a relationship, and that Amanda Peet's network suit character was based on former NBC and ABC executive Jamie Tarses.[35] Of course, as a show set behind the scenes at a television production, concerned with the struggles of creative artists to produce good content, the audience would be primed to see the representation as Sorkin's own reflections on being in charge of his earlier efforts, *Sports Night* and *The West Wing*.

David Chase's authorship of *The Sopranos* was lent much authority by his Italian-American identity, but discourses positioning Chase as *auteur* would often go much further in identifying Chase's experiences as sources for his storytelling. The protagonist's mother, Livia Soprano, was apparently inspired by Chase's own mother, and the show's North Jersey settings were his youthful stamping grounds. When asked if he researched psychotherapy in preparation for writing scenes set in Dr. Melfi's office, Chase often offered his own years of therapy as the only background necessary to create this aspect of the show. Positioning the drama of the program as the expression of Chase's own experience confirms that television is indeed a personal medium in which one individual's vision can be realized, making TV shows subject to the same kind of interpretive strategies that have long functioned as means of making sense of artistic works.[36] "Personal" narratives, furthermore, are implicitly opposed to comparatively impersonal forms of TV like formulaic crime procedurals, reality shows, and soap operas around which we seldom find such powerful authorship discourses.

The auteur*'s works constituting an* œuvre

If the showrunner-*auteur* functions as a guarantee of value within discourses of legitimation, the identity of the artist should transfer from one production to the next. This helps the television networks promote their new programs ("from the creator of . . .") and it helps the audience identify signature styles and meanings. One essential component of authorship discourses is the unification of vision across works, which may include consistency of themes, motifs, verbal and visual styles, settings, and genres. Sarris identifies one premise of *auteurism* as "the distinguishable personality of the director as a criterion of value."[37] Marc and Thompson take this to be the most important part of the TV *auteur* formula, finding consistent thematic preoccupations among the writer-producers of television history of the time before the rise of the showrunner to public and industry prominence, including Jack Webb, Sherwood Schwartz, Susan Harris, Spelling, and Bochco, among others.[38] Contemporary showrunner-*auteurs* cultivate individual styles as marks of their authorial identity. In the eyes of discerning consumers of television, Joss Whedon, Aaron Sorkin, and David E. Kelley shows could never be mistaken for one another, as each writer has a personal voice recognizable across several series. Sorkin and Kelley, moreover, are notorious for hogging writing duties, having more of an active hand in scene-by-scene storytelling than many a showrunner.

As with so many characteristics of Quality TV in the 1990s and beyond, *Twin Peaks* established a model to be widely followed both in production and promotion and in critical reception. When it began on ABC in the spring of 1990 the series was positioned discursively as a new entry in the *œuvre* of David Lynch, whose authorial signature, familiar from earlier works including *Blue Velvet*, was all over the new program. This was essential to the show's positioning as an alternative to ordinary TV that would appeal as original and artistic—*Time* magazine wondered if the show "may be the most hauntingly original work ever done for American TV."[39] A profile of Lynch in the *New York Times Magazine*, for instance, identified a catalog of Lynchian motifs and stylistic ticks, including "slow dissolves, spotlighting, extreme close-ups, figures who emerge out of darkness, shots held an extra beat to catch the sound and texture of a place or thing" as well as "an interest in facial deformities, exaggerated noise, sick puns and comically banal dialogue," all of which would be familiar from earlier works to the cine-literate *Twin Peaks* viewer.[40] *Blue Velvet* was an especially significant point of reference for critics locating the new series in the terrain of Lynch's obsessions, as the film and television series shared not only a star in Kyle MacLachlan, but also a concern with uncovering the surrealistic, violent undercurrents beneath façades of genteel Americana. Amy Taubin, writing in the *Village Voice* about the *auteur*'s move to the small screen, identified several Lynchian traits to be found as much in the TV series as the film, such as a fixation on the 1950s, associative and elliptical editing, erratic pacing, and displays of bold emotion. "His most indelible characters are ruled by unsublimated, infantile rages and desires. His villains are powerhouses, his heroes are obsessed with evil, driven to uncover the perversity beneath the wholesome surfaces of small towns."[41]

Joss Whedon's *œuvre* is so identifiable and distinct that a term, the "Whedonverse," has been coined to describe this uniquely Joss sci-fi/fantasy world of vampires and demons (Figure 3.6). Books have been published explicating the philosophical underpinnings of his narrative representations, which naturally assume that his stories have meanings in common across the genres, series, and media in which he has worked, and which issue from his distinctive genius. His slangy, neologistic dialogue is instantly recognizable and his representations in particular of gender relations share common threads in a number of different series. The construction of an *œuvre* is especially salient when new works are released, and in the discourses surrounding Whedon's

FIGURE 3.6 Joss Whedon with Lorne, soul-raiding demon and host at the Caritas
karaoke bar, on the set of *Angel*

Source: The WB/Photofest © The WB

Firefly and *Dollhouse* we see instances of the power of authorship in shaping
popular understanding of television texts. A *New York Times Magazine* profile
of Whedon in 2002 made clear that *Firefly* would pick up many threads from
Whedon's earlier shows. Like Buffy Summers, Nathan Fillion's Mal Reynolds
is "a singularly thorny pop creation: a mordant, dark-humored fellow with
bile boiling just beneath the surface." Further continuities emerge: "Much in the
way Buffy is a demon-killer obsessed with the morality of killing, Mal is a man
of action frozen by his conviction that nothing really matters, a man forced to
choose his morality at each juncture."[42] Reviews routinely introduced *Dollhouse*
not as "Fox's new series *Dollhouse*" or as "the new Eliza Dushku series *Dollhouse*"
but as "Joss Whedon's *Dollhouse*," and presented Whedon as the *auteur* responsible
for *Buffy*, *Angel*, *Firefly*, and, most recently, *Dr. Horrible's Sing-Along Blog*.[43] While
certain of Whedon's personal affectations and interests are undoubtedly present
in the series—futuristic fantasy scenarios, genre storytelling with plenty of action
and suspense, concerns with gendered notions of power and identity—the
tone and moral tenor are also darker and more troubling than in *Buffy*, and the
dialogue generally lacks the knowing, slangy, referential appeals of the earlier series.
Even in instances of departures from earlier personal styles, however, the power
of authorship shines through, as the cultish audience is guided by its *auteurism*
to pay attention to such things and so to read them as significant departures.

The identification of authorial marks across an *œuvre* functions as effective commercial branding; the fan loyalty to Joss Whedon was undoubtedly a factor in the show's renewal after a first season of low ratings. And this identification is essential to the circulation of discourses of artistry in television, as the unitary vision of a solitary artist is best appreciated across a whole body of work.

Attribution of artistry to the individual rather than a collaborating team

Like film production, series television is a massively collaborative endeavor, and despite the rhetoric within production circles of respecting the vision of the showrunner-*auteur*, myriad choices and decisions are made every day a TV show is in production, and many or most of them are outside of the purview of even the most hands-on showrunner. Even in considering only leadership roles, many series have multiple producers, writers, story editors, and others in positions of authority. Furthermore, showrunner duties are often shared among teams of partners. And yet even in instances when critical and fan discourses are well aware of these situations, individuals are inevitably promoted as solitary sources of meaning. *Hill Street Blues* and *Twin Peaks*, arguably the most influential Quality TV series of recent decades, were led by partnerships rather than solitary geniuses, and yet Michael Kozoll and Mark Frost, respectively Steven Bochco and David Lynch's partners, have largely been forgotten amidst the mythologizing surrounding their more famous counterparts' authorship. Like many aspects of TV *auteurism*, this construction is an inheritance from film culture. Andrew Sarris understood that cinema is collaborative and that roles other than the director might have a greater claim on the status of *auteur*, and thus he was being self-consciously polemical in asserting that "It is when the director dominates the film that the cinema comes closest to reflecting the personality of a single artist."[44] Sarris saw Hollywood studio directors as struggling in tension with their material rather than fully controlling it, and yet those rising to the status of *auteur* could be considered in critical terms used to describe more legitimately solitary artists such as painters, composers, and novelists. In its effort to isolate showrunner-*auteurs*, the culture of Quality TV distinction—like the film culture of *auteurism* before it—obscures the conditions of industrial media production and substitutes for collaborative notions of authorship a Romantic vision of the autonomous individual.

An example of this process at work is the series of commentary podcasts recorded by Ronald D. Moore to accompany new episodes of *Battlestar Galactica* beginning in 2005.[45] Moore was the *BSG* showrunner, but the production of the series was typically collaborative. Moore's partner David Eick could certainly claim a central creative role in developing and executing the show, and yet Eick is never considered on par with Moore in critical or fan discourses celebrating *Battlestar*. Moore worked on writing and editing the show in California, but the production was centered in Vancouver, and thus the showrunner was generally absent from the set. The podcasts, commentary tracks made available well before the DVD releases of the show's seasons, function to unify the vision of the *BSG* world in Moore, and though he often describes collaborative creative processes in his narrations, the unitary voice of the commentaries and the status of Moore as a kind of TV author star in his own right function to push an *auteurist* notion of creativity.[46] As Allison McCracken argues, in these paratexts, Moore's showrunner identity functions to "remystify conditions of television production."[47]

Discourses surrounding the authorship of David Simon's HBO programs *The Corner*, *The Wire*, and *Treme* offer an emblematic case of how the popular press frames Quality TV in terms of highly individualized authorship and showrunner-*auteur* control and authority. These shows are products of collaboration among many writers and producers, and Simon, himself a former journalist, seems especially adept at building teams of writers that bring together figures from the world of crime fiction rather than relying on old television hands. Novelists such as George Pelecanos, Richard Price, and Dennis Lehane scripted episodes of *The Wire*, and the participation of so many established names from the world of books would seem likely to mitigate the singular genius ideal of showrunner-*auteurism*. And yet Simon is typically figured in just this identity. In a long *New York Times Magazine* profile in advance of the premiere of *Treme* in 2010, the many various contributions of a team of writers are regularly noted, and yet the article carries the title "The HBO Auteur" and goes out of its way to portray Simon as the ultimate genius-boss of his productions, continually attributing essentially total storytelling agency to the showrunner. He "works on every script by every writer of every show he produces," the profile goes. Pelecanos says that Simon would rewrite entire scripts of his. Price observes, "You really need a single sensibility at the top, a writer-producer who's a ruthless rewriter."[48] The fact that articles such as this one appear in advance of new series and seasons of television demonstrates the mutually reinforcing nature of promotional and critical discourses of authorship, which together shape the popular imagination of legitimated forms of television.

In the era of heroic *auteurism* best exemplified in American film criticism by Sarris, the idea of Hollywood directorial authorship was a matter of intellectual controversy. The film *auteur*'s tentative status was signaled in the term "auteur theory," with "theory" here acknowledging the problematic status of individual authorship in a collaborative, commercial, industrial mass medium. In the intervening years, Hollywood authorship has become a central strategy of branding and publicity, and the discourses of authorship adapted from film to television culture make this promotional dimension essential to conceptions of the television artist. Now rather than struggling to produce art in the context of a ruthless commercial machine, the audiovisual artist is as much brand manager as lonely genius. This identity has only been intensified under convergence culture, as Denise Mann argues; now showrunners like Damon Lindelof and Carleton Cuse of *Lost* preside over not only the production of episodes of television, but of a whole raft of transmedia products, many of which blur lines of product and promotion.[49] As Mann explains, the "2.0," convergence culture context of *Lost* and similar blockbuster television series requires numerous executive producers to oversee and manage production, making it impossible for one or two individuals to function effectively as authors of a unified brand and text. Despite this, an image persists of Lindelof and Cuse as "the brain trust" ultimately responsible for the series' narrative.[50] The Ron Moore podcasts function in this same context: as authorship extending not only to the primary text but also to the various ancillary paratexts that help sustain contemporary media franchises. The visibility of the showrunner in these paratextual discourses further reinforces the trope of *auteurism* in which participation of a team of collaborators is obscured by the promotion of the *auteur* genius. The legitimation of television through tropes of authorship extends from the shows themselves, to the promotions and ancillary products made to sustain transmedia properties as branded franchises, to the critical sites so central to the shaping of the popular imagination of television as a newly respectable medium.

The auteur *as celebrity*

In September 2010, Kurt Sutter, the showrunner of *Sons of Anarchy*, a basic cable hit about a motorcycle gang, was profiled in the *Los Angeles Times* as an example of a "celebrity showrunner," i.e., "a writer-producer who's become almost as famous as the series he or she oversees."[51] The article noted that the visibility of television's creative personnel is a new phenomenon:

> While as recently as five or 10 years ago average fans knew little or nothing about the people who made their favorite programs, celebrity showrunners have become vital in a TV world packed to the rafters with niche programs and fans connecting through social media.[52]

This claim may be overstated; television producers and writers like Jack Webb, Rod Serling, Norman Lear, Larry Gelbart, and Steven Bochco have been public figures for decades. But it does indicate a change toward a greater role for the television creator within a culture that celebrates creative individuals in numerous areas of endeavor, from architecture and painting to fashion design and cuisine. It also serves as a token of how the rise of showrunners as famous personalities functions as another way of understanding television to be renewed and improved. It might not be accurate to deny the historical visibility of television writers and producers, but it is undeniable that the convergence era has brought Quality TV writer-producers new public roles, new opportunities to perform their function authorizing the artistic appreciation of television. *Variety* reported in 2010 that the celebrity showrunner "is changing the way networks tubthump their shows and deepening the way fans connect with shows."[53] This new conception of the television creator's role marks the convergence of the function of the author as guarantee of art with the complementary function of the author as the most critical node in the commercial promotion of legitimated culture.

In this new role, television showrunners become only the latest entrants in a now well-established tradition of the artist as celebrity. The idea is perhaps most often associated with Andy Warhol, who cultivated his own public image as a form of artistic creativity in its own right, and as a way of adding value to his work. As Stuart D. Hobbs writes, Warhol "deliberately courted fame, as if being famous as an artist was the same as being significant. In a culture of consumption, he was probably right."[54] In 1971, Robert Hughes, *Time* magazine's art critic, gave voice to a common cynical conception of celebrity in assessing Warhol's public persona: "Warhol is not so much famous for doing something—he rarely turns out any paintings beyond a few commissioned portraits a year, and no longer directs his own films—as for being someone named Andy Warhol."[55] But Warhol did not invent the idea of the artist as celebrity, and Hughes names Picasso and Dalí as his betters in this status. Authors such as Ernest Hemingway also fit this idea as famous public personages, recognizable even to those unfamiliar with their work, and beginning in the 1950s and 1960s, courtesy of Sarris's importation of French film criticism as the *auteur* theory, film directors were also candidates for this kind of place in highbrow culture. It might trivialize art when creators become media personalities and even quasi-stars, promoting themselves for vanity and personal gain, but it also affirms cultural hierarchies when novelists and painters can more easily attain such a status than can television creators. The creation of "showrunner" as an identity has made television's participation in the discourse of the artist as celebrity more likely and more meaningful, as it isolates unique individuals for the public to appreciate. The appearance of television showrunners like David Simon as artists with a public face, profiled in serious magazines like *The New Yorker* and interviewed on NPR's *Fresh Air*, establishes a brand of high value, and marks the ascent of television to respectability.[56]

In addition to the popular press, official promotional texts such as podcasts, and more DIY media like message board postings, Twitter has been an especially significant site in which celebrity showrunners have maintained their visibility and promoted themselves and their works. Among the prominent Twittering TV *auteurs* during the 2010–2011 TV season were Shonda Rhimes of *Grey's Anatomy* and *Private Practice*, Josh Schwartz of *Chuck* and *Gossip Girl*, Dan Harmon of *Community*, Hart Hanson of *Bones*, Steve Levitan of *Modern Family*, Carter Bays of *How I Met Your Mother*, and Seth MacFarlane of *Family Guy*, *American Dad*, and *The Cleveland Show*. This use fits within a larger phenomenon of celebrities of all kinds taking to online sites such as Facebook and Twitter to project their star texts and interact with audiences, offering a sense of authentic and perpetual access to fans, seemingly bypassing the more polished images filtered through publicists.[57] Although this might appear to be a kind of unmediated representation of celebrities' authentic selves, as Nick Muntean and Anne Helen Petersen argue, celebrity Twitter postings function ideologically in the fashion of earlier forms of star image-making as the construction of a mediated identity.[58] The showrunners who tweet regularly unify their shows' meanings under their own personal brands and appeal to followers to watch. They work to fashion an image of themselves as witty or brash or down-to-earth, and to give fans an impression of immediacy and availability. Using the hashtag ("#") and at-reply ("@username") conventions of tweeting, showrunners are able to follow conversations about their shows and engage in back-and-forth dialogue with viewers and critics. As Myles McNutt observes, on Twitter, showrunners can become facilitators of fan communities while also opening themselves up to negative feedback from viewers who might find plot twists unsatisfying.[59]

Whether received positively or negatively by their public, showrunners participating in social networks serve at once to promote the Quality TV programs associated with them and to reassert themselves as the unifying forces behind their narratives. As Jonathan Gray observes, the proliferation of digital audience-created paratexts such as discussion boards makes possible the building of rapport between creators and fans, with the author potentially functioning as a kind of mediator between audience and media industries.[60] New media might offer a sense of novel access but they also remediate old media functions of publicity and promotion, and like Andy Warhol and other artist-celebrities, the showrunners whose names become well known gain significant value from their fame. This value is not merely economic; it is also a form of cultural cachet, and the distinction between television shows that come to us courtesy of an author and the vast majority of shows that do not is one product of this phenomenon.

Authorship as Elevation

Legitimated forms of television, in particular scripted prime time narrative series, are aestheticized in numerous ways, including textual appeals (narrative form, dialogue, audiovisual style) and those arising in discourses of the media industries and of media promotion and publicity. The centrality of authorship to legitimation is a good example of the interplay of these discourses, as the textual and contextual or paratextual meanings converge around the author as a source and anchor of meaning. The status of television as art is an effect produced through the elevation of certain instances of television over others, thereby legitimating not just the television texts at hand but also the efforts and tastes of those who create and consume them. By making some television conspicuously authored, the culture of television's legitimation—from production to reception—aligns some forms of scripted prime time series with cinema, literature, painting, and other forms of serious, highly respected culture.

In these other art forms, one mark of distinction is the extent to which individual identity can be read in the text. We have seen that Sarris saw the distinctive personality of the director to be a criterion used for judging films. The production practices making showrunners into powerful and important TV industry figures have made Quality TV shows likely, in many instances, to exhibit the marks of authorship, or to be ready-made for authorship as a reading strategy. Thus it is not some arbitrary body of television work that has come to be understood as the work of authors, but certain kinds of serialized, long-form narrative. In various ways, this kind of storytelling matches the conspicuously authored forms of literary and cinematic culture, whether by being sprawling in the manner of a nineteenth-century novel or deliberately paced and enigmatic in the manner of a 1960s art film. But television cannot be understood as the work of an author without the availability of information from outside of the text about production practices and interpretive conventions. Authorship in any medium is both a fact of production and an effect of publicity. In convergence-era television, authorship is central not only to the textual appeals of Quality TV, but also to the culture of television appreciation and fandom in the niche audience segments to whom legitimated programs are addressed.

4

UPGRADING THE SITUATION COMEDY

The dusty sitcom has caught up to the modern mind.
New York Times[1]

During the early 2000s, the situation comedy, with its reliable comedic tropes, its conventions of storytelling and style enduring since television's early years, underwent a significant transformation. Without exception, the critically admired and culturally validated comedies of the convergence era have rejected some of the once-defining traits of the genre. In this period, this quintessentially televisual form has morphed into a version of itself positioned to be more legitimate than the traditional version purportedly left behind by aesthetic progress.

The historical reputation of the sitcom has been curiously two-faced. Many of American TV history's most admired programs—shows such as *The Honeymooners*, *The Mary Tyler Moore Show*, and *The Cosby Show*—have worked within the familiar conventions of the genre, often winning the status of Quality TV and marrying remarkable commercial, critical, and popular success. But as a genre taken as a whole rather than as a select roster of beloved classics, the sitcom is often regarded contemptuously as among the most conservative, formulaic, and artless of narrative forms. For instance, film reviewers might compare big-screen comedies like *My Big Fat Greek Wedding* or *Little Miss Sunshine* unfavorably to sitcoms, implying that works of serious merit avoid television comedy's hackneyed tropes, and that cinematic comedy ought to distinguish itself from an association with mass-market television style.[2] Efforts at the legitimation of the situation comedy genre have occurred against the backdrop of this split reputation, with new shows regarded as worthwhile and artistic set off against the genre as a whole, and thus positioned as rising above the sitcom's status.

Around the turn of the millennium, American sitcoms began to show changes in some of their most basic conventions. Despite frequent, cyclical declarations of the death of TV comedy and a general absence of sitcoms from Nielsen top 10 lists in the years following the endings of *Friends* and *Everybody Loves Raymond*, in the 2000s and early 2010s we have seen a new movement in the American sitcom that has found many champions. Shows emerged, like *Malcolm in the Middle*, the lone new hit sitcom of the 2000–2001 season, which conspicuously reject many of the genre's production norms and storytelling conventions and prove that bold and prominent visuals and sound can make for a successful network comedy.[3] Following the impressive influence of *The Simpsons*, many animated sitcoms have explored styles of humor diverging from those of traditional live-action comedies, and in turn have offered models to creators of live-action shows like *Malcolm* looking to explore new dimensions of screen comedy. The best comedy Emmy Award went to *Ally McBeal* in 1999, the first time an hour-long show took the honor, and this surely encouraged comedy producers and networks to think about expanding the conception of sitcoms to include different styles of shooting and humor.

In the years to follow, comedies such as *Arrested Development, Curb Your Enthusiasm, 30 Rock*, and *Modern Family* have explored forms of style and storytelling rarely seen in American TV comedy. *My Name is Earl* debuted in 2005 as the only new comedy to be even a modest hit, and along with *The Office*, which found a technologically adept audience through iTunes downloads and became a cultural sensation, it pushed the networks toward more half-hour shows that depart from tradition and appeal to desirable young and affluent viewers.[4] NBC's Thursday night schedule in the 2006–2007 season of *My Name is Earl, The Office, Scrubs*, and *30 Rock* offered two hours of comedies in its historically significant "must-see TV" program block with nary a laugh track or proscenium set among them. Beginning midseason, in January 2011, NBC filled all three hours of Thursday primetime with half-hour shows in the new style: *Community, Perfect Couples, The Office, Parks and Recreation, 30 Rock*, and *Outsourced*.

In industry and press discourses, such sitcoms are usually called single-camera shows for short, to contrast them against the multiple-camera format of traditional TV comedies, though the differences are not mainly a matter of how many cameras are shooting. By 2009, among the broadcast networks only CBS was airing hit multi-camera comedies (though cable channels like Disney also profitably maintained the style); the other networks had turned mainly to single-camera shows, and ABC and NBC had almost entirely abandoned multi-cams. Although rarely really big hits, single-cam sitcoms win awards and accolades, appeal as cult or Quality TV to upscale audiences, and have found some enthusiastic viewers in popular press critics like *Time* magazine's James Poniewozik who admire them for being "more ambitious" than traditional comedies.[5] Television creators like *The Office*'s Greg Daniels look to the new style as an opportunity to "expand the creative terrain for scripted shows on broadcast TV."[6] In discourses of television criticism both popular and scholarly, as well as those of television production, the style of these new programs is positioned as an upgrade on the sitcom formula—as a welcome improvement to an otherwise exhausted genre.

One of the key strategies used in justifying the legitimation of the single-camera comedy is to connect its audiovisual style to cinema's. We can observe this cinematization of the sitcom on two levels. First, it is a product of the adoption of production practices conventionally associated more with cinema than television, such as setting up shots one at a time rather than shooting entire episodes staged like a play in front of a live audience. Of course, no sitcom production practice is naturally more cinematic or televisual. These media are constructed culturally as belonging to distinct categories, but they overlap considerably in their technologies and industrial practices. Second, the cinematization of the sitcom is a product of comparative discourses that associate the single-camera show with more legitimated cultural forms and distance it from less legitimated ones. In this instance, the more respected forms are feature films (as well in some instances as literary works and Quality TV dramas, which themselves gain legitimacy by comparison with movies), while the less legitimated ones are traditional multi-camera television comedies. According to such discourses, traditional TV comedy is positioned as inartistic and thus as having lesser cultural value because of its putatively televisual character. By contrast, the new style is figured as an advance on the grounds of its similarities to feature filmmaking.

Two Styles, Many Options

This history of American television comedy is more heterogeneous than it may seem from the dichotomous rhetoric of champions of the new sitcom style. It serves the interests of those disparaging the multi-cam comedy to present it having an unchanging formula, but actually it admits variability. Styles vary according to shooting format (film or video, black and white or color), the use of the live audience (not all multi-cam shows are filmed or taped before an audience, not all have audible laughter, and not all laughter is the live audience's), and the number of cameras and size and other qualities of sets (older shows used three cameras and more spare sets, while more recent shows shoot with four and are visually more expansive). Performance and writing styles range from the broad, low, or ethnic humor of *Married . . . with Children* or *The Nanny* to the more sophisticated, witty style of *Will & Grace* and *Frasier*. Moreover, single-camera comedies are hardly a recent innovation, and have been made for decades. *Leave it to Beaver*, *The Andy Griffith Show,* and *The Brady Bunch* were all shot in the single-cam style before it became more artistically distinguished.

Rather than two fixed formulas with rigid characteristics, we can understand single- and multi-camera television comedies in terms of clusters of formal options within two identifiable formats. Any one program's style is comprised of a number of distinct choices made in production, and there will be some variation among individual comedies within each larger group style. For example, multi-camera shows are usually shot in front of studio audiences, but not in every instance; *How I Met Your Mother* is shot without a live audience. Many single-camera shows eschew the sound of audience laughter in favor of other comical sound cues, but there are exceptions here as well. *Coupling*, a 2003 NBC remake of a British hit comedy, used a laugh track in combination with single-cam style shooting, and American single-camera comedies of the 1950s, 1960s, and 1970s used laugh tracks virtually without exception. Both multi- and single-camera styles have histories, with developments over time such as a move from three to four cameras in traditional productions in the early 1980s. Especially among single-camera shows, there is room for considerable variability in the devices employed for comical effect, and the many options tend to cluster into identifiable varieties of the style, but the functions of these devices in the different shows still overlap considerably.

The traditional sitcom like *All in the Family* is shot on a three-wall set with the cameras, crew, and audience taking the place of the fourth wall (Figure 4.1). The action is performed like a play, scene by scene, with three or four cameras shooting simultaneously. This production style, which Jeremy Butler calls the

FIGURE 4.1 A typical multiple-camera setup in *All in the Family* frames the characters from a distance in the familiar proscenium set, illuminated by bright, flat lighting. This theatrical style suits its production convention of filming or taping before a live audience

"multiple-camera proscenium schema," is one comedies share with soap operas, another genre with radio origins, as well as many genres of live TV such as local news and talk, and this common visual approach serves to link the traditional sitcom to these oft-degraded TV genres.[7] The "three-headed monster" originated by Karl Freund for *I Love Lucy* in 1953 was among other things a way of preserving television programming by shooting live on film (and later sometimes tape), and of making the production of regular programming efficient. This production style is in some ways more economical and much faster than setting up one shot at a time, but it requires bright, flat, even lighting to make shots from many angles workable (a look generally considered visually cheap, uninteresting, and non-naturalistic, especially by cinematographers and other craft professionals). Camera, lighting, and audience positions necessitate fairly shallow staging against familiar standing sets oriented more horizontally than in depth, like the bar in *Cheers* with the front door at the left, the table seating and bar itself in the center, and the office door at the right. Given the constancy of our orientation in scenographic space and the reliance on a small number of regular sets, as an audience we become so familiar with the settings of a multi-cam show that we might wonder whether we have actually inhabited them ourselves.

The multi-camera sitcom also typically follows familiar norms of storytelling and scene construction. Dramatic development depends on the verbal pattern of setup–punchline, setup–punchline, and actors pause while the audience's laughter (or a laugh track, also known as "canned laughter") makes clear whether a joke is merely amusing or full-on hilarious. Plots follow the "hilarity ensues . . ." format of setting up ill-advised schemes or comical misunderstandings that resolve in lessons learned. Music is reserved for credit sequences, transitions, montages, and laugh-free message moments, as when on *Happy Days* Howard or, later, Fonzie, would offer Richie one of his wise lessons. This basic sitcom structure has always been good at showcasing both verbal and physical comedy and it encourages a broad, theatrical performance style characterized by pronounced gestures and facial expressions, and loud, distinctive, and even obnoxious voices. Both the writing and performance style of the multi-camera show emphasize bold doorway character entrances and exits, and the live audience further commands our attention to these moments when they applaud and cheer characters notable for their signature appearances, like Kramer bursting through Jerry Seinfeld's apartment door. The multi-camera style has a venerable history closely associated with the comic artists whose talents it has foregrounded, from Lucille Ball and Jackie Gleason to Roseanne Barr and Bill Cosby.

Single-camera shows, by contrast, are staged and shot quite differently. Many shows of the 1960s were shot this way, allowing for special effects in *The Munsters*, *The Addams Family*, *Bewitched*, and *I Dream of Jeannie*, and for portraying the exotic setting effectively in *Gilligan's Island*. But, by comparison to more recent single-camera shows, the programs of previous decades are relatively restrained stylistically, at least in terms of staging and editing; newer shows tend to have

FIGURE 4.2 By contrast to the more traditional *All in the Family* style, the new single-camera shows like *Malcolm in the Middle* frame characters from a closer distance in more shadowy lighting, using dramatic angles and, in this case, a convention-defying glance at the camera

more aggressive and frantic use of sound and image (Figure 4.2). But whether more conventional or more adventurous, single-camera shows have no implicit proscenium, and the camera may be placed in many positions, such as high and close angles, where it would not go in a typical multi-cam shoot.

The single-camera style also includes no audible live audience. Old single-camera shows used a laugh track, but this is exceedingly rare in the more recent wave of shows. New single-camera programs typically use camerawork and editing much more prominently than multi-cam shows, often as sources of humor as in their frequent flashback or fantasy shots, or as tone-setting techniques in *verité*-inspired shows like *Arrested Development*. Mockumentary sitcom cinematography often includes noticeably jerky zooming, reframing, or refocusing, which calls attention to itself as a mark of authenticity. Like conventional feature filmmaking (as well as television dramas and movies), the single camera can penetrate the space of the scene and shoot from any angle. Shots are set up one at a time even if "single-cam" productions employ more than one camera (*Arrested Development*, for instance, used two), which allows for more depth, contour, and contrast in lighting, though comedies are shot more high-key than dramas whether for theatrical features or for TV.

Distinguishing themselves from those comedies with laugh tracks, many single-camera shows prominently use music or sound effects to punctuate scenes and transitions and establish a comical tone, as in the folky strumming of *Arrested Development*, the jazzy woodwinds and brushed drums of *30 Rock*, and the aggressive snare fills and electronic whooshes on *Scrubs*. An episode of *30 Rock* ("Black Light Attack!" originally aired January 14, 2010) uses overly dramatic music ironically, with minor-key low-pitch brass instruments indicating danger and fear to mock the exceptionally vain character Jenna Maroney when she discovers she has been cast in the role of a mother. *My Name is Earl* uses considerable scoring for a sitcom, mainly bluesy rock to establish the "redneck" character and setting, with occasional stings of Jew's harp, harmonica, slide guitar, and other appropriate instruments to punctuate humorous lines and scene transitions. Many single-camera shows use a voice-over, often in some register of irony as in *Arrested Development*'s Ron Howard deadpan readings, or in *Everybody Hates Chris* as a central source of humor in Chris Rock's standup-style narration. In both of these shows, the soundtrack highlights the contrast between the straight and the comical, with dramatic tones in tension with those of the spoken narration. In *Arrested,* the dramatic tone is much broader than the matter-of-fact style of the voice-over, while in *Chris*, it's the drama played straight while the narration pushes the comedy. By contrast, *Sex and the City*, *Scrubs*, and *Malcolm in the Middle* use a sincere character-narrator establishing a sympathetic guide to an often wacky narrative world in which secondary characters are drawn much more broadly than the protagonist. These various sound practices generally function consistently in two ways: to differentiate this newer style from the familiar chuckles and guffaws of the multi-cam soundtrack, and to support and emphasize the comical elements of the narrative. Even in shows that avoid aggressive sound tricks, the functions of their sound practice are evident. For instance, *The Office* and *Parks and Recreation*, working in a faux-documentary style, make comical use of "realistic" awkward silences to achieve an understated, knowing tone.

In place of a theatrical performance aesthetic with longish scenes, entrances and exits, and scene-ending dramatic reactions (picture Jack Tripper's expression as we cut to a commercial on *Three's Company*), we find many very short scenes. An act of *All in the Family* might play out in uninterrupted real time in the Bunker living room as a single scene, but today's sitcoms cram numerous shifts in place and time into a typical commercial-to-commercial act. Many single-camera shows offer frequent cuts to absurd visual jokes offered as characters' wild fantasies, miniature parodies, or preposterous flashbacks and flashforwards. For instance, *30 Rock* frequently shows us quick, embarrassing hits of Liz Lemon and Tracy Morgan in their earlier years (Figures 4.3 and 4.4), and often travesties television conventions through clips of fictitious programs like *MILF Island*, *Dealbreakers*, and *The Hot Box with Avery Jessup* (Figure 4.5), which are effective not only for establishing a hyper-inventive, allusive comical style but also for repurposing as promotional web videos. *Scrubs* makes regular use of absurd

FIGURE 4.3 Tracy Jordan reminisces about his novelty party hit and viral sensation, "Werewolf Bar Mitzvah," in "Jack Gets in the Game," *30 Rock*, NBC, October 11, 2007

fantasy moments taking us inside J.D.'s over-imaginative mind. In place of setup alternating with punchline, every bit of dialogue can be meant to be funny and the absence of a laugh track means no pause is needed between jokes. The laughs-per-minute tally can be amped up and up, like virtually everything else in the style of contemporary media: faster, more impact, more energy. It used to be enough to be incisively funny; in the new single-camera style, it's often necessary to be outrageous. Once *The Simpsons*, a cartoon, had become the *ne plus ultra* of contemporary comedy, many live-action shows started to seem more like cartoons, defying the conventional sitcom's limitations in space and time. Creators of live-action comedies recognize that the style of *The Simpsons* is in some ways the same as shows like *The Office*: shifting visual perspectives, no laugh track. Greg Daniels, creator of the American version of *The Office*, notes that, by using a single camera and no laugh track, his show has the same basic style as an animated program's.[8] *South Park*, *The Family Guy*, and Comedy Central's stable of programs have continued to push at the limits of edgy television comedy while working in this format.

Single-camera sitcoms employ other means of distinction, as well. Some defy the laughs-per-minute formula in the other direction, preferring to be smart and observant rather than depend on never-ending streams of jokes and gags. *The Larry Sanders Show* pioneered this mode of TV comedy, using dry, dark humor that flatters its audience by not making jokes too obvious, and amuses in part by making viewers feel uncomfortable. The British and American versions of

FIGURE 4.4 A teenage Liz Lemon flubs a field goal, raises her arms skyward, and cries, "Yeah, feminism!" enjoying her victory in the law suit that allowed her to play high school football. This flashback in time was inserted into "Ludachristmas," *30 Rock*, NBC, December 13, 2007

FIGURE 4.5 *The Hot Box with Avery Jessup*, a parody of cable news channel style, introduces Jack Donaghy's new girlfriend in "Anna Howard Shaw Day," *30 Rock*, NBC, February 11, 2010

The Office as well as *Curb Your Enthusiasm* work in this tradition, and in their own ways so too do *Sex and the City*, *Weeds*, *Entourage*, *The United States of Tara*, and other premium cable comedies (aside from the failed *Lucky Louie*, all of Showtime's and HBO's comedies have been single-cams). If *The Simpsons* pushed manic shows like *Scrubs* to cram more jokes in each segment, to find more visual sources of comedy, and to show off their comical inventiveness, the looser-style *Larry Sanders* and its progeny have nudged the sitcom in the opposite direction, toward more dramatic, wry, understated forms of humor.

Premium cable comedies are also key texts in the other major innovation in the past decade of sitcoms: serialization. Most of these single-camera shows have in common with many TV dramas that they tell arcing stories that stretch across episodes and seasons, and this trend has suffused many formally traditional sitcoms too, the shows like *Friends*. All of these arc sitcoms shift some of the emphasis away from the comic situation and onto the characters' ongoing romantic entanglements, and in doing so also shift the narrative emphasis to some degree against traditional, episodic sitcom storytelling. By shedding the total reset convention of earlier sitcoms, more serialized shows inch closer in their narrative format to primetime dramas, which are of course among the most legitimated of contemporary programming. A key historical text in this shift is *Cheers*, which threaded its will-they-or-won't-they romance arc through several seasons of Sam and Diane's tempestuous relationship, including a much-publicized season-ending cliffhanger. At a time when serial primetime storytelling was gaining legitimacy, the sitcom's efforts to integrate ongoing stories mark a significant departure and potentially function as an "improvement" on the implausible formula requiring a kind of character amnesia whereby events of one week's episodes are seemingly forgotten the next week. The combination of sitcom and serial story formats also adds the influence of romantic comedy to the formal mix, and in particular the screwball comedies of classical Hollywood.

Within the single-camera shows we can identify a number of overlapping but distinctive trends. *Arrested Development*, *The Office*, and *Modern Family* exemplify a style that Brett Mills and Ethan Thompson have analyzed as "comedy vérité," hybrids in some sense of sitcoms and reality shows or documentaries, borrowing the visual vocabulary of observational non-fiction and merging it with the fictional storytelling conventions of half-hour comedy.[9] Other shows like *Scrubs* and *My Name is Earl* have a more cartoonish visual style (Figure 4.6), indebted to movies like *Raising Arizona*, which shoot live-action but in an exaggerated comical vein both aggressively visual, with inventive and attention-seeking use of short lenses, high and low angles, and mobile camera (Figures 4.7 and 4.8), and aural, with often goofy or broad applications of scoring—music begging for notice.

Both the reality TV-inspired comedy *vérité* style and the live-action cartoon offer new forms of high-energy comical outrageousness, which comes as a contrast to the familiar rhythms, imagery, and sounds of the 30-minute comedy format. A final trend, the understated dramatic comedy in the *Larry Sanders* vein, is by contrast more laconic and witty than the broad, crowd-pleasing network sitcom. Whatever the style, new single-camera shows have sought to expand the range of stylistic and narrative options available to American television comedy and thereby position themselves as an upgrade on this familiar form.

"Like a Movie"

In explaining the distinction between traditional and new sitcom styles, the most frequently employed analogy is to feature filmmaking. While many Hollywood films actually do shoot with multiple cameras (like many "single-camera" comedies on TV), with the possible exception of films made during the early days of sync sound in the late 1920s and early 1930s, it's hard to think of any feature films that use the multiple-camera proscenium schema, and the aural presence of a studio audience in the form of a laugh track would be quite jarring in a movie. Discursively, the distance between Hollywood film practice and traditional sitcom practice is ripe for exploiting when the new single-camera style is offered as an upgrade. The cultural status of film vis-à-vis television adds cachet to the new sitcom style when its characteristics are understood as cinematic, and thus anti-televisual.

Invariably in descriptions of single-camera shows, cast members, producers, network executives, and journalists explain the style as being "like a movie": each shot has its own setup and the shooting schedule is thus longer and in some ways

FIGURE 4.6 Earl framed from a low angle for comical effect, capturing his exaggerated facial expression, a style *My Name is Earl* owes to animation and outrageous film comedies like *Raising Arizona*

FIGURES 4.7 AND 4.8 *My Name is Earl* uses visual effects and a camera free to occupy any space in the scene to create absurd comical situations, as when a champagne cork flies across a garden party to strike Earl in the eye. When we see Earl's reaction, it is from a bird's-eye view

more challenging.[10] Rather than several days of off-camera read-throughs and rehearsals followed by an evening of filming or taping before the live audience, an episode of a single-camera show might shoot over five long days in which dozens of setups are filmed, which is reminiscent to craft professionals and actors of feature film practice. Greg Garcia, the creator of *My Name is Earl*, believes that this pays off in aesthetic terms: "We try to give it a look that feels more like an independent feature film. To the extent that we're successful doing that, it feels like a movie rather than a TV show." Jason Lee, the show's star, describes his thought process in deciding whether or not to appear in the show in terms of a clear hierarchy of value, placing movies above TV:

> It's TV, TV can be pretty corny, and this is something that I would see in a film if done right . . . how much can you take a show that's going to be on mainstream network television and make it feel like a movie?[11]

Creators of *Arrested Development* likewise analogize their production practices to those of legitimated forms of cinema. Mitchell Hurwitz described the production having "an independent filmmaker guerilla mentality" as a product of the show's frequent directors, Joe and Anthony Russo, having come from the world of indie cinema.[12] Several of the series' creative team have insisted that the show's style was meant to be unlike familiar television comedy formats. On the pilot episode's DVD commentary track, one of the Russo brothers claims that they intended to avoid having the show look like television, and to break the mold of traditional comedy. In a behind-the-scenes feature, Jason Bateman, the show's star, distinguishes the series against the "multi-camera family hi-jinksy crap" he had previously done on television. Ron Howard, referring to the innovative dimension of incorporating reality TV or documentary style into half-hour comedy, explains:

> I kept watching television and it just occurred to me that you could use that new style, that grammar, to create a different kind of situation comedy that would be packed with more jokes, more funny situations, and a less traditional feel than you get with a normal half-hour sitcom.[13]

Making clear that the single-camera style is not merely an alternative to the traditional sitcom but a rejection of its premises, Greg Garcia says, "It's a comedy that comes out of character and not out of a set-up and a punchline."[14] In an episode of the Trio cable channel's *Brilliant But Cancelled* series dedicated to the short-lived Fox sitcom *Andy Richter Controls the Universe*, the network executive who championed the series observes that when you shoot "like a movie," you can use music to punctuate and give form to the comical progression of the storytelling, replacing the laugh track in performing that function and upgrading the aesthetic to make for innovative and edgy programming. A writer for the show praises the single-cam format for opening up the possibility of using editing as a comical device, as when fantastical images from Andy's wild imagination would be inserted into scenes. Suzanne Martin, a writer-producer who has worked in both multi-cam and single-cam styles, notes new possibilities opened up by single-camera production: "You can get more into the characters' heads. You can use voice-overs. You can have scenes where dialogue can be a little more natural and not necessarily punctuated by a joke."[15] Using editing and music to signal humor is deemed more cinematic than using verbal jokes and pratfalls, and perhaps the stylistic departure most welcome within the discourse of upscaling television is the absence of a laugh track. The explanation for this is always put in terms of respect for the audience, which is complimented for being smart enough not to need to be told when to laugh.[16]

The stylistic influences on the single-camera sitcom are multiple and various, but in enumerating them, champions of the style generally avoid naming the traditional sitcom or anything associated with it. The cartoonish style of a show like *Earl* owes much to animated TV comedies, but Garcia emphasizes his debt to the Coen brothers' bold visuals and outlandish situations.[17] The multigenerational dysfunctional family situation of *Arrested Development* is similar to that of *The Royal Tenenbaums*, a title named in the DVD making-of feature. The observational mockumentary style of *The Office* and *Modern Family* recalls Direct Cinema as well as films like *This is Spinal Tap* and *Zelig*. Reality TV is another influence, though we might see these shows lampooning the conventions of reality and documentary programming, as Brett Mills argues, challenging the authoritative discourse of non-fiction media.[18] The more understated dramatic style of many of the premium cable shows positions them discursively alongside the prestige programming of the same channels' dramas, as well as the feature films which are still those channels' bread and butter. Some critics have also noted literary affinities for the single-cam style, such as one *New York Times* columnist who likened the digressive cut-away humor of *30 Rock* and its ilk to the postmodern metafiction of Pynchon, Coover, and Barth.[19] Whatever the actual influences on these single-camera shows, those most often highlighted in industrial and critical discourse are those that boost the sitcom's respectability and distance the genre from its roots in a theatrical television style of which the laugh track and the three-wall set are remnants. Quality TV has shifted far from the theatrical conception of the first few decades of television comedy; in sitcoms of the era of convergence, anything too reminiscent of live performance is a challenge to legitimation and is thus strongly refused.

Class vs. Mass: Costs and Benefits of Upscaling

For all of the single-camera style's appeals, its perceived edgy or sophisticated qualities may also be the obstacle to these shows breaking through to become as commercially successful as earlier generations of beloved sitcoms. *Two and a Half Men* and *The Big Bang Theory*, traditional multi-camera shows, have been hits for CBS in the late 2000s and early 2010s, but no single-camera program has approached their ratings and many of the more aestheticized and critically admired shows, from *Andy Richter* to *Parks and Recreation*, have struggled to find audiences impressive enough to make for a highly successful network run. Since this single-camera production cycle began in the early 2000s, TV comedies winning accolades and awards tend to be the single-camera shows, including premium cable programs. Since 1999, in addition to *Ally McBeal*, a number of single-camera shows have won the outstanding comedy Emmy, such as *Sex and the City*, *Arrested Development*, *The Office*, and *30 Rock*. But these achievements have not translated into Nielsen ratings anywhere near those of bona fide network hits like *American Idol* and *CSI*, and some single-camera shows languish with very low ratings even as they get glowing reviews and find passionate niche followings. The cancellation of *Arrested Development* despite its numerous accolades and its cult status was a sign that the vanguard of TV comedy would be at odds with the economic logic of network programming, and that the aesthetic value of an innovative program could be measured by the mass audience's rejection of it. The upscaling of the situation comedy form through stylistic innovation is matched by the upscaling of the sitcom audience from "mass" to "class."

The single-camera sitcom thus appears to be a more narrowcast format compared with traditional sitcoms of the network era and into the early 2000s, which appealed as widely as possible, functioning as a common popular culture. The largest audiences do not follow the new comedy style, but critics and affluent viewers—those most likely to be viewing using DVRs, DVDs, iTunes, and other new convergence technologies—elevate them above the old-fashioned multi-cam style aesthetically by identifying them as having sophisticated and cinematic qualities. Industry professionals believe that critics tend to favor single-camera shows because of their preference for the sophisticated; their role demands discernment and fashionable taste. It is arguably harder for a multi-camera pilot to get a positive review. According to TV industry conventional wisdom, audiences are not likely to be paying much attention to stylistic difference between traditional and new sitcom styles—the proverbial average viewer does not categorize shows according to how many cameras are used—and yet large audiences still seem more likely to find the traditional style appealing. The single-camera shows are constructed within contextual discourses as edgy and smart, but as *Variety* reported in 2007, "edgy may find critics, but it often struggles to build an [audience] of significant size."[20] A similar distinction between multi-camera shows as primitive and single-camera shows as vanguard obtains in the creative side of the industry, as cinematographers, directors, and many actors claim to prefer shooting "like a movie." For the cinematographers, single-camera shooting allows for more careful lighting and allows them to avoid the flat, even illumination that multi-camera shooting demands.[21] The look of a single-camera comedy is typically still bright, colorful, even cartoonish, but the possibilities of expression in this style appeal more to the aspirations of craft professionals whose identities depend on displaying technical skill and artistry.

The broadcast networks thus face a challenge in programming and marketing single-camera comedies, hoping at once to appeal broadly in network prime time and to find favor with critics and upscale segments of the audience as well as to satisfy the aspirations of creative workers. On the occasion of *My Name is Earl*'s debut in 2005, NBC struggled to play the show two ways, as an adventurous and creative comedy in the same vein as the much admired *Arrested Development*, but also as a warm, crowd-pleasing sitcom capable of wide appeal. In presenting the show to critics, Kevin Reilly, the network president, described *Earl* as a "redneck show that was also upscale."[22] Wary that a "quirky" show too much like *Arrested Development* would turn off the desirable mass audience that NBC still hoped would find its most recent modest single-cam success, *The Office*, Reilly insisted that *Earl* would connect with ordinary viewers but understood the challenge of satisfying many constituencies. "You hear from the audience that they want something more than 'stupid' sitcoms. The young audience wants different form-breakers, but it's hard to get a mass-appeal show that breaks the form too much."[23] The dichotomous status of the single-camera style, caught between the old ideas of television as the least objectionable programming for the largest possible and thus unsophisticated audience and the new narrowcast appeals of a convergence-era medium, makes clear that the social positioning of the audience figures strongly into the construction of aesthetic categories and their uses.

This has been especially evident in the reception of the CBS hits of creator and showrunner Chuck Lorre, in particular *Two and a Half Men* and *The Big Bang Theory* (Lorre's earlier work includes *Grace Under Fire* and *Dharma & Greg*). With its familiar multi-camera style and low humor often centered on sexual jokes and gags, *Two and a Half Men* has come to epitomize the mass/class divide in American television. At a time when few comedies are hits, it is the most watched sitcom on television. The show is also widely despised by elites, whose distaste for it—however authentically felt—effectively marks their social and cultural positioning. Its network, CBS, seems comfortable with its reputation as the safest and stodgiest of the networks in its programming strategies, content to have old-skewing, generic programming as long as its ratings are favorable.[24] The show's reputation among fans of Quality TV as more or less unwatchable tripe is a stark contrast against its embrace by the largest audience for comedy on television. As one emblem of this division, consider the comment given by the actress Lizzy Caplan of the cult favorite *Party Down*, a comedy that aired for two seasons on the premium cable channel Starz in 2009 and 2010, upon the program's cancellation:

> Our fans . . . were exactly the type of people we were hoping to impress: smart and vocal and funny and almost snobby about their comedy preferences. You look at hugely rated shows like *Two and a Half Men* that get like a gazillion viewers—I have the sneaking suspicion that not one of them watches *Party Down*. I think if a girl who liked *Party Down* found out that her boyfriend liked *Two and a Half Men*, she would break up with him. I wish we could have reached a larger audience, because more people would have seen it and we might still be on, but it always sort of felt like the appeal for our fans was that the show felt like it was theirs. It belonged to them, and they discovered it, and they told their circles of friends. It was like a secret club of people in the know.[25]

A similar notion surfaces in a blog called *Essays on Sucking* that riffs on a *New Yorker* profile of Chuck Lorre published in 2010. The *New Yorker* profile presents Lorre as a naturally talented comical populist with a special gift for making retrograde TV for mass audiences, the sort of people assumed not to read *The New Yorker*.[26] The blogger, eschewing the polite tone of the highbrow magazine, insults Lorre by referring to him as a hack and comparing his work to unhealthy and cheap fast food and top 40 radio. *Two and a Half Men* is "a program for people who want to watch television but don't care what they want." *Two and a Half Men* is contrasted unfavorably with supposedly more worthwhile and intelligent shows such as *Community* and *Arrested Development*, which "inspire love" by having "emotional depth."[27] To an extent, in these discourses Lorre and his hit show are merely synechdoches for the traditional sitcom, but they also function as a central example for champions of the single-camera style, an easy shorthand for the form of sitcom that appeals broadly but without the aspirations to higher cultural value more typical of the upscale versions of television comedy.

Sitcom Distinction in Practice: Soundtrack Negotiations

The significance of the single-camera style as a model for newly legitimated, "classy" TV comedy is crystallized especially in discussions of the most loathed convention of the traditional multi-cam style: the audience's audible laughter. The dichotomous discourse surrounding convergence-era sitcoms seizes on the laugh track as the epitome of the multi-cam style's poverty, which is tied to its appeal to a lowest-common-denominator audience. Single-camera comedies understood to shoot "like a movie" avoid the laugh track not only to explore the comedic use of voice-over, music, and sound effects, but also to follow the style of feature films, which include no audible audience sounds. The avoidance of the laugh track in single-camera shows is seen as a sign of respect for the audience's intellect, judgment, and sense of humor. A highbrow critic like *The New Yorker*'s Nancy Franklin might liken the laugh track to a cattle prod, dehumanizing the audience for unfashionable shows like *Two and a Half Men* that continue its use, and blaming television producers for insulting their consumers.[28] Chuck Klosterman, an essayist and intellectual pop culture commentator, describes the laugh track as "incredibly idiotic" and adds that "It's pretty clear all the sophisticated situation comedies are dropping the laugh track."[29] TV fans participating in online discussions routinely disparage the laugh track as beneath them. An emblematic statement by Ser Greguh in a thread entitled "Single Cam vs. Multi Cam: Fad or Television Revolution" on the Entertainment forum of the site A Song of Ice and Fire reads: "I can only hope I live to see the day where [sic] laugh tracks are fully and completely obliterated from the face of television."[30] Implicit in all such discussions is contempt for the traditional sitcom audience's taste, and for the television industry for pandering to it. Also implicit is the suspicion that recorded laughter is likely to be inauthentic, an insecurity felt by broadcast audiences since the days of radio. Uncertainty and suspicion of undue artifice and manipulation have marked discourses surrounding the sound of laughter on television since the 1950s, when it was often intended to unite the fragmented television audience as one community.[31]

Journalists and television industry workers alike typically refer to the lack of a laugh track as among the first traits of the single-camera style when describing it, telling us that this is among its essential characteristics. Categorization works not only by inclusion of some traits, but also by negation of others; central to the single-camera style is its negation of the traditional TV comedy soundtrack, in which an audible audience figures so prominently. The audience's laughter, which Brett Mills calls "the convention which has traditionally most simply and effectively defined the [sitcom] genre,"[32] now defines not the sitcom *per se* but just the old style, and by virtue of that also defines the new style through its absence. Sometimes this creates clashing expectations and textual conventions, as in the case of shows whose laugh tracks might seem at odds with their aspirations to legitimated status.

Admirers of the Quality TV, cult favorite *Gilmore Girls* were largely disappointed by Amy Sherman-Palladino's subsequent effort, *The Return of Jezebel James*, a multi-cam sitcom starring Parker Posey and Lauren Ambrose that ran for three episodes before it was pulled. When a few scenes were posted online in the spring of 2007, many months before the show's debut, reactions were harshly negative. One article, posted at *The Onion A.V. Club*, carried the headline, "Parker Posey Gets the Laugh Track She Never Wanted."[33] A write-up at the website film.com found the pilot episode hugely disappointing:

> So why doesn't *The Return of Jezebel James* work? For one thing, it's mostly shot as a multi-camera traditional sitcom, complete with an obnoxious and off-putting laugh track that literally makes you not want to laugh; it's disconcerting and awkward and doesn't match at all with the sort of smooth dialogue and character interplay that would be much more at home in a single-camera comedy.[34]

When the series finally debuted in March 2008, reviews were likewise scathing and ratings were low. Among its most despised aspects was the sound of audible laughter from its studio audience, which the critic for the *New York Times* compared to peanut butter on pizza.[35] It was the show's misfortune to have arrived at a moment in television history when most of the comedies seen as aesthetically advanced had abandoned the audience laughter that had been part of the sitcom format since radio days.

Jezebel James was attempting to fit into the old-style set of conventions that had worked so well for classics like *Cheers*, which Amy Sherman-Palladino named as an influence on her show.[36] But by 2007 and 2008, these had become too familiar, especially after having seen them so effectively defamiliarized by a new generation of television comedies appealing to smaller but more upscale audiences. In many ways *Jezebel James* came across as aiming for aesthetic sophistication. It was a product of the same creators who had made the beloved screwball *Gilmore Girls*, renowned for its erudite and referential dialogue and engaging, fully human characters. *Gilmore Girls* had become many viewers' favorite, and expectations were thus high for its successor, which mimicked the *Gilmore* fast-paced, culturally literate verbal style. The casting of Lauren Ambrose, veteran of HBO's family melodrama *Six Feet Under*, and Parker Posey, identified so much with indie cinema, suggested that *Jezebel James* would be highbrow TV. The associations the creative team's previous work evoked would not seem to jibe with the conventions of the traditional sitcom, a genre so wanting in cultural legitimacy. It would be unfair and shortsighted to peg the failure of *The Return of Jezebel James* squarely on its soundtrack, but the discourses surrounding the show's style make clear that the sound of the audience's laughter was a point of significant dissent for the creators and audience of the show, and that this dissent centered around matters of taste and cultural status.

Another telling episode in the popular understanding of sitcom style began in January 2010, when YouTube user internettoday posted a 43-second clip of *The Big Bang Theory* with its laugh track edited out. This video was viewed more than 600,000 times in its first half-year online and discussed widely in blogs, forums, and other sites of online social media.[37] *The Big Bang Theory* is a significant show to figure in discussions of television style and cultural status, given its address to "geek" audiences—young, male, and technologically adept. In terms of gender and class, this audience is likely to appreciate legitimated forms of television and to participate in the taste culture of television's upscaling. At the same time, it is a CBS multi-cam comedy created by Chuck Lorre, sharing many of the same stylistic and comedic qualities as *Two and a Half Men*. This positions the show as caught in between the mass and class positions sketched so far. The responses to this video were something of a Rorschach test, revealing many divergent attitudes about comedy style, as well as this show in particular. The absence of laughter functions to interpolate awkward silent pauses after each punchline, which the *Vulture* blog described as a surreal effect.[38] Some commenters on the video on YouTube interpreted the video to reveal the show's lack of humor ("and now you realize that this show isn't funny its [*sic*] just the audiences [*sic*] laughter triggering a response"[39]), while others found it to be a commentary on the laugh track itself ("laugh track is for retards that don't know when to laugh"[40]). A commenter on the *Geekologie* site responded sarcastically, "i for one am a goddamn moron and like to be reminded when something is funny."[41] The frequent use of insulting terms to disparage the intellect of the traditional sitcom's audience speaks clearly to the loaded politics of sound style in these shows. Many YouTube commenters admiring of *The Big Bang Theory* pointed out that, as a show filmed in front of a live audience, the laughter is authentic rather than fake, insisting that "laugh track" is the wrong term to describe the show's sound style and suggesting that the audience is not being told when to find the show funny. In these defensive comments, the status of the laugh track as a cheap device to manipulate a credulous audience must be challenged to maintain the legitimacy of viewer taste for a questionable format of programming. In comments at many sites, comparisons to *Scrubs*, *The Office*, *30 Rock*, and other single-camera shows abound, and unvaryingly these are held up as standards of more taste-appropriate sitcoms. The discussion surrounding this brief viral video, like the reception of *The Return of Jezebel James* a few years earlier, makes clear that the negotiation of meaning around shifting TV comedy styles produces clear distinctions between formats of programming. These align with social distinctions: the upscaling of television programming legitimates the audience for culturally upgraded shows no less than it does the programs themselves.

Audience Fragmentation, Aesthetic Progress, and the Revaluation of the Sitcom

Changes in television comedy offer another example of the interconnection of textual and contextual appeals in the process of determining cultural value. Production, promotion, and reception discourses feed into one another such that the cultural implications of the sitcom text can hardly be understood without grappling with qualities of surrounding discourses. These changes in television comedy also remind us that constructions of progress in the realm of aesthetics, no less than in the realm of technology, tend to serve the interests of those who profit from change, such as cultural elites whose tastes are affirmed when new styles and fashions can be distinguished against old ones. Progress cannot be appreciated naively as steps forward, as improvements, moving us toward better and better forms and experiences. Formal changes are always to some extent responses to social, economic, and technological conditions, and the rise of the single-camera style in the convergence era is not merely the evolution of the sitcom. We must see it, rather, as the development of a niche subgenre within the broader category of situation comedy to serve certain audiences. The narrowcasting economics of the television industry and the needs of social groups for culture to mark their distinction explain the rise of the new style better than the idea of natural progress. Thus the transition in the media industries toward targeting narrower and more fragmented target markets is essential background for understanding shifts in textual forms of convergence-era television. It is certainly at play in the distinction between CBS's more "mass" and NBC's more "class" offerings, as CBS and NBC pursue divergent strategies and conceptualize the value of the audience differently, with CBS taking a more traditional strategy. NBC's attempt to win over the segment of the audience it hopes will be most desirable to advertisers, which is a young and affluent demographic, has led it to prefer the "edgy" style understood as aesthetically advanced, but which has not scored the biggest sitcom hits for the network in the later 2000s and early 2010s.

At the same time, as part of this same audience fragmentation, the market for original television comedies has expanded beyond the broadcast networks to basic cable. Disney Channel original shows aimed in particular at tweens, and tween girls especially, such as *That's So Raven*, *The Suite Life of Zack and Cody*, *Hannah Montana*, *Wizards of Waverly Place*, and *Sonny with a Chance*, are ultra-traditional multi-cam comedies, created by some of the same personnel as worked on 1980s network comedies like *Who's the Boss?* and *Diff'rent Strokes*. Some Disney shows like *Lizzie McGuire* and *Jonas L.A.* have been single-camera, as are some other tween comedies like Nickelodeon's *Zoey 101*. But the "teen sitcom" subgenre has tended to be stylistically quite conservative, following *Saved by the Bell* and *Saved by the Bell: The New Class*, fixtures of NBC's Saturday morning lineup in the 1990s. As the traditional sitcom comes to be associated with less legitimated audience segments (young and female viewers), the legitimacy of the prime time single-camera show is reaffirmed. Similarly, in the early 2010s, basic cable channels such as TV Land and CMT have begun to program "broad-appeal," original, multi-camera comedies aimed for older adults (they say 40–50 years old) less served by network fare.[42] *Hot in Cleveland* and other shows in this vein likewise degrade the aestheticized appeal of the traditional sitcom by associating it with a culturally less valued audience. The original CMT sitcom *Working Class*, which debuted in 2011, makes clear the association between audience and aesthetics. In its first episode, the show's lead character, a single mom, jokes about the customers at the fancy grocery store where she works buying pastries for their pets while she cannot afford milk and cereal to feed her children. These "working-class" characters and humor are central to its appeal as a folksy show on a channel whose identity is still connected to its original format of airing country music videos. In all of these examples, the way the media industries have made room for the young and affluent adult demographic to appreciate the new form of sitcom functions ideologically, according to distinctions of age, gender, and class.

As with so many of the sites of television's legitimation, the cinematized single-camera sitcom is invested with value by differing from a past ideal of television, one associated with the period before convergence. This ideal is of television made for a broad audience, an audience made up of viewers less highly valued than those addressed by legitimated programming and technologies. Television and the sitcom are upgraded by being unlike television, or by being better than television, or by being a new conception of television to replace the old one. The multi-camera comedy is not just one style of TV, but in some sense it is *the* emblematic genre of the traditional small screen, one unique to television, incredibly familiar to anyone who has spent a lifetime being entertained by TV. By relegating this kind of show to the past, or to the realm of the juvenile, feminine, or *passé*, the culture of television's legitimation seeks a new identity for the medium.

5

NOT A SOAP OPERA

In the same way that men are often concerned to show that what they are, above all, is not women, not "feminine," so television programs and movies will, surprisingly often, tell us that they are not soap operas.

Tania Modleski[1]

No form of television programming has been more celebrated in the era of media convergence than prime time serials, which occupy a primary site where discourses of distinction circulate. Such programs are valued most highly of all forms and genres of television in industry, popular press, and fan discourses alike. The last time a strictly episodic or procedural drama won the Emmy Award for best dramatic series was in 1997, when *Law & Order* took home the statue. Since *Hill Street Blues'* first win in 1981, each year but one the Emmy-winning drama has had at least some significant serial elements. Popular press writers routinely highlight serialized programming as television's best. *Entertainment Weekly* points to the "rebirth" of the "art of serialized drama" in the past decade as evidence of television's aesthetic renewal.[2] The canon of cult TV favorites of recent years is made up largely of serialized primetime dramas like *Buffy the Vampire Slayer* and *Lost*, which invite immersive and passionate engagement, spin off transmedia adaptations, and sell well on DVD. The reputation of HBO's original programming as upscale and artistic rests on the appeal of the long-form storytelling of its hits and critical favorites, such as *Sex and the City*, *The Sopranos*, and *The Wire*. Original premium cable series have accrued more prestige than other programming in the convergence era, and the form, style, and thematics of these shows are widely imitated in basic cable and network shows seeking distinction.

Intellectual culture seizes on serials as the most artistically advanced form of television, as in this statement in the highbrow journal *n+1* charting the fortunes of TV narrative following *Hill Street*: "Through serialization, a medium of popular entertainment became a medium of popular Art."[3] While discourses elevating the serial might acknowledge the tricky economics of such television fare, which can be a challenge to sell in syndication, this can be constructed as an unfortunate reality against which the best of television struggles to flourish. Since the 1980s, as we have seen, any highbrow brief for television's artistic respectability has made long-form, novelistic storytelling central to claims of legitimacy. Taking a broad narrative scope and parceling out storytelling in regular installments function to elevate television above its historical status as intellectually worthless mass culture.

Within production circles, serials and episodic programs are not merely a pair of equal options; they have distinct ideological characteristics tied to conceptions of the television audience in terms of its presumed passivity and activity. Episodic crime shows are seen as less demanding of the audience, which might tune in only once in a while, while serials are seen as more engaging, addressing a committed and passionate viewer who likes to see every episode in order and invests more emotionally in the ongoing narrative. The appeal of procedurals, speaking generally, has more connotations of mass audiences viewing in a casual, distracted mode, while serials might be more likely to find upscale, active, and fan audiences.[4] As FX president John Landgraf has said of the serialized programs on his channel, "We can't just do case-of-the-week stuff . . . We have to make more adult, more original, more idiosyncratic, higher-risk, edgier shows," thereby aligning the serialized (or at least the non-episodic) with the adult, original and edgy.[5] The recurrence of terms such as "original," "edgy," "complex," and "sophisticated" in such discourse functions to privilege serialized storytelling above other kinds of TV narrative. This rhetoric flatters the audience for serials and slights the audience for procedurals even as many shows—at varying levels of prestige—strive to balance appeals to both kinds of viewer by weaving episodic and serial narratives artfully together.

Despite the excitement over the value of serialization, this discourse rarely makes positive reference to the television genre that pioneered serialized narrative and which has perpetuated it to this day: the daytime soap opera. This is a highly significant omission given the centrality of serialization to historical conceptions of feminized popular culture, and the centrality of feminized qualities in constructions of pre-convergence television as mass culture. When soap opera is mentioned in reference to primetime serials, it is typically done in one of two ways. Soaps might be introduced quickly but dismissively, as a brief acknowledgement that serialization has existed on TV for many years. Or a reference to daytime drama can be made as a way of establishing relative value, as another means to distinguish good TV from bad. A negative review of *Mad Men* published in the *New York Review of Books* in 2011 calls the show a soap opera as a term of cutting derision, going on to explain that its storytelling is melodramatic rather than dramatic and arguing for its lack of aesthetic worth on these grounds.[6] The soaps' longstanding association with the feminine is central to such distinctions, for much of what gets praised about prime time seriality is framed in masculinist terms that work to distance such programming from its feminized other. Differentiating the artistically legitimated prime time serialized programming from soap opera is a chief means of establishing that legitimation.

Although such distinctions are at the heart of convergence-era legitimation discourses, daytime soap opera and prime time drama have a long, intertwined history. Since the 1950s, serialized narration has appeared in American prime time, its intermittent presence hinting at its unstable status. We begin here with a sketch of this history to illustrate the checkered path that prime time serialization has taken toward legitimation and the myriad ways in which prime time drama has been compared to soap opera throughout its existence. This history demonstrates that the serialized narration in convergence-era TV is not as new or revolutionary as it is often made out to be. From there, we examine the three key strategies of distinction that differentiate the legitimated prime time serials from soap opera, primarily as manifested in the programs themselves, as well as in the extra-textual discourses that accord them their high status. By placing immense importance on endings, by constraining their degree of seriality, and by distancing themselves from "soapy," feminized subjects, the legitimated serials of the convergence era masculinize a denigrated form, negating and denying the feminized other upon which their status depends.

Historicizing the Prime Time Serial

The history of serialized narratives in prime time TV has been repeated relatively frequently in both scholarly and popular forums. This story typically acknowledges the existence of *Peyton Place* (ABC, 1964–1969) in the 1960s, then suggests that serialized tales vacated prime time until the appearance of *Dallas* in the late 1970s, followed by the turn to serialization in the Quality TV phase of the 1980s, beginning with *Hill Street Blues*.[7] While such a history is accurate as far as the most influential instances of serialization go, it relies upon a presentist assumption that the contemporary form of serialized drama is at the apex of a long climb towards television's best. Such an assumption is problematic not only in its self-serving privileging of the present and of prime time over daytime but also in its inability to account for the range of different ways in which serialization has entered prime time, and the range of ways it has been culturally valued as a result. In other words, serialized narratives have not always been seen as the most original, edgy, or sophisticated that television can offer. As Angela Ndalianis has pointed out, as early as the 1960s, a number of series began to be structured around a central narrative goal, much as in many of today's heralded serial dramas.[8] Yet the programs that included such continuing questions in the 1960s tended to be more disparaged than heralded. Consider the castaways' quest to be rescued from Gilligan's Island, or Jeannie's drive to marry her master, both cases that involved some degree of serialization, at least in the form of character memory, but that were categorized more as wasteland fare than as sophisticated narrative experimentation.

Programming that matches the more typical conceptualization of serialized drama appeared in prime time even before the 1960s, and suggests that the distinctions between daytime and prime time serialization were less significant in television's early years. As the broadcast networks transitioned from radio to TV, some radio serials got prime time try-outs. Radio hit *One Man's Family* first came to TV as a weekly prime time serial (NBC, 1949–1952) before transitioning to daytime (1954–1955). And the Dumont network debuted TV's first original serial, *Faraway Hill* (1946), in the evening. Producer David P. Lewis hoped that the program would eventually move to daytime (it never did), indicating that prime time was not seen as an inherently more desirable spot.[9] Another serial, *The World of Mr. Sweeney*, began as a weekly sketch on the daytime *Kate Smith Show* (NBC, appearing 1953–1954), then moved to prime time (1954) before returning to NBC daytime (1954–1955).[10] In the early days of TV, as in network radio, serialization was not strictly aligned with daytime, and included some comedic as well as dramatic storytelling.

After these early experiments, serialized storytelling settled into daytime, but the debut of *Peyton Place* in 1964 again began to trouble these divisions. Behind the scenes, executives at ABC openly admitted that the program was a serial, functioning much like those in daytime. As ABC programming vice-president Edgar J. Scherick wrote to producer Paul Monash, "*Peyton Place* is a serial, whatever we may call it in our publicity releases!"[11] Meanwhile, Monash and ABC's Douglas Cramer discussed the intricacies of serial plotting and performer contracts, with Cramer hoping to take a page from daytime in how to handle the latter.[12] Yet, publicly, both Monash and the ABC executives sought to distinguish their series from daytime soaps. As Caryn Murphy has shown, Monash attempted to distance himself and the show from daytime serial creator Irna Phillips, whom ABC had hired as a consultant, claiming he had neither met her nor received any advice from her.[13] ABC's sales department described the program as a "continuing drama" in its pitch to advertisers, while print ads used the same terminology, as well as labeling it a "television novel."[14] Star Dorothy Malone emphasized the program's filmic production values, claiming that working on it was "really more like making a movie than a soap opera."[15] And ABC's Edgar Scherick changed his tune when speaking to the press, where he insisted that "the daytime soap operas were many levels below" the quality of *Peyton Place*, emphasizing, "*Peyton Place* is definitely not a soap opera."[16] At this early point in the history of serialization in American prime time, distinguishing the evening efforts from the soaps of daytime was standard practice, even when the program in question was widely read as a serial.

Whether despite or because of these efforts to separate it from daytime drama, *Peyton Place* was a ratings success. Soap or not, those ratings inspired other attempts at serialized drama in the 1960s. At one point, Irna Phillips was to write a *Peyton Place* spin-off, *The Girl from Peyton Place*, to feature the character of Betty Anderson leaving the eponymous small town for New York City.[17] Instead, ABC aired the semi-serialized *The Long Hot Summer* for the 1965–1966 season. NBC also tried to join the serial trend, announcing plans to broadcast *Dr. Kildare* twice a week and stretch stories over multiple episodes.[18] Meanwhile, CBS openly brought soap opera to prime time with *Our Private World*, a spin-off of daytime's *As the World Turns*, which followed the example of *Peyton Place* by airing two nights a week in the spring and summer of 1965. When *Peyton Place* ended in 1969, ABC quickly followed up with another serial, *Harold Robbins' The Survivors* (1969–1970), which pioneered the glitzy backdrop and corporate intrigue that would eventually become central to prime time soaps. None of these efforts had the staying power of *Peyton Place*, but their existence across the latter part of the 1960s points out one way in which serialized fare had a place in prime time television well before the Quality turn of the 1980s, even if that place was not especially valued either economically or aesthetically.

Yet serialized storytelling did begin to show some promise as both a commodity and a cultural marker during this period, in that during this time PBS began to air several serialized mini-series imported from Britain, among them *The Forsyte Saga* and *The Six Wives of Henry VIII*. The success of this programming led the American networks to program their own mini-series, which followed a serialized structure and form, albeit with a limited number of episodes.[19] Reviews of one of the first such efforts, ABC's *Rich Man, Poor Man* in 1976, labeled the drama as "soap opera," yet still worked to distinguish it from daytime drama. *Newsweek* called it "a modest departure from TV's stale, overworked forms," and acknowledged that the characters "grow visibly older and psychologically more complex with time," suggesting "something beyond soap opera."[20] With *Rich Man, Poor Man* and the mini-series that followed, a specific kind of serialization (adapted from a novel, historically oriented, limited run) became a television institution, and a well-respected one, at that. As Elayne Rapping has argued, such fare was "used as cultural capital in television's battle for serious attention."[21]

The 1970s also saw some faint efforts to introduce serialized elements into ongoing series. Jane Feuer has pointed out the moves toward serial form in MTM sitcoms such as *Rhoda* (particularly around the character's divorce) and dramas such as *Lou Grant*, as when the character Rossi refers to the time he went to jail for refusing to name a source, an event that had occurred in the previous season.[22] Non-MTM shows of the 1970s also wove in some serialized instances. For example, in the drama series *Family*, Willie Lawrence's girlfriend Salina Magee, whom he met in season one when she was pregnant with another man's child, returns to town in three separate episodes of season two, baby in tow, and reignites her relationship with Willie. Yet *Family* episodes more typically tended to raise and resolve situations episodically, with a visiting relation or a problem with a friend creating conflict and never being heard from, or of, again.

Despite this hesitant approach to serialization, *Family* and various series of the 1970s were crucial forerunners to *Dallas*, the first wholly serialized drama to succeed in prime time post-*Peyton Place* and the program that set the stage not only for the prime time soap boom of the 1980s but also for the embrace of serialization in the Quality dramas of the period. In series such as *Family*, *The Waltons*, *Little House on the Prairie*, and *Eight is Enough*, storytelling revolved around domestic life and family dynamics. Unlike the "franchise" or genre series (cops, docs, etc.) that had wholly populated prime time drama previous to this, these new series necessarily allowed for and represented characters that changed over time. Thus, for example, when John-Boy Walton went to college, the narrative had to accommodate this shift in the character's experience, including the fact that he no longer lived at home. These programs still told episodic stories, but they allowed for character development across episodes. *Family*'s producer, Nigel McKeand, offered a scripting formula for this new kind of TV narrative: "Resolve the situation, don't solve the problem."[23] In approaching the prime time family drama in this way, *Family* and similar shows of the 1970s sought to manage and contain the economically and culturally risky aspects of serialized storytelling.

The economic risks had been clear since the days of *Peyton Place*. Despite its successful network run, the serial had fared poorly in off-network syndication, a key space for the recuperation of production expenses, especially in the network era.[24] Bound up with this was the industry's explanation for the failure of the serialized dramas that debuted after *Peyton Place*. In their wake, network logic insisted that audiences wanted to see characters that stayed the same from week to week, as in episodic cop and doctor series. The networks also liked the flexibility that strictly episodic programs allowed—episodes could be run in any order and audiences could tune in to any given episode without risk of narrative confusion, another business imperative of an era of exclusively live, rather than partially time- or space-shifted, viewing.[25] When a few more attempts at serialized drama during the 1970s were ratings failures, this network mindset was even further reinforced.[26]

But there also remained some anxiety both within the industry and in the culture at large about "soap opera" *content* appearing in prime time. This anxiety is especially clear in the case of the one pre-*Dallas* serialized program that had some staying power in 1970s television, the serialized sitcom, *Soap* (ABC, 1977–81). The concerns about soap opera's prime time presence—and about *Soap*—had more to do with the culturally questionable status of daytime drama than they did with the economics of serialization. By the mid-1970s, daytime soap opera was increasingly understood to be television's most sexually explicit site. The introduction of a number of new daytime serials in the late 1960s and early 1970s brought with them an appeal to younger audiences. The new soaps featured younger characters, more bedroom scenes, and more explicit discussion of contemporary social issues, including sex-related matters such as venereal disease, abortion, and rape.[27] As a result, allusions to soap opera during this period referenced not only the low budget production and *sturm und drang* historically associated with the genre but also a risqué representation of sex.[28] The soaps' location in the daytime kept them relatively unnoticed by the moral crusaders of the 1970s, but the possibility of soap-like sexual content appearing in prime time benefited from no such protection.[29]

Thus when ABC announced that *Soap* would debut in the 1977–1978 season, protests and boycotts spearheaded by religious groups targeted the program, with concern centered primarily on its sexual storylines.[30] Jason Mittell has detailed the ways in which the controversy over *Soap* drew upon contemporaneous generic assumptions about both sitcoms and soap opera.[31] But the particular associations with soap opera activated in the controversy—and in the program itself—are telling indicators of the problematic status of soap opera for prime time TV more generally. Not only was the sexual content of *Soap* seen as objectionable, but also the serialized nature of its storytelling, which led to characters not feeling the repercussions of their actions for multiple episodes and episodes ending with unresolved conflicts. As Mittell explains:

> For detractors of the program, the soap opera narrative form itself con-
> tributed to the questionable moral content of the program, as the ongoing
> storylines could never provide the ideological equilibrium that they desired
> from their sitcoms, furthering a linkage between the soap opera genre and
> assumed moral uncertainty.[32]

While the controversy over *Soap* eventually simmered down and the program managed to run for four prime time seasons, the intense response to its debut reveals the problematic cultural standing of any material with a connection to soap opera.[33]

Both the economic and the cultural anxieties associated with soap opera and prime time TV help to explain the very tentative approach to serialization and the "prime time soap" label taken by *Dallas* in its five-episode "pilot season" in 1978 and its second, full-length season in 1978–1979. In these early stages, *Dallas* more closely resembled progenitors such as *Family* or *The Waltons* than it did daytime soap opera or even *Soap*. Creator David Jacobs has declared that this was a deliberate strategy, a way of moving the program gradually toward serialization: "We always knew that *Dallas* would have to be a serial. The problem was *starting out* with it as a serial."[34] With the past failures of serialized dramas and the controversy around *Soap*, it is no wonder that *Dallas* initially avoided serialization, even while planting the seeds for its future flowering. As a result, in the five-episode first season, central conflicts such as those between the Barnes and Ewing families and between brothers J.R. and Bobby are raised and left unresolved. But each episode introduces and concludes a situation that is never referenced again in future episodes. This technique carried over into the second season, wherein some serialized strands were threaded through the later episodes, but were still not allowed to direct the weekly narrative. For example, in the fourth episode of season two, "Bypass," patriarch Jock Ewing suffers a heart attack and requires bypass surgery. We learn that Jock has come through successfully during that episode, but his heart condition and recovery do not resurface as plot points until five episodes later, when his wife, Ellie, tries to hide from Jock the news of their sons' plane crash, concerned about his precarious health. Interspersed are wholly episodic stories, such as one in which Ewing niece Lucy is taken hostage by a con man or another in which Pam's first husband surfaces, looking to scam the Ewings out of money. As the season progressed, serialized elements began to be planted almost surreptitiously within otherwise episodic stories, functioning so intermittently as to barely even qualify as third-tier "C" plots. So began Sue Ellen Ewing's extramarital affair with Cliff Barnes, which we see begin in a sub-plot of one episode and which is referenced for a while thereafter only briefly, as in Sue Ellen's half of a phone call (Figure 5.1) and sly departure and arrival at the Ewing homestead, presumably before and after a tryst ("Fallen Idol," December 3, 1978).

By the end of season two, *Dallas* was finally following a more serialized format, and by the end of season three it was a major cultural sensation, assisted by the

FIGURE 5.1 Sue Ellen Ewing phoning her lover, Cliff Barnes, who also happens to be her husband's nemesis. Such moments provided the first glimmers of serialized storytelling in the second season of *Dallas*.

season's cliffhanger "Who shot J.R.?" ending. *Dallas'* ratings power encouraged the networks to schedule more and more serialized fare. Lorimar Productions, *Dallas'* home, was responsible for a number of other serialized dramas debuting in *Dallas'* wake. The most successful of these were *Dallas* spin-off *Knots Landing* (begun in the 1979–1980 season, even before *Dallas* became such a popular craze) and *Falcon Crest* (begun at the end of 1981), which both followed *Dallas'* lead in introducing serialized storytelling quite slowly and gradually. Lorimar's less successful efforts, including *Kings Crossing* (ABC, 1982, a reboot of Lorimar's *Secrets of Midland Heights*, CBS, 1980–1981) and *Flamingo Road* (NBC, 1981–1982), were more fully serialized from the start, perhaps suggesting that episodic storytelling was still a more effective way of capturing viewers unused to serialization in prime time.[35] Yet ABC's entry into the prime time soap business jumped right into its serialized tale, with great success. *Dynasty* (1981–1989) became the only real competitor to the Lorimar CBS shows. With *Dynasty*, the "prime time soap" trend became widespread enough to become widely recognized, with more spin-offs and imitators to come into the mid-1980s.

At the same time as these overtly "soapy" series were becoming the most popular in prime time, NBC, the network that had had no success in generating a prime time soap hit, began a new kind of serialized drama, one that told continuing stories and concerned itself with soap-like interpersonal relationships, but that embedded these features within the setting of the decidedly non-soapy cop show. While *Hill Street Blues* was slow to build an audience, popular and scholarly critics loved it, helping to canonize the series as the initiator of a new kind of Quality TV—central to which was some significant degree of serialization, of character memory and development from episode to episode and of open-endedness. Although the program's debt to soap opera was openly acknowledged, *Hill Street* was most often appreciated for being *unlike* television anyone had seen before, as in Joyce Carol Oates' praise of the program for being "as intellectually and emotionally provocative as a good book."[36] Todd Gitlin studied the program as the exception to prove the rule of the drive toward mediocrity in network TV.[37] And Michael Pollan argued that "The show is one of those rare events in television history: a genuinely new form."[38] Because *Hill Street* had this "newness" going for it, it did not need to be strongly differentiated from soap opera to achieve its legitimated status. It was only once the *Hill Street* Quality TV formula became a prime time staple that such distinctions were more heavily activated.

Yet, as Jane Feuer has pointed out, *Hill Street*'s arrival alongside the ongoing presence of *Dallas* and its followers led to the development of a two-pronged approach to serialization in American prime time, with Quality drama at one end and prime time melodrama at the other.[39] These two forms of serialized narrative were differentiated from each other in the 1980s, as now, both textually and extra-textually. Perhaps the most significant strategy of differentiation was in the labeling of these two forms, with the melodramas—*Dallas*, *Dynasty*, and eventually such series as *Melrose Place*—being openly labeled as soaps or serials while the Quality dramas were more typically and simply called dramas. By the mid-1980s, industry and popular discourse began to suggest that the prime time soaps were on the decline. As one ad agency executive put it in January 1986, "Serials are not hot. My guess is that we won't see as much in the way of serials next season."[40] While the networks did not add any programs that might be classified as prime time soaps to the 1986–1987 schedule, they did add new Quality dramas with serialized elements. Thus, *Falcon Crest* squared off against *L.A. Law*, the new series from *Hill Street* creator Steven Bochco. Also on the fall schedule was the serialized *Crime Story*, created by *Miami Vice*'s Michael Mann. And the networks continued to program Quality serialized dramas in the subsequent seasons.

While the Quality kind of serialization became a valued prime time staple, the prime time soaps were increasingly seen as has-beens.[41] Thus, in 1988, it was rumored that both *Dallas* and *Falcon Crest* might drop their serialized narratives and become more episodically driven and, for the 1989–1990 season, *Falcon Crest* was handed over to a new production team with credits "in every genre but soap opera," who pledged to drastically reduce the serialized elements.[42] When *Twin Peaks* premiered in the spring of 1990, it was widely labeled as "soap opera," but the term was always qualified and enhanced with such additional labels as "art television," "subversive," and "soap-opera-like-no-other."[43] *Twin Peaks* solidified a shift that had been underway since the arrival of *Hill Street Blues*, a shift that distinguished between the two poles of prime time serialization and that made one—the arty, *Peaks*ian kind—the best that TV could offer while relegating the other—soon to be embodied by such fare as *Beverly Hills 90210* and *Melrose Place*—to nothing more than fluffy soap.

The Gendered Distinction of the Contemporary Serial

The distinctions drawn between recent instances of prime time serialization and soap opera that came into place by the early 1990s have occurred both in discourses surrounding these shows and within the texts themselves. Thus, we are led to think about and understand contemporary serialized dramas as fundamentally different from—and, in most instances, better than—soap opera, both daytime and prime time. There are three key points around which such distinctions get made: (1) an emphasis on endings; (2) a "management" of the extent of seriality these programs employ; and (3) an avoidance or rejection of story content identified as "soapy." In each of these instances, the prime time serialization that is most highly valued is that which marks itself as most unlike soap opera.

The Essential Ending

A key trait of the daytime soap opera is its never-ending story. While many a daytime serial has ended its run and thus seemingly come to a conclusion, it is rare even in those cases for every story to definitively conclude. Many have considered the soaps' lack of closure to be a defining feature of the genre, one that brings particularly feminized pleasures to viewers. As John Fiske argues in *Television Culture*, soaps' "endless deferment" can be seen as "an articulation of a specific feminine definition of desire and pleasure that is contrasted with the masculine pleasure of the final success."[44] Whether we see these gender constructions as abiding is beside the point; most important here is the widely held cultural assumption that soaps feature never-ending stories, with complications spinning off from even the resolutions that do occur, and that this kind of narrative trajectory reads as feminine.

In contrast to these conceptions of soap opera, across the history of prime time seriality we see a repeated valuation of the serialized narrative that successfully concludes. One of the earliest such instances was that of the television mini-series as begun in the 1970s. The fact that the mini-series could present a serialized tale, but do so with a set timeframe for conclusion, enhanced the respectability of the genre, even when critics bemoaned some of its "soapy" content. But the importance of the ending to the aesthetic legitimacy of serialized programming is especially evident in more recent times, as seen in the discussion leading up to the conclusion to *Lost*. Before ABC and *Lost*'s creators agreed upon an end date for the series, novelist Stephen King argued that determining a concluding point was essential to any "story . . . perfectly told." Indeed, he insisted that the question of whether *Lost* would have a clear conclusion was a matter crucial to the "soul" of what he calls "the new TV."[45] Media scholar Ivan Askwith essentially agreed, pointing out that he and others attuned to the series—both its fans and its anti-fans—believed that the worth of the show depended upon whether the writers had a long-term narrative plan, with a conclusion therein.[46] In such discourse, not only is the serialized *Lost* figured as the epitome of a new, aesthetically elevated kind of television, its need for a definitive conclusion, an ending, is seen as determinative of its legitimized status. Without it, the twists and turns of the plot would be read as "pointless," manipulative efforts to keep the story going, akin to the soaps' stories of evil twins, long-lost offspring, and characters killed off coming back to life.

At the heart of the discourse about the vital importance of *Lost*'s ending is a wariness and caution, a concern that a bad or "failed" ending to a serialized drama will forever ruin that program's aesthetic status. The incredible weight placed upon the ending is again indicative of how such series are differentiated from soap opera. Most commonly referenced here are *Twin Peaks* and *The X-Files*, each of which comes under critique for its problematic ending, although the debate over *The Sopranos*' finale is also telling in this regard.[47] *The X-Files* is widely considered to have gone on too long, past its ideal point of conclusion and thereby failing to function satisfyingly as a unified aesthetic whole.

But the supposed failure of *Twin Peaks*' ending may be more specifically related to its connection to soap opera. *Twin Peaks*' creator David Lynch has insisted that he and co-creator Mark Frost never intended for the Laura Palmer murder mystery to become the focus of the series. Instead, they envisioned the murder as a background story, against which they would explore a range of different characters' tales (Figure 5.2). They did not intend to solve the murder for a long time, instead hoping, as Lynch put it, that "The progress towards [solving the murder], but never getting there, [would be] what made us know all the people in Twin Peaks."[48] In this respect, the intended direction of *Twin Peaks* quite closely matched a standard conception of soap opera. As Jennifer Hayward describes, "Soap structure encourages accumulating knowledge of character relationships [and] subplot complications . . . not as a set of 'keys' that will eventually buy narrative resolution, but as part of an intricate game with no teleological purpose."[49] The narrative pleasure of a soap is not so much in the lack of an ending, rather it is in the reveals and complications along the way that provide insight into the characters and their world. Feminist scholars have identified these pleasures as closely related to those social competencies seen as feminine: reading faces, interpreting relationships, contemplating the impact of events on feelings.[50]

Eager to capitalize on the popular interest in the murder mystery, ABC pushed Lynch and Frost to focus on the mystery and reveal Laura's killer. As Lynch has explained, "The pressure was just so great that the murder mystery couldn't be just a background thing any more."[51] Once that mystery was solved, the serial

FIGURE 5.2 David Lynch directing an episode of *Twin Peaks*.

Source: Lynch/Frost Productions/Photofest © Lynch/Frost Productions

seemed directionless to many viewers, who quickly lost interest. Yet Mark Dolan has argued that this was not necessarily the creative failure it is often made out to be. Instead, it might best be understood as a shift in narrative structure, away from a mini-series-like "episodic serial," complete with an ending, and toward a more open-ended, continuous serial.[52] In essence, after the murder was solved, *Twin Peaks'* narrative structure more closely resembled that of soap opera—the lack of a definitive ending, as well as the absence of a clearly defined and central narrative question, may be what most lessened the series' status in the eyes of its critics. Ultimately, *Twin Peaks* failed to respect the sanctity of the ending, and thus trod too closely to the indeterminacy of the devalued daytime soap.

Managing Seriality

The supposed problems encountered by *Twin Peaks* are infamous within the television industry and among the journalistic and scholarly critics who have sought to understand its failings. Thus, David Lavery argues that *Buffy the Vampire Slayer* "learned lessons about the liabilities of multiple-season story arcs from the forever incomplete *Twin Peaks*," resulting, in that case, with a drive toward narrative closure in each TV season.[53] *Lost* showrunner Carlton Cuse refers to *Twin Peaks* as a "cautionary tale."[54] And Mark C. Rogers, Michael Epstein, and Jimmie L. Reeves describe *The Sopranos* as admirable for being "serial, but not too serial like *Twin Peaks*."[55] These sorts of comparisons suggest that serialized dramas must necessarily seek ways to manage or contain their seriality, to keep that seriality and its associations with feminized excess from overrunning the narrative. There is little doubt that many, if not all, of American television's serialized dramas over the past 30 years combine episodic and serial storytelling as a means of managing the imperatives and constraints of the commercial television system.[56] We do not dispute this; rather we contend that it is serialization in particular that is seen as the problem to be managed, a problem that is regularly articulated to the feminized soap form. By managing or containing that feminized element, serialized dramas are able to achieve a kind of masculinized aesthetic and economic legitimacy. At the same time, they avoid being categorized with more mass appeal episodic dramas, even while they draw upon many of the same narrative techniques.

Scholars frequently reference *The X-Files* as a prototype for this sort of narrative negotiation, a pioneer of the combined episodic/serial form.[57] Creator Chris Carter was quite vocal about his desire to keep the series from becoming "too soap opera-y" and his feelings on the matter were echoed by a cluster of fans who dubbed themselves the "NoRomos," a group defined by their opposition to a romance between series leads Mulder and Scully (Figure 5.3). Christine Scodari and Jenna L. Felder have argued that the combination of the episodic and the serial in *The X-Files* "marries masculine and feminine in a manner [that] provokes conflicting expectations among viewers" in that "elements

FIGURE 5.3 The will-they-or-won't-they romantic status of *X-Files* agents Mulder and Scully was the source of a dispute between "shipper" fans who wanted the two to become a couple and "NoRomos," who strongly opposed this "soapy" development

Source: Photofest © Fox Broadcasting

of melodrama and emotional realism within the character-driven serial narrative inject a feminine sensibility into the program despite the intentions of creators." In other words, they see the feminized soap element as a disruptive force in the series, one that is embodied in the battle between the "shipper" fans, those who want to see Mulder and Scully in a romantic relationship, and the NoRomos.[58] Alternately, the persistence of episodic storytelling across the run of the series, as well as the fact that Mulder and Scully never became a full-fledged couple, can be seen as keeping the more serialized elements in check.

Many scholarly and lay critics have argued that recent series such as *24* and *Lost* are more wholly serialized. As Jason Mittell contends, "Unlike nearly every other television series, *Lost* features no stand-alone episodes, and no 'monsters-of-the-week' that offer reprieves from the serialized mythologies."[59] Yet such programs nevertheless rely quite heavily on episodic storytelling as a "cheat," a way to manage and constrain the undeniably difficult and unwieldy work of more fully serialized narration. They thereby use some of the same narrative techniques as do more admittedly episodic programs, even though they get characterized as wholly unlike these more mass-targeted shows. *Lost* is certainly structured around a narrative enigma or puzzle, as typically characterizes a serialized cult series,[60] and yet most of the narrative in most of its episodes is occupied by a largely episodic "story of the week" structured as a flashback, flashforward, or flash-sideways. Thus we spend one week on the story of Locke's relationship with his con man father, one on the story of Jack and his wife, one on the early days of Jin and Sun's relationship. While these stories may provide insight into the characters' motivations and goals, they are hardly crucial to the central enigma of the island and its mysteries; they are more diversions from the central serialized narrative than a perpetuation of it.

In this respect, *Lost* manages its serial storytelling in ways much like *24*. In *24*, as showrunner Joel Surnow explains, "Most of [the weekly] stories could be done as two-hour movies . . . [the episodes feature] these little lateral arabesques that aren't on the spine of the story."[61] For example, in the program's fourth season, counter-terrorist agent Jack Bauer spends a full episode pretending to be a robber holding the customers of a gas station hostage, since one of the customers is a terrorist he is trying to detain. While this incident is introduced at the end of the third episode, the majority of the fourth episode is focused on this event. The incident is resolved in the fifth episode, when the terrorist in question martyrs himself by dying in a car crash. As a result, Jack's desperate effort to keep the terrorist at the gas station is for naught. The situation ends up having no relevance for the season as a whole and is not mentioned again. Instead, it provides a suspenseful *episode* that has no consequences for the longer story arc. These sorts of episodic arabesques help to stretch the storytelling across the season, providing a means of managing the challenges of more fully serialized narration. In this way, these prime time dramas distinguish themselves from soaps by becoming more like the episodic dramas against which they also seek separation. Yet they escape the denigrated status of an episodic procedural by articulating such instances to movies, as in the description offered by *24*'s Surnow. (David Chase has made similar claims, often referring to the season one episode "College" as the perfect "little movie" of an episode.[62]) The legitimated serialized dramas thereby manage the challenges of serialization while still distinguishing themselves from the delegitimated world of episodic and procedural drama.

Rejection of the Feminine

Perhaps the most overt effort to manage or constrain serialization and its feminized markings can be seen in *The Sopranos*, which was regularly praised for its use of serialized threads. Creator David Chase has repeatedly expressed his disdain for television—"I loathe and despise almost every second of it"[63]—and declares his personal goal to be "making episodes that could have been made as a stand alone feature film . . . self contained."[64] According to David Lavery and Robert J. Thompson, Chase worried about replicating the errors of *Twin Peaks* and was "determined from the start not to make a soap opera or serial of any kind."[65] Such denials and protestations reveal the intensity with which highly valued, aestheticized television works to distinguish itself from soap opera. Yet, Cindy

Donatelli and Sharon Alward argue that it is in fact a soap, even comparing the narrative function of the program's standing sets—Satriale's, the Bada Bing, Dr. Melfi's office—to that of The Tuscany restaurant on *Days of Our Lives*.[66]

Perhaps because of the contradictory mix of these soap-like qualities and Chase's anti-television vehemence, *The Sopranos* spends quite a bit of narrative time resisting its status as soapy TV. Within the on-screen world, the program comments upon the domestication and feminization associated not only with soap opera but with television itself, especially in comparison to the public, masculinized, culturally legitimated world of cinema. Glen Creeber argues that "*The Sopranos* implicitly critiques the 'televisionization' of the gangster genre—parodying its gradual development (Chase might say decline) from cinematic epic to standard video or television fare." The awkward fit of Tony and his crew with their suburban, domestic milieu and the private and personal concerns that pervade it allows the series to comment on the ways the once great cinematic gangster has been felled.[67] At the same time, Tony's tale offers a metaphor for the ways that cinema itself has been felled by television, as well as the ways that the masculinized world has been hobbled by the increasing presence and power of the feminine. Tony is at once an object of ridicule and a site of identification for the masculinized viewing subject, to be mocked but also pitied for his failure to live up to the masculine ideal of the cinematic gangster, padding around his house in his underwear and raiding his well-stocked suburban refrigerator for leftover lasagna (Figure 5.4).

FIGURE 5.4 Tony and Carmela Soprano in their suburban New Jersey kitchen
Source: HBO/Photofest © HBO

In these respects, it is not just soap opera that Chase and his series seek to avoid or television that they disdain. Rather it is the predominance of the feminine in these realms and in the culture more generally that *The Sopranos* comments upon and resists.

Many of the most culturally elevated of the contemporary serialized dramas share this resistance toward the feminine, although *The Sopranos* surely perfects this effort. This manifests itself most often in the fact that many of the aesthetically legitimated instances of serialization avoid, reject, or de-emphasize the very subject matter of soaps—that of domestic family drama and romance. The most overt case of this resistance is the "NoRomo" stance of some *X-Files* fans and creator Chris Carter, their opposition to a romance between Mulder and Scully. In this case, the "NoRomos" are not simply resisting serialization and its assumed problems, but more specifically the feminized world of romance narratives. Scodari and Felder argue that the resistance to the Mulder/Scully romance is inherently patriarchal, not only in its avoidance of a feminized romance plot but more specifically because of the nature of Mulder and Scully's relationship. They point out that the Mulder/Scully "shipper" fans are drawn to the couple precisely because of the ways their relationship defies conventional gender roles and norms of heterosexuality, with the characters coming to each other as equals. The effort to keep the two apart reads to such fans as an "adolescent idea" that sex is necessarily separate from love and friendship, that a sexual relationship is inherently different from one of true feeling between equals.[68]

Chris Carter claimed that he was unwilling to make Mulder and Scully a couple because doing so would detract "from what makes the show so good, which is the stories,"[69] a claim that sets "stories" apart from romance, as if the latter treads too much in the soap world of meaningful glances and endless rehashing, a world opposed to one of narrative momentum. Carter was also likely dissuaded by other series that had tried to manage a romance between leads. Matt Hills points to the case of *Moonlighting*, in which the consummation of the "will they, won't they" relationship between David and Maddie harmed the series' culturally elevated status and cult loyalty. Once the couple got together, Hills explains, "*Moonlighting* entered the world of soap opera, in which the resolution of one narrative thread opened up a new set of possibilities, and thereby sacrificed the focal point of its own endlessly deferred narrative."[70] *Moonlighting* tried to rectify this step by breaking up the couple in the end, but it had arguably already "fallen" from its culturally valued status. Christine Scodari has asserted that the failure to sustain a romance between a formerly will-they-or-won't-they couple in TV dramas and comedies perpetuates a "culturally masculine subjectivity," in that it rejects the possibility of an ongoing, heterosexual, romantic and sexual pairing of equals who challenge each other. Thus, for example, she references the failed relationship of Sam and Diane in the 1980s sitcom *Cheers* (a comedy, rather than a drama, but one that drew upon some serialized elements). She asserts that, as a result of their break-up, "male bachelorhood [was] valorized and the opportunity for Sam to continue his predatory ways [was] preserved. Any positive memory of Sam and Diane as a couple and their promise of an egalitarian, spirited, and challenging union [was] delegitimized."[71] Scodari's argument suggests that television's serialized narratives of sex and romance tend to uphold masculinist conceptions of heterosexual pairings, in that they are often unable—or unwilling—to offer stories of complicated, ongoing, and egalitarian sexual relationships between men and women. Such relationships might be seen as the central fodder of soap opera storytelling, and thus the inability or refusal to explore their dynamics in prime time narratives may be another way in which such programs distinguish themselves from soap and the feminized concerns associated with it.

Of course, there have been many instances of prime time serialization that do explore ongoing romantic relationships, so Scodari's argument cannot be universally applied. But if we think carefully about those instances, we find that they are circumscribed generically, and that the degree of prominence of relationships in their storytelling potentially degrades their Quality status in relation to the most distinguished serials. Some instances of shows with prominent relationship narratives would be programs whose soapiness is never under dispute—think of Pam and Bobby's relationship across the many years of *Dallas*' run, or Gaby and Carlos's on *Desperate Housewives*. The classification of such programs as nighttime soap operas feminizes their appeal and sets the shows apart from those serialized dramas that have been more culturally legitimated. More telling may be the case of *thirtysomething*, a drama that Jane Feuer has argued distinguished itself from the prime time soapy melodrama but was not in the mainstream of the new, Quality dramas begun in the 1980s and featuring serialized elements. In part, Feuer claims, *thirtysomething* was distinct for taking "its generic material from the daytime soap opera."[72] In its exploration of marriages, friendships, family dynamics, and romantic entanglements, *thirtysomething* addressed matters similar to those under exploration in daytime, albeit without some of daytime's more melodramatic complications. Yet, unlike early instances of Quality serialized drama such as *Hill Street Blues* and *St. Elsewhere* and their reimaginings of prime time staples like the cop and doc dramas, the more soap-like *thirtysomething* has had relatively little influence on the television programming that followed it. Feuer argues that only in other series produced by the *thirtysomething* production team of Edward Zwick and Marshall Herskovitz such as *Once and Again*, and in the occasional cable drama (she cites *Six Feet Under* in particular), have we seen a real continuation of *thirtysomething*'s influence as a Quality series centered on the soap-like content of familial and romantic relationships.[73] We can further add to this roster programs run by Jason Katims, a veteran of Zwick and Herskovitz productions, namely *Friday Night Lights* and *Parenthood*. *Brothers and Sisters* fits this conception as well.

The presence of soapy elements such as domestic settings, drawn-out family and relationship narratives, and heightened emotional sensibility helps determine a given program's place on a scale of distinction within the category of Quality

TV. The most soapy of prime time shows, those like *Gossip Girl* and *Desperate Housewives*, might still find a place on the cultural hierarchy above the most debased genres of television like basic cable reality competitions and daytime talk shows and dramas, and perhaps above or alongside some procedurals. But they suffer in reputation next to the more adult, masculine, and legitimated serial programs like *The West Wing* and *The Wire*. Serials located in professional settings—the *Hill Street/L.A. Law/St. Elsewhere* tradition of Quality TV—balance their ongoing relationship arcs with more masculinized cop, lawyer, and doc storylines, helping to legitimize their storytelling by locating it within public work settings where characters often face life-and-death conflict. But to the extent that such shows emphasize their relationship storylines, they might feminize their appeal. We can see examples of such dynamics in convergence-era medical dramas like *Grey's Anatomy*, whose female (even feminist) narrative perspective and emphasis on characters' love lives produces more of a "guilty pleasure" reputation than ever attaches to more masculinized Quality TV.

"Soapy" elements like will-they-or-won't-they relationship plots find their way into a wide variety of serials without necessarily diminishing those programs' status as highly legitimated. But the scale of Quality TV legitimacy depends on the relative significance or intensity of focus on such feminized narrative content. The Donna–Josh romantic subtext on *The West Wing* might seem soapy in the abstract, but the larger narrative counterbalances this kind of material with the show's engagement with politics and society. The Jack–Kate–Sawyer love triangle on *Lost* is a point of great interest to some passionate viewers of that show, but its relative importance in comparison to many other appeals, from island mythology to character backstory to narrative structure itself, saves the show's overall reputation from feminization.

As *Lost* demonstrates, prime time dramas in the convergence era have brought new generic material into the Quality canon. In particular we might think of the science fiction and fantasy elements typical of many so-called cult series, including Joss Whedon's shows, *The X-Files*, and *Battlestar Galactica*. Cult series historically have been valued for their "anti-mainstream" status, with the mainstream constructed as a feminized other.[74] Because the "other" of serialized prime time is so often daytime soap opera, itself a feminized form, serialized cult series and their dedicated viewers may also construct themselves as the non-feminine. As Joanne Hollows argues regarding the gendering of cult, "the mainstream 'Other' of the cult fan is characterized using a familiar image of the distracted female television viewer . . . cult is naturalized as masculine and the mainstream as feminine."[75]

These distinctions arguably play out in the texts themselves, as neither the re-imagined conventional genres nor the sci-fi-influenced cult series make romantic or familial relationships the driving materials of their narratives. Instead, in the reimagined genres, the dynamics of whatever professional world marks the series' setting is the central narrative focus (e.g., *ER* and the trials of modern medicine), while in the cult series, the "defining narrative enigma or puzzle that is bound up with their creation of fantastic narrative worlds" plays that role.[76] Within such frameworks, romantic and familial relationships have their place, but are always secondary in significance to the central narrative focus, at least in dominant readings of these series.

Soap opera's typical concern with the romantic and the familial does find its way into prime time serial narrative in one last type of show. Apart from the prime time soaps, the key place for the exploration of such matter in contemporary serialized TV has been in so-called teen series, dramatic (and sometimes comedic) programs with serialized elements that focus on teen characters (as well, sometimes, as adult ones) and are frequently targeted at young audiences. Prominent examples include *Dawson's Creek*, *The O.C.*, and *One Tree Hill,* and the teen genre overlaps as well with other categories in instances such as *Buffy* and *Friday Night Lights*. As Rachel Moseley has described, "At the imaginative centre of the teen drama, as in soap, are place, character and relationships, and emotional drama."[77] Such programming tends to be at two removes from the most valued and legitimated of contemporary TV. For one, its association with youth brings to these series "the associated negative perception of youth culture as commercialized and conformist," and the ways in which the adult world tends to devalue that which is associated with the young.[78] But such programming is also kept away from the most legitimated sites of contemporary TV through its association with the feminine. Sharon Marie Ross and Louisa Ellen Stein point out that such fare is often derisively labeled as "teen soaps,"[79] and Matt Hills, writing about *Dawson's Creek*, points out that, despite intense fan involvement, such shows are "relatively delegitimated and denied cult status" due to their proximity to "culturally conventional female interests (including soaps)."[80] Thus, soap-like concerns appear within certain prime time venues, but remain delegitimated and outside the kinds of serialized TV that helps give contemporary television a greater degree of cultural validation.

In the discourses of the contemporary serialized television that is most typically praised, valued, and legitimated, we find a persistent process of distinction. Much of what we identify as Quality, complex, and sophisticated in American television since at least the 1980s achieves that status in part through its ability to mark itself off from soap opera. Whether through an emphasis on the crucial place of a narrative conclusion, through persistent efforts to "cheat" the degree of serialization in favor of more episodic storytelling, or through a resistance to soap-like subject matter, this programming manages to carry the banner of serialization while rejecting the label of soap opera. These distinctions are about much more than determining generic boundaries; they are thoroughly and fundamentally gendered ways of imagining and validating the television narratives we consume, and they sadly, if not surprisingly, keep the feminine at the bottom of widely accepted hierarchies of value and taste.

6

THE TELEVISION IMAGE AND THE IMAGE OF THE TELEVISION

Perhaps the 21st century will prove to be the golden age of TV, a time in which the handsome possibilities of high-definition digital programming allow television to become an art form every bit as adventurous as cinema.

Mark Kermode[1]

In the early 1960s, Marshall McLuhan theorized that cinema is "high definition," filled with data that absorbs the full visual attention of its spectator, while television is so meager as to make it "not so much visual as audile-tactile."[2] Cinema was hot and TV was cool, and their sensory appeals were at the heart of the distinction. Putting aside the overreaching and essentializing rhetoric, we must see that to media consumers of McLuhan's era, the difference between cinematic and televisual images was pronounced. And the cultural identities of these media were distinct even as both delivered similar audiovisual representations, including television broadcasts of movies and telefilms and series made in the Hollywood studios following the classical style. One unavoidable difference between cinema and television at that time was to be found in their pictures—both their size and quality. Over the past half-century, not only have cinema and television converged as forms of digital media, but both the television image and our ideas about it have undergone metamorphosis. Among the changes to television is the introduction of larger and wider pictures with sharper resolution, accompanied by Dolby 5.1 surround sound. Given these changes in television's technologies, today's would-be McLuhans would have difficulty making such radical distinctions between media.

"Television" means many things. Depending on context it may refer to programs, to the institutions that produce and distribute them, and to the devices we use to access this content. It can be used to mean culture, industry, or technology. These meanings are always interconnected and interdependent, such that the legitimation of television programming will necessarily have causes and consequences among the other ways in which we can think of television as medium and as experience. We might talk specifically of TV as shows or as networks or as hardware, but ultimately it is all of these and more, and to talk of one assumes much about the others. Many uses of "television" are metonymic references extending beyond the hardware, the set itself and the technologies that constitute it. The shifting cultural status of television has occurred at every level at which we can identify television, but one especially significant site of convergence-era legitimation has been the status of the television set (*the* television) as an image machine, and by direct consequence, of formats of content made to fit its picture. We might regard the television to be a technological base upon which television's many meanings are built, and on which these meanings are imprinted.

In the era of convergence, the television set has been remade in the image of the film screen, so much that the new standard of television picture is known by the same term McLuhan used to describe hot media like cinema: *high definition*. In concert with this transformation, all of the cultural associations of film and television—as distinct and opposed audiovisual media, as cultural forms with differing visual and experiential status, as media of greater and lesser cultural import, as masculinized and feminized—have been opened to negotiation. Such negotiation occurs at multiple sites, such as the retail environments in which the new television sets are sold to consumers, the domestic spaces in which the new sets are experienced in the context of everyday life, and the formats of programming created to match the demand for a technologically improved and culturally upgraded form of television hardware, each of which this chapter considers. All of these sites share a discursive agenda of making television new and improved through the construction of the television picture as more distinguished, aesthetic, formally pleasing, and cinematic than it had been before. By legitimating the television itself, flat-panel sets articulate a fresh identity for the medium, revising its class and gender associations by emphasizing affluence and masculinity. In the process, legitimation functions to reinscribe the same class and gender hierarchies that have worked historically to perpetuate television's cultural degradation.

Introducing the Flat-Panel Screen

Changes in the television have not happened all at once, but they rapidly intensified in the second half of the 2000s, when a new kind of set was adopted by millions of consumers just as television producers, networks and stations, and cable and satellite providers hastened to offer content made to fit it. Flat-panel, digital, HDTV sets with their bright, colorful, and high-resolution picture, their broad 16:9 shape, and often room-dominating size were not to be found in American homes at the beginning of the millennium. By the end of its first decade, plasma, LCD, and LED televisions in particular had become common sights not just in family rooms but in restaurants and bars, airport departure lounges, hotel rooms, supermarkets, and fitness centers. Along with other digital devices used to select content to view on them, flat-panel TVs have been essential in creating a sense of television's renewal and improvement as a technology and as a medium. This has arisen not only by positive associations with the putatively cinematic qualities of HDTV image and sound, but also by negative comparison with the old standard-definition 4:3 sets, which the new televisions usher into obsolescence.

The years 2007 and 2008 in particular saw steadily growing adoption of flat-panel HDTV sets as prices fell sharply in the U.S.—20% to 30% in a year—and they entered the mainstream rather than merely the early adopter and luxury markets.[3] Sales of LCD sets were projected to be only 3% of the world market in 2003,[4] but global sales of LCDs surpassed cathode ray tubes (CRTs) during the fourth quarter of 2007 to reach 47% of all sales.[5] By the end of 2008, Nielsen found that more than 23% of American households had an HDTV, more than double the number of a year previous, when Nielsen began to track this figure.[6] According to a 2009 Nielsen report, one-third of American homes then owned an HDTV set, which was identified as the most rapidly adopted new television technology since color.[7] By early 2011, news reports citing electronics manu-facturers asserted that almost two-thirds of American households had a flat-panel set.[8] Anyone who visited an American electronics store like Best Buy or a discount retailer like Target or Costco during these years was likely overwhelmed by the size, number, and vividness of these new products, the new "consumer electronics pop stars," but before long grew accustomed to seeing them all the time.[9]

When first introduced into the American market in the late 1990s, high-definition televisions were not flat-panel televisions, but projection or perhaps picture-tube sets of enormous size and cost.[10] Little programming was available in high definition, and what was would be found only in big cities.[11] At that time, LCD displays were becoming familiar in homes and offices as space-saving but expensive computer monitors, not as television screens.[12] When they began to penetrate the American market, LCD as well as plasma televisions had the advantage over CRT sets of coming in larger sizes and appealing in terms of design elements such as shape, volume, and line. Picture-tube sets would seldom get much bigger than 34 inches, but plasma displays could get 50 inches or larger without needing substantial space behind the screen for a tube. During the holiday season of 2003, reports described a "mania" for the new flat sets, driven in part by "the popularity of DVD players, games consoles and digital cable, all of which produce clear, sharp images that look particularly good on a big screen."[13] Standard rhetoric introduced the new flat-panels in contrast with CRT sets in terms not just of picture quality (actually high-def picture-tube sets were available with images no worse than those of the flat screen)[14] but of size and shape, and consequently of novelty and ineffable qualities of gadget cool. CRT sets would be called "boxy," "bulky," and "hefty," while flat-panel HDTVs were "sleek," "svelte," and "thin." Unlike a traditional set, a flat-panel TV could be mounted on a wall like a large framed artwork, an unthinkable site for the home screen in the pre-HD era. In distinction to familiar CRT sets, flat-panels were of widescreen dimensions but only inches deep, and thus broad but not voluminous. This newly trim and chic image *of* the set is often as important as the image produced *by* it in establishing a renewed identity for television.

But picture is central to the appeal of the new television. The consumer of the new technology would instantly recognize its shape in comparison with a traditional CRT set as wider, which popular press discourses invariably have described in terms of a widescreen movie image. By the 1990s, most film viewing was occurring in the home on television screens, and now the television set was seen to be advancing closer to reproducing the experience of theatrical cinema exhibition, fitting well within the home theater phenomenon as analyzed by Barbara Klinger.[15] While HD resolution still is not visually as rich as 35mm film, the high-def image has several times more pixels than standard-definition NTSC, and on a large screen more detail is observed.

Popular press discourses around the introduction of HDTV often seized on the television set's newfound ability to picture previously unrepresented imagery, such as the stitches on a baseball or the pores and lines on a face.[16] First-time viewers, the *New York Times* reported in 1998, describe high-definition television as "looking through a window rather than looking at a picture."[17] Sports broadcasts in HD "neatly transplant the viewer out of the living room and into the stadium, minus the obnoxious drunks," promised *Broadcasting & Cable* in 2004.[18] High-def pictures would be more lifelike and present, less like a representation of reality and more seemingly unmediated—what *Wired* magazine in 2006 called "realer than real."[19] High-def was to make us behold what previously was impossible to see. Facial blemishes, wrinkles, lines, and blotches would be newly apparent, while deep-set eyes and shine on the skin would look more unappealing in HD, a challenge to makeup artists.[20] According to this renewal of the "hyperrealist" discourse that Lynn Spigel found to characterize the advertising of television as a new domestic technology in the 1950s, television would conquer its status as a mere medium and offer direct access to a world of vivid and detailed images with the advent of high-def pictures.[21]

We can locate a number of desires animating the consumer to invest considerable sums in a new television set during the era of convergence. Considering only the picture, a desire for a more cinematic image and a desire for a more lifelike or natural image together make for a collective aspiration for a new conception of television that is basically un-television-like. As a domestic appliance with its own distinct formal qualities expressing fresh cultural connotations, the flat-panel television set likewise functions in distinction to the old idea of TV, offering itself as a newly desirable commodity. To remake the television means to abandon what the medium and technology once were, to relegate the old idea of television to a backwards past from which we have progressed. As this old idea of television is left behind, television's identity shifts from one set of social class and gender associations to another. This process occurs on many levels, including the presentation of new televisions as consumer goods in retail spaces and marketing discourses.

Selling HDTV

While historically TV has been seen as a medium associated both with the feminine and the underclass, the discourses surrounding HDTV challenge these constructions. In such discourses, television becomes technologically sophisticated, masculinized, and both economically and aesthetically valued. Much of the cultural legitimacy lent to television by the rise of flat-panel HDTV sets is a product of the gender and class value ascribed to the technology. Wide and flat HD screens are constructed as objects of technological sophistication and in a culture in which "technical competence is an integral part of masculine gender identity," we experience a "historical and cultural construction of technology as masculine."[22] The discourse of masculinized technological superiority articulated to HDTV sets precedes their widespread adoption, most clearly in the rise of home theaters in the 1990s. In pre-HD home theater technology, the massive size of the image and especially the use of surround sound promised an escape from the "inferior" technology of (feminized) television. As Klinger has argued of this phenomenon, "By reproducing the big picture and big sound associated with cinema's conditions of exhibition, home theater 'rescues' the family television from what promoters depict as its lack of spectacle and technological refinement."[23] Along with Klinger, William Boddy recognizes the ways in which gender informs the home theater's transcendence of mere TV. As he notes, early 1990s ads for big-screen televisions, "seek to reassure the male television consumer that he remains uncontaminated by the traditional emasculating associations of television viewing," a discursive move that assists the broader "remasculinization of the television apparatus through fantasies of power and control."[24]

The remasculinization of the television apparatus to which Boddy refers has reached its apex in the convergence-era context, in which the plasma and LCD high-definition screens that now dominate the marketing, sales, and purchase of TVs have achieved the status of being technologically sophisticated and masculine by virtue of their distinction from the old analog sets with their cathode ray tubes and squarish 4:3 screens. When flat-panel HDTVs first appeared in electronics stores in the early 2000s, retailers explored different means of showcasing the technology. Initially, this meant displaying the single HDTV in the store alongside an analog model, each playing the same prerecorded content. Side-by-side presentation would be the surest way to show off the new technology to its best advantage and to make clear the rapidly approaching obsolescence of the old screens. But as HDTV prices dropped and interest in the technology grew, retail displays became dominated by these sets.[25] At that point, TV manufacturers and retailers sought new ways to use technology as a selling point, in particular by highlighting the different degrees of technological sophistication one can gain through such sets, as in the distinction between 720 and 1080p (these numbers refer to the lines of vertical resolution the set offers; both versions are considered HDTV). In big box retailers such as Best Buy, this has meant playing different content on differently priced TVs and using different kinds of connectors to push purchasers toward the more expensive models. Thus, the 1080 models of higher-end brands will play Blu-ray DVDs and connect the DVD player to the set with component or HDMI connections while less expensive and 720p sets will play a prerecorded loop of over-the-air HD content and use lower-quality composite video connectors.[26] The consumer electronics industry thereby emphasizes the technological distinctions between HD sets not only to push sales of the more expensive versions but also to sustain the discourse of technological sophistication that makes the TVs seem a preserve of exclusive, masculinist understanding, a set of distinctions all the more pressing as the technology is embraced by a broader market.

The masculinization of television underway in HDTV retailing encompasses more than the strategic deployment of technological distinctions between sets. The choice of content displayed on HD sets in retail spaces also masculinizes the new television. HDTVs are almost universally marketed as devices for displaying such "non-TV" content as feature films (in keeping with the home theater discourse) and video games, while sports programming is the only content created for television broadcast that is regularly highlighted in HDTV marketing. A print advertising campaign for Sharp's Aquos line of LCD televisions circa 2007 pictures the set framing a baseball player sliding headfirst into a base, specks of dirt vividly frozen in air. Samsung partnered with Microsoft's Xbox gaming platform as a way to showcase the "12 millisecond pixel switching speed" and ability to overcome any "motion artifacts" of its LCD TVs, as well as becoming the lead sponsor of the World Cyber Games.[27] Samsung brokered a marketing deal with the National Football League, and Mitsubishi became the "official HDTV" of the PGA Tour, while Sharp partnered with both Major League Baseball and Nascar as the sports' "official HDTV."[28]

Dealers of consumer electronics are urged to choose content for floor models such as high-definition cable or satellite feeds of ESPN, HBO, and HDNet; Blu-ray or HD-DVD discs; or Xbox or PlayStation 3 games; none of which offer the kinds of content most associated with the old image of the television.[29] The emphasis on sports is in response to a widespread belief that consumers who purchase HD sets typically see sports viewing as the key appeal of the new technology.[30] For instance, many prospective buyers in 2006 were apparently enticed by the promise of watching Super Bowl XL, the Turin Winter Olympics, and the Germany 2006 FIFA World Cup in high definition.[31] As Jeff Joseph, a vice president of the Consumer Electronics Association, told retailers in 2006 in the pages of the industry trade journal *Dealerscope*: "Since you began selling HDTV some nine years ago, you probably noticed very quickly that sports programming drove sales of HD displays and receivers." This fact was to help sales staffs adopt a strategy for influencing customers, expecting that many prospective buyers would have sports viewing in mind. "The key is leveraging the excitement of HD content to those still on the proverbial purchasing fence."[32]

The logic informing the marketing of HDTVs via masculinized media forms has been rooted in research into the interests and motivations of early adopters, and the assumptions about masculinity that result. Thus, survey research from 1999 indicates that "Innovators and early adopters of HDTV receivers will likely be younger, have higher income, be frequent moviegoers, watch sports programs, and express a keen interest in high-resolution, large screen televisions."[33] More recently, Samsung identified its "male-dominated" target of the "young-minded consumer" as particularly passionate about sports and gaming.[34] Meanwhile, a number of different set manufacturers hawk their products on gaming websites. For example, the UGO Lifestyle for Gamers site touts that gaming on the Panasonic TH-42PX600U plasma TV will make you "feel as though you could catch that long pass from the forty yard line or get hit by Jeff Gordon's car when it spins out on the track."[35] Indeed, as Bernadette Flynn has argued, gaming platforms promise their users the experience of escaping from the confines of the domestic sphere, even as their play is by definition rooted in the space of the home and the interface of the TV screen.[36] The media content most often used to market HD sets not only positions these screens away from over-the-air (or cable) television and the domestic confines with which it is associated. It naturalizes the link between HDTVs and the masculinized realms of feature films (especially genres like action blockbusters), hard-core gaming, and professional spectator sports, as if these are the inevitable and exclusive purposes of television. In the even more recent emergence of 3D television and televisions offering applications for accessing web-based content, we see a further distancing of TV use from the pre-convergence era's broadcasting status quo.

Associations between flat-panel screens and masculinity are also reinforced in the marketing of consumer electronics such as the circular advertisements bundled with Sunday newspapers. In circulars for stores like Best Buy and Target, flat-panel HDTV sets are routinely cross-promoted with other media goods such as video game consoles and titles; delivery technologies such as satellite or cable services and TiVo; and especially newly released DVDs of Hollywood films, which might effectively bring in a regular stream of customers to admire the new televisions on conspicuous display at the store entrance. The widescreen sets in the circulars are usually pictured filled with content, and this content is almost never the typical feminine, juvenile, or "low-class" TV fare of the pre-convergence era such as talk shows, comedies, cartoons, or soap operas. Sometimes circulars picture sports images framed in the televisions, for instance, during football playoffs when the appeal of watching "the big game" on a new TV set can help sell the hardware to a masculine audience (Figure 6.1).

More often, the images seen in the HD sets in these marketing sites are largely those of console games and Hollywood movies, further reinforcing distinctions between old and new conceptions of TV, and emphasizing the function of the flat-panel set in extending the use of television to myriad un-TV-like activities such as watching films and playing a Nintendo Wii. The movie titles typically advertised are of the genres that best show off the technical advances of widescreen high-def and home theaters more generally—films with high concept visuals and sound, with elaborate CGI effects and action sequences. In other words, films of more masculine genres, like *Iron Man 2*, which Klinger notes have been the justification for the creation of masculinized home theaters in the first place.[37] In the retail space as well as the advertising space, the identity of the television set as a broadcast receiver as in the network era diminishes as the medium is nudged toward fuller convergence with gaming and cinema.

Gaming and action blockbusters offer one set of fresh cultural associations for television, but marketing discourses can also make more sophisticated appeals to upscale (or aspiring) consumers based on the aesthetic possibilities of the new sets. The national brand advertising for these TVs regularly associates

FIGURE 6.1 A Best Buy Sunday circular promotes flat-panel televisions with images of football players, selling sets as the ideal means of watching sports

them with the art world, emphasizing striking, even poetic, visuals and evocative music. Commercial spots for Sony's Bravia line thus feature explosions of color overtaking city streets, set to such taste-assuring music as Swedish indie folk artist Jose González's "Heartbeats," announcing, as Lynn Spigel has observed, that the sets are "not just high-tech but also high art."[38] Similarly, ads for Sharp's Aquos line have featured the music of Jonathan Elias, a classically trained composer of film scores, and depict a cityscape of people moving about their lives with their eyes closed. The last shots of the diegetic world are of a massive painting covering a wall in an art museum and a vaguely ethnic, hip, and young woman opening her eyes before this stunning sight. The image then dissolves to a title screen declaring "see more," the words subsequently dissolving out as a rotating image of the Aquos set reveals itself to us. The set promises a kind of vision we never knew we were missing, access to a world of beauty and art we could not see before Sharp's HDTV opened our eyes. In such ad campaigns, HDTVs are represented as elite objects; as a result, our potential and actual acquisition of them is meant to confirm our knowing and elite tastes. These sets are thereby differentiated from the "plastic black boxes" of the 4:3 analog era and their owners are differentiated from the masses unable to appreciate the artistic potential of the new TV.[39]

The New Television in the Home

The masculinization and high class status of HD display technology have been a major factor in the new sets' adoption, and have also been important in determining where their place should be in the home. The television set in the home has always been a site of gendered tension, and familiar conflicts and contradictions resurface with the emergence of these new screens. A 2009 *Today* show segment on the integration of electronics into décor, for example, illustrates how the new set introduces a gendered tension between hardware and the domestic sphere. Host Natalie Morales introduces the placement of the new flat-panel television as a matter "that men and women feel very differently about." Her guest, a male home improvement expert, agrees, and Morales elaborates:

> I know that when we did this in my house recently it was like, OK, where's the flat screen gonna go? Over the fireplace! Huge focal point! But yet, for the women, I know a lot of us are like, I don't know if I want that to be . . . that takes away from the fireplace!

As this segment shows, decisions about the location of a flat-panel television in a living room are not just matters of style but opportunities to examine the changing cultural positioning of television itself. The fact that HDTVs become a problem in updating prevailing standards of "good taste" in home décor bespeaks their status as a masculine intruder into a feminine realm. Decorating

FIGURE 6.2 Sharp LCD TV 2007 catalog illustration

makeover programs on HGTV might dramatize choices about a new flat-panel TV in a redesigned domestic space as a conflict between a heterosexual couple over the inclusion, size, location, and significance of this hardware, treating it as a marital issue or a battle of the sexes to be overcome through creative design. (One senses that the designers would prefer to avoid having a television in any room, so there is also often a tinge of conflict between clients and experts over the television, with designers aligned with both femininity and class, no matter their identity.) As the owner of Frame My TV, a company that creates frames to mask flat-screens, describes the conflict between husbands and wives over flat-panels in the home, "We'll get a frantic call from one spouse who can't believe the other brought home this giant thing that looks like it's out of Star Wars."[40] An image from a 2007 Sharp LCD catalog (Figure 6.2) captures the gendered tensions around the introduction of the new television into the domestic sphere. A white, adult, heterosexual couple in a modern living room of tasteful straight lines and muted colors watch a baseball game on their new Sharp TV, the man's arm around the woman holding her close as they enjoy sports together. The image at once encourages female consumers to see the new TV as a sleek design feature that promises to domesticate masculinity while also masculinizing the domestic sphere through the integration of the new television hardware and its male-skewing content.

One persistent design approach of the pre-HD period banished the television from view entirely, and we still sometimes see the desire for the suppression of the television's presence. In the 1990s and early 2000s, when the sets in question were larger 4:3 CRTs, the solution of hiding a television set behind the doors of a wooden armoire was one way of negotiating the place of a large electronic appliance in a well-designed living space. But cabinetry of this sort is ill suited to concealing a wide but shallow screen, and to owners of a new flat-panel set concealment might defeat the purpose of conspicuous or aspirational consumption. Perhaps more importantly, total concealment might be undesirable if the new set is regarded as an object of visual appeal in its own right. Consumers of new televisions who seek to integrate them well into living spaces might want to make them visible but with restraint and subtlety, avoiding attracting excess attention to a large electronic appliance which could easily disrupt or overwhelm a design aesthetic. A wide but shallow flat-panel television can be integrated into shelving systems but a large screen of 42 inches or more takes up considerable space. One example of a "solution" is the "Bestå" unit (Figure 6.3), whose sliding door panels conceal or reveal the set, integrating it into a larger minimalist concept of stylish cabinetry. As in this aesthetic from Ikea, the play of concealed and revealed hardware is a common theme in designs for integrating the new television into

BESTÅ/BOÅS
TV/storage combination
with sliding doors
$420

FIGURE 6.3 An Ikea Bestå media cabinet advertised in the 2011 catalog

the home, carrying over some of the functions of the television armoire. TV technology is still at times constructed culturally as ugly and shameful; the concealment of the television is a denial of the extent to which leisure time is spent in a blue glow. But high-def television technology is also a reinvention of TV as modern, drool-worthy gadgetry, as a must-have upgrade on the old, boxy CRT console. This masculine ideal of the new television sits uneasily within the gendered aesthetics of an affluent family's living room, where a large-screen high-def set is most often pictured. A desire at once to hide and display the flat-panel bespeaks a tension between the excitement over television's reinvention as masculinized, legitimated HDTV and ambivalence over the incorporation of massive hardware into feminized domestic spaces. Of course, the question of where to place the television set has arisen in the more distant past as well, most notably upon the introduction of television to American homes.[41] The contemporary era of flat-panel HDTV adoption more explicitly intensifies the gendered negotiations between the masculinized home electronics technology and the feminized domains of taste, style, and interior design.

The two options most often chosen for integrating a flat-panel TV into a living room are mounting it on a wall and placing it on furniture such as a media console, cabinet, or shelving system. Home design magazines caution—in both their words and images—that, however it is displayed, the television should not attract excessive attention. Terms such as "discreet" and "disappear" signal that tasteful integration of the set can be achieved through design choices that minimize the TV's disruptive potential by integrating it within a particular aesthetic ensemble. A feature in *House & Home: Condos, Lofts, & Apartments* proposes ways to distract from the flat-panel TV by making it "blend into its backdrop" of a gray built-in cabinet or by wall-mounting it between bookcases and above seating (a rather non-utilitarian arrangement) to give it "grounding and further distraction."[42] Mounting on a wall or integrating into bookcases are both options that make possible hiding the TV in plain sight, emphasizing its status as aesthetic object to be looked at rather than its presence as an appliance. Making the TV blend in can be accomplished in a number of ways, in particular by concealing cables behind walls and cabinetry—symbolically denying the television's status as electronics—and by treating the television as "wall art." In one episode of the HGTV program *Color Splash: Miami*, designer David Bromstad frames a wall-mounted flat-panel television in thick, dark wood, explaining: "We're putting a frame around the TV and this way it's going to blend in and look like a piece of art. This is a great design strategy."[43]

In some instances, fashionable, upscale design shows off the new television as a formal appeal in harmony with a larger modern aesthetic. An image of a mid-century modern living room in the pages of *Atomic Ranch* magazine places a Sony flat-panel with a black-and-white medium close-up of George Clooney in *Good Night and Good Luck* in a room of furnishings with straight lines and right angles (Figure 6.4). The rectilinear form of the HDTV is balanced perfectly with the

FIGURE 6.4 In this mid-century modern interior from *Atomic Ranch*, the form of the HD television set blends naturally into its surroundings

FIGURE 6.5 A living room pictured in *House Beautiful* represents a flat-panel TV display hung on the wall like a framed artwork

lines and angles in the credenza on which the set rests, as well as the coffee tables and sofa cushions. An electrical outlet sits just below the TV but no cable connects one to the other, and the image on the screen might well have been Photoshopped in, as no DVD player or cable box is visible.[44] A *House Beautiful* spread of an "oh-so-sleek" elegant-modern cottage shows a pristine white living room in which a flat-panel displaying a black-and-white image of studio-era Hollywood glamor hangs above a fireplace, flanked by framed drawings (Figure 6.5). Here the television is integrated as artwork, and of course no cables allowing for the image to be powered or for a source to convey content are visible.[45] To integrate the television as an object worthy of looking at rather than as an appliance to be concealed from view reorients our understanding of TV and aestheticizes the hardware itself.

Many of the solutions that the commercial sphere has generated to resolve the gendered debate about fitting the flat-panel set into the home ultimately help to maintain the masculinist associations that flat-panel HDTVs accrue as sophisticated technologies. In fact, such solutions often depend upon a technological fix, one that shifts the feminized puzzle of interior design into the masculinized realms of construction and gadgetry. Thus, when the décor compromise is to mount the flat screen to the wall, there often ensues a discussion of the careful mounting technique one must follow (stud finders, support brackets, etc.). In instances of new home construction or remodels, contractors engage in elaborate problem-solving processes to create built-in spaces for the TV, speakers, and components.[46] Sometimes "gadget" solutions are sought to resolve the conflict, such as lift technologies that raise and lower the TV into a cabinet, reversible media centers that feature the TV on one side and bookcases on the other, and panels of various kinds that can be remotely triggered to lower over the TV when it is mounted to a wall. While each of these solutions addresses aesthetic concerns, they do so by way of a technological wizardry designed to amuse and amaze those who value the flat screen for *its* technological prowess. Such devices thereby mollify feminized aesthetic worries while also enhancing the masculinized pleasures to be found in clever gizmos.

However, the meanings of television generated around flat-panel HDTVs are not marked only by gender; they are also discourses imbued with conceptions of class and taste, in which television has the potential to leave behind its more mass and lowbrow associations. In such discourses we can see still more of the cultural struggle that arises in the process of television's legitimation. The home décor question is centrally concerned with these matters of class and taste. While contemporary efforts to hide the flat screen may seem to place the set within the realm of the *déclassé* and the tacky, this has not always been the case. When the sets were first introduced and purchased, their high cost made them available to only the wealthiest of customers. As a result, owning one at all was a status symbol to be flaunted. Media coverage of the new TVs in 2001 and 2002 declared that "the svelte new sets seem designed for display," and spoke glowingly about the "stunning," "elegant" objects. These early adopters placed "interesting architectural elements around the TV to add to its importance," hung multiple framed, matted photographs around it, put it on a pole like a flag.[47] Because the aesthetics of the flat-panel sets were so different from 4:3 analog TVs, those with the money and privilege to be early adopters could readily refute the 1990s common decorating wisdom that televisions should be hidden when not in use.

Yet, as flat-screen HDTVs have dropped in price and broadened in reach, their status within the home has become more ambiguous. The initial flurry of decorator interest in mounting the sets on a wall, usually above a fireplace, has given way to doubts about the comfort of watching a TV significantly higher than eye level as well as to the safety of placing electronic equipment above a heat-generating source like a fireplace.[48] All agree, however, that hiding the wires that feed into the TV is essential if one is to mount it above the mantel. Even if the problem of the wires is resolved, still others see the industrial plastic, glass, and metal materials of the television as unattractive focal points, hence the number of products that have sprung up in order to disguise it. Chief among these are the TV frame, which literalizes the metaphor of HDTV as artwork by treating it like an oil painting, not only in the sense of being hung on the wall or even framed as on *Color Splash*, but actually used to display artworks when not in use for watching television or movies. To achieve such an effect, Comcast offered subscribers Gallery Player, a video-on-demand service of still images of paintings or photographs, shown for about a minute at a time and accompanied by music, to integrate the flat-panel set as an art display medium.[49] In these instances nothing conceals the flat-panel set while it is in not in use, but a frame may also be employed as a device of concealment employing a mirror displayed when the set is off. The "art screen" is a television-hiding solution in which a painting or other artwork raises, lowers, or unfurls over the set.

These instances, along with those devices that physically lift the TV itself in and out of the viewing space, suggest a revitalization of the stigma around television that seemed to disappear—albeit briefly—with the initial arrival of flat-screen HDTVs. These various devices evidence enough technical wizardry in and of themselves to make them match the TV as markers of masculine pride and technological sophistication. They also institute more conventional, conservative markers of taste in place of the set (especially in the case of the art screen) in such a way that suggests more a middle-class striving for an imagined ideal of upper-class refinement than a valuation of the masking artwork in and of itself. While some companies will build such systems using custom artwork, most are dealing with a stock set of reproductions, largely of traditional landscapes, religious scenes, and still lifes. These systems are not targeted to the serious art collector or the significantly wealthy. Instead they target what marketers call the "new mass affluent" demographic, those with enough money to purchase expensive consumer electronics and furnishings to cover them up but whose money is earned, not inherited, and whose tastes are more "mass" than "class."[50] The desire among a certain segment of the population to hide the flat-screen TV may have more to do with their own (misplaced) economic and social striving than with any specific distaste for TV. Clearly, ambivalence about the cultural status of TV persists, given the proliferation of these hide-the-set devices, but the everyday struggles to determine just how ashamed of TV watching one is supposed to be these days reveals that, at the very least, the medium's status is in flux. Indeed, in some ways the flat-panel HDTV carries so much cachet that other household appliances are being fashioned under the influence of its design aesthetic. Wall-mounted electronic fireplaces using plasma, LCD, or LED technology have emerged, mimicking the look of the new television, with roughly 16:9 dimensions and black plastic frames, suggesting that the negative connotations of a large, high-tech gadget in the domestic sphere are being overcome thanks to discourses of television's legitimation.[51]

Widescreen TV Content

Just as television hardware itself has old and new iterations—bulky CRT sets and sleek flat-panel HDTVs—the content made for these televisions has its before and after too, a distinction not only of picture quality but also of aspect ratio, i.e., picture dimensions given in terms of the ratio of width to height. In particular, the widescreen 16:9 image standard on flat-panel HD sets has pushed the identity of television closer to cinema, marking convergence by making television displays more suitable for watching movies and by making television shows more movie-like, at least in terms of aspect ratio. The transition from squarish to wide rectangular television images actually predates the wide adoption of HDTV sets, anticipating the transition from old to new hardware. Viewers became familiar with widescreen, televised images in the late 1990s and early 2000s, when they watched almost exclusively on 4:3 CRT sets. The ubiquity of widescreen images on television before the flat-panels went mainstream would serve to demonstrate the inadequacy of viewers' existing televisions, demanding upgraded equipment to match an upgraded image.

NBC's medical drama *ER* was in its seventh season, and in first place in the Nielsen ratings in November 2000, when it became the network's first program to air in a widescreen aspect ratio, with horizontal black stripes along the top and bottom of the 4:3, standard-definition picture, a format known as "letterbox."[52] Popular press discussion of the new format praised its visual appeal in rather lofty terms. To a reporter from *USA Today*, the show's supervising producer, Richard Thorpe, boasted that the newly wide image is a "more appealing shape to the human mind," comparing it to the forms of Greek architecture.[53] In describing the difference between the conventional 4:3 television frame and the wider frame within the frame, the *Washington Post*'s television critic Tom Shales explained that many viewers would be familiar with the new format from watching widescreen movies on DVD, laser disc, and VHS cassette. Shales made clear an aesthetic preference for the wider ratio, asserting that it "is more satisfying and compelling to the eye, perhaps simply because it's closer to the human field of vision."[54]

ER was not the first television show to switch to a widescreen format for broadcasting. It was preceded by a number of programs, including *The X-Files*, which on November 22, 1998, aired an episode, "Triangle," which picked up a narrative strand from the movie *The X-Files: Fight of the Future* of the previous summer, with split-screen and other sequences in widescreen evoking the visual style of the cinematic spin-off.[55] Even if some were not yet familiar with widescreen video versions of movies, television viewers at the turn of the millennium were certainly becoming familiar with the letterbox look from advertising and music videos.[56] In 1999, *Advertising Age* described the letterbox as advertising's "look du jour" and explained its appeal by evoking associations with foreign, independent, and "important" films.

One of the main motivations, agency creatives say, is that:

> [It makes their work more] "cinematic"—that is, it imbues the spot with the look and feel of a feature film. This was the case with a spot from the Kaplan Thaler Group, New York, for Clairol's Daily Defense shampoo; the commercial parodies the high-energy trailers of action-adventure films. To mimic the genre, the agency turned to a feature film cinematographer to orchestrate a series of wild stunts such as explosions and car chases, which were shown in letterbox form.[57]

In all three of these examples, a switch from full-frame television images to shrunken, letterboxed ones is motivated by a connection between the shape of the frame (in combination with the blacked out areas top and bottom) and the cultural status of the content. This distinction between ordinary and elevated content rests on the associations between a wider rectangular format and theatrical motion pictures, and between a squarish format and the typical content produced for television. Even as some kinds of programming were going widescreen, the vast majority of TV shows at the time—talk, news, sports, sitcoms, cartoons— were filling the 4:3 frame.

Many television viewers were also familiar with the letterbox format from cut scenes, the non-interactive portions of immersive narrative video games such as *Halo*.[58] Here the presence of horizontal black stripes is not so much a means of distinguishing games from television as it is the signal of shift out of play and into spectatorship. The connotations of a cinematic, rather than televisual, image in a hard-core shooter video game identifies gaming and cinema alike with masculinity, and reinforces the superiority of widescreen over full-frame as a standard of sophisticated audiovisual composition.

The switch to wider images on television was underway by the late 1990s, and as the 2000s unfolded more and more television programming was being presented in aspect ratios that had only a few years earlier been used exclusively for movies. This shift is a product of increasing convergence between movies and television, and television aspect ratios have developed historically in relation to cinema aspect ratios, with cinema leading and television following. Since television's emergence as a mass medium, the two media have always to varying degrees been symbiotic and convergent industrially, technologically, aesthetically, and socio-culturally. It is generally accepted wisdom that, despite many efforts at innovating and promoting widescreen technologies, beginning in the days of Thomas Edison and W.K.L. Dickson, it was the steep decline in cinema's audience in the 1950s that stimulated the American film industry to adopt new formats as standard. This decline is attributed to various causes, but prominent among them in the film industry's self-understanding is the challenge of television as an alternative to moviegoing. The TV image in the 1950s was small, monochrome, and squarish. In an attempt to win the mass audience back to the movies, Hollywood introduced CinemaScope, VistaVision, and a host of other technologies which in combination with color cinematography would produce an image much more visually impressive and imposing than one would see in a domestic space.[59] The aspect ratio standardized by the Academy of Motion Picture Arts and Sciences at the beginning of cinema's sound era in the early 1930s— the "Academy ratio" was approximately 1.37:1. The National Television System Committee (NTSC) standardized the aspect ratio of American television sets at 1.33:1, or 4:3, in 1941, not long after the Academy ratio was adopted. Thus movie and television frames were roughly the same size when television emerged as a mass medium in the 1940s and 1950s. This is why movies made during Hollywood's studio era play well on television in their original dimensions, without needing reformatting such as noticeable cropping or letterboxing.

CinemaScope, the first widely adopted anamorphic widescreen technology, is typically projected at a ratio of 2.35:1. Many widescreen processes have competed for Hollywood's business since the success of 'Scope epics like *The Robe* (1953), settling in the contemporary period on two common aspect ratios for Hollywood films: 2.39:1 for anamorphic widescreen films shot with Panavision lenses and 1.85:1 for widescreen films whose aspect ratio is produced using matting (typically in projection) of the full-frame image to obscure the top and bottom of the standard 35mm frame (Figure 6.6). Convergence-era television programs have been shot on various formats, from magnetic videotape to 16mm, 35mm, and super 35mm film, to digital and 24p high-def video. Any of these can produce widescreen images, whether by anamorphic processes that squeeze and stretch an image captured on a frame of film or tape, by masking the top and bottom of the image, or by shooting on a format such as three-perforation super 35mm film or 24p, which both expose a frame with a 1.78:1 (16:9) ratio.

Until the 1990s, it was rare for Americans to see non-4:3 images on their television screens. Television shows were shot in the aspect ratio in which they would be seen, but movies had to be modified. The two techniques most

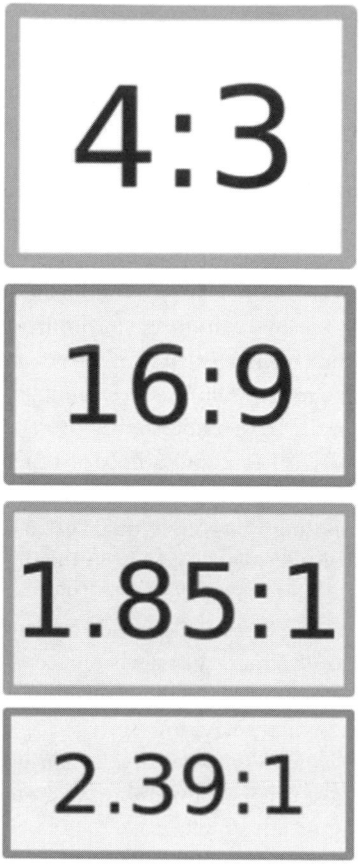

FIGURE 6.6 Four common aspects ratios are 4:3 (standard-definition television), 16:9 (high-definition television), 1.85:1 (typical non-anamorphic film projection in the U.S.), and 2.39:1 (typical anamorphic film projection)

commonly applied are cropping and letterboxing, but neither one is ideal as a way of representing the original cinematic image. Cropping a 2.35:1 image to fit a 4:3 screen ("fullscreen") means a loss of almost half the picture. In order to preserve the meaning of each shot, a video transfer might introduce cuts from one portion of the frame to another that were not in the theatrical version of the film, or pan across unnaturally to include all of the characters in the shot ("pan-and-scan"). By contrast, letterboxing preserves almost the whole image (some cropping may be inevitable in video transfer) but at the cost of shrinking the image considerably. Depending on the size of one's TV set, details just visible in a 4:3 crop may no longer be discernible to the viewer if that film is presented shrunken between black stripes.

Fullscreen versions of films were the standard on network and cable television and on VHS cassette, the dominant formats for home viewing of movies, through the mid-1990s. The laser disc format introduced in the early 1980s never caught on with a wide audience but was the preferred medium of home video for technophiles and cinephiles. To appeal to connoisseurs, laser discs, unlike VHS tapes, were often released in letterboxed widescreen versions.[60] In the 1990s especially, a discourse of aesthetic discernment attached itself to the letterbox format as an alternative to pan-and-scan, which held that it more faithfully adhered to the artist's intentions for how a film was to be viewed.[61] Filmmakers—in particular, directors and cinematographers—were active in promoting this distinction, asserting that the preservation of the full frame in its original ratio is essential in reproducing their work for the small screen. The inclusion of directors' commentaries on letterboxed laser disc editions helped establish among cinephile viewers that the widescreen ratio is the authorized way to watch a movie on a television screen. Thus, widescreen and fullscreen video transfers were not considered equally problematic compromises in adapting movies for home video. Rather, they were set up as a hierarchy, with one option for connoisseurs and another for everyone else.[62] Criterion Collection laser discs were essential in setting the terms of cinephile home video consumption. By including extra features such as commentaries and by preserving theatrical aspect ratios, Criterion releases in the 1980s and 1990s authorized an appreciative, aestheticizing mode of home viewing, and this has transferred to the more widely accessible DVD and HDTV formats in the 2000s.[63]

When the U.S. Congress and the FCC were planning television's digital future in the 1980s and 1990s, among their considerations were proposals for advanced television (ATV) displays that would improve on the resolution of the NTSC format. The HDTV format and its FCC-mandated technical requirements were the product of negotiations among the FCC, the U.S. Congress, and groups representing various interests (e.g., the computer and electronics industries). Descriptions of HDTV would typically boast of its superior picture quality, "as crisp and sharp as movies in a theater."[64] The dimensions of the HDTV frame would "have the rectangular proportions of a movie screen rather than the boxy proportions of a television set."[65] The FCC's own descriptions of HDTV make the comparison between the 16:9 aspect ratio and the look of movies.[66] A TV industry advisory committee's report claimed that with HDTV "the viewing experience is more encompassing, in the matter of a film," backing this up with the erroneous assertion that 16:9 has "the same dimensions as 35-millimeter film."[67]

Among the interested parties in this deliberation was a group of Hollywood directors and cinematographers who lobbied the FCC to adopt an aspect ratio for high-definition television that would be greater than the proposed 16:9 (1.78:1), which was based on a Japanese advanced television technology invented in the 1970s. The American Society of Cinematographers (ASC) argued that a television display with a ratio of 2:1 or greater would better preserve the dimensions of most movies without the need for letterboxing.[68] An ASC presentation at the Artists Rights Symposium in 1994 noted that 2.4:1 would be a preferable standard for ATV, as it would accommodate the widest screen standard then in use for motion pictures. But the cinematographers settled on 2:1 as "an adequate, if not ideal, standard ratio" to propose to the FCC.[69] A ratio of 16:9 would require more compromise, as 2.39:1 films would still not easily fit the format and require considerable shrinkage to fit a letterboxed image. Eventually the ASC withdrew its recommendation and the FCC decided not to specify an aspect ratio in its guidelines; the 16:9 format became standard without the force of regulation based on its previous adoption in other countries and its suitability as a compromise between various options, especially in its similarity to the most common cinematic aspect ratio of 1.85:1.[70] What is telling in this history, however, is that the need to improve on television's translation of cinema to the home viewer was a central factor in the choice of an aspect ratio for advanced, high-definition broadcasting. By the 1980s, it had become common sense that one primary function of television is to screen theatrical motion pictures in the home. The development of high-definition television and widescreen television are not connected by any technological necessity, and any aspect ratio including 4:3 could have been developed for HDTV. But the cultural logic of cinema's superiority over TV naturalized the marriage of high-definition and widescreen images, marking the newly improved television in relation both to the movie image and to the image of the picture tube set left behind by advancing technology.

The emergence of widescreen television around the time of the letterboxed *ER* was part of a larger phenomenon of rising public awareness of aspect ratios and the desirability of their preservation in transfer of films to video. The introduction of DVDs into the American market in 1997 was attended by considerable publicity and promotion in the form of popular press articles touting the advantages of the new technology. Among these was the possibility of offering a choice of versions, full or wide, and of encoding both widescreen and fullscreen versions of a film on a single disc (on either side of a two-sided DVD), thus giving the consumer a choice of format. Like Criterion laser discs, DVD "extras" often include commentaries by directors and other creative personnel. In many ways, the DVD format allowed for the Criterion Collection's mode of appreciative consumption to spread beyond its small, devoted audience. This included the discursive construction of the letterboxed image as culturally distinguished and aesthetically superior. When television series such as *ER* and *The Sopranos* began to letterbox their images, they were striving for inclusion among the forms of audiovisual culture to be considered in terms of aesthetic value. The black stripes were pleading for a new degree of cultural sanction not for television *per se*, but for the forms of television eager to be validated as culturally legitimate. Thus television's adoption of letterboxing—especially for shows addressed at upper- and middle-class, adult, male viewers—functions ideologically, privileging masculine and upscale tastes.

In addition to aesthetic rationales, however, the new widescreen television pictures were also products of more strictly economic logics. Around the same time that 16:9 TV sets were becoming available to consumers, television productions increasingly shifted toward widescreen framing (as well as toward production in formats that would transfer well to HD), though networks were exceedingly cautious about airing widescreen images in standard-definition broadcasts. This was future-oriented: producers knew that their programs would be seen on video and in syndication in widescreen formats on new television sets. One function of letterboxing content to be seen on 4:3 displays would be to prepare the audience for an upgrade in hardware to match the upgrade in picture.

The move toward widescreen TV thus must be seen within a number of contexts. One is technology: television programming shot on film or high-def video can be framed in a number of aspect ratios, most commonly the 4:3 of NTSC and the 16:9 of HDTV. Actually most programming shot in the convergence era for 16:9 is also "protected" for 4:3, meaning that the production is framing for multiple aspect ratios. Another context is economic: television producers since the late 1990s have seen the 16:9 framing as "protecting their future" (i.e., producing content for eventual syndication and DVD sales at a time when the 16:9 set is standard) while appealing to a desirable audience. Within the culture of TV production, many creatives (directors, cinematographers) preferred to shoot widescreen even well before the emergence of HD broadcasting, not only because this aspect ratio is closer to that of contemporary films, but to fit the dimensions of the more "cinematic" 16:9 screens of the future.[71] Indeed, the 16:9 HD frame was designed to fit widescreen films on TV (ironic, since Hollywood adopted widescreen to distinguish its image from television's) and is always promoted as more movie-like. Within the culture of TV consumption, many viewers prefer to see widescreen images that fill their new 16:9 sets. But the distinction between squarish 4:3 and widescreen 16:9 is one centrally defined as a contest of connotations: the old, boxy image is televisual; the new, expansive one is cinematic. Cinematic here means classy, artistic, and sophisticated. Although there is nothing inherently better or worse about either ratio, in the discourse surrounding the move to widescreen TV, one rarely hears a kind word about 4:3.

For a number of years in the 2000s, network television programming varied from hour to hour in its aspect ratio. Even with HD sets becoming more standard, many viewers still use 4:3 CRT sets on which the image is not letterboxed; in part this is why so many TV productions frame for more than one aspect ratio. They keep important action and graphics in a "safe" zone away from the frame edges. In the early 2000s, programming was shot with widescreen framings in mind and the network would have the option to air a program in either ratio. Cinematographers and television showrunners alike tended to prefer widescreen, but networks were reluctant to letterbox. *The Sopranos* aired full frame for its first two seasons until David Chase prevailed upon HBO to letterbox the series.[72] HBO's viewer surveys had convinced them that the audience was opposed to letterboxing in 1999; perhaps that had changed by 2001.[73] *Alias*, which debuted in 2001, was framed in 16:9 but broadcast in 4:3. Everyone involved behind the scenes in making the show, from editors to network executives, watched its rough cuts and final masters in a letterbox format, but the largest audience saw a squarish frame because ABC would not air a widescreen version.[74] Similarly, cinematographers and other creatives on quality dramas of the same period like *Felicity*, *The West Wing*, and *Boston Public* advocated for widescreen composition but were constrained by their networks from doing so out of a fear of annoying and alienating consumers.[75] Bob Zitter, an HBO vice-president, told *Variety* in 2001, "People don't like smaller pictures."[76]

Those shows that did air with the black bands were the ones that were successful enough to risk turning some viewers off, and also those with an audience deemed sophisticated enough to understand the upscale significance of widescreen. Jeff Zucker said that NBC could get away with a letterboxed *ER* because the show is "in a class by itself."[77] John Wells said letterboxing marked his program as classy and distinguished, an effect that contemporaneous advertising achieved using the same device.[78] *The West Wing* began to air letterboxed in 2001, as did *Angel*. It is significant in such instances that it is not the composition of the image in a different shape that marks the improvement in status, but the reshaping of the television frame with black bands, a more noticeable effect to most viewers. The letterbox, now familiar from DVDs, carried the connotations of cinema, art, and legitimacy. *The Sopranos* appealed along these lines as well, not only by letter-boxing its image beginning in 2001, but by flaunting its cinematic qualities in a number of ways. Its cinematography was often said to be inspired by Gordon Willis's work on *The Godfather*, just as its main narrative influences were gangster and mob movies including *Goodfellas*. In first-season dialogue, one mafioso, Paulie Walnuts, even discusses the framing and composition of an execution scene from *The Godfather*.[79]

By the late 2000s, the 16:9 frame had become standard as the shape of sophisticated visual content, whether on an HD set, a web video frame, or a mobile device. The standardization of widescreen video has been central to the aesthetic convergence of film and television, making distinctions between the two on a visual level less likely to persist. Hulu, iTunes, official TV network sites, YouTube, and other internet-based distributors favor the widescreen image for film and television pictures alike. TV on DVD box sets present seasons of shows such as *ER* in a widescreen format even if they were never seen this way in their original airing, proving that "protecting the future" was a prescient strategy even in the 1990s. Many mobile video devices have widescreen dimensions. Apple's iPhone and iPod touch have a wide 1.5:1 ratio (though not quite as wide as 16:9), and when Apple's hotly anticipated iPad was unveiled in 2010, technology enthusiasts lamented its 4:3 display as a possible "dealbreaker."[80]

While gadget-loving techies, cinephile aesthetes, and home theater aristocrats all might prefer widescreen displays on the basis of their preservation of artistic intent as well as a more general sense of cachet, to many less elite consumers a more important consideration is likely the maximization of value from investment in consumer electronics. The same audiences who saw letterboxing as picture shrinkage rather than as a means of maintaining aesthetic integrity prefer to see widescreen pictures fill the frame of their expensive new flat-panel televisions. This undoubtedly explains the familiar sight of 4:3 images stretched horizontally or cropped vertically to fit a 16:9 display, often fattening faces and distorting compositions. In the era of convergence, the cinematic shape of the picture is ultimately as significant to many viewers as the qualities of its content.

Content in High-Def

The shift from 4:3 to 16:9 images beginning with advertisements, music videos, cut scenes, and Quality prime time dramas like *ER* anticipated a more substantial shift in television programming, mainly during the century's first decade, from standard analog NTSC to digital high definition. This change was expensive and technically complex, necessitating the acquisition of sophisticated new equipment for staging, shooting, editing, and transmitting programs at both the network and local levels. High-definition broadcasts were important in motivating the acquisition of HDTV sets, and the wide adoption of this technology was necessary for the move from standard-def to high-def content in virtually all genres of television programming, from sports to drama and comedy to game shows and local news. In this instance, the consumer electronics and media industries functioned to promote each other's interests for mutually beneficial ends. The switch to high-definition signals had long been anticipated, the promising future of television in numerous writings in the scholarly, trade, and popular press. The most typical framing of this switch was as an improvement not just of the television picture but of television itself as a medium, rising above its low cultural status to rival cinema in legitimacy. In the rollout of this new format of content transmission we see parallel discourses to those of the retailing, domestic, and content creation spheres. The way in which high-definition has been introduced to the public privileges masculine and upscale genres and formats as a means of affirming a new concept of legitimated television at the expense of an old idea of a more degraded version of the medium rooted in the past.

Just as the retailing of flat-panel sets has appealed first of all to the male early adopter intoxicated by the novelty of the latest and most advanced gadgetry, many of the earliest forms of HD content were masculinized in comparison with the abiding feminized identity of television. Movies were among the earliest available forms of high-definition programming, first on cable outlets such as HDNet and new HD channels offered by upscale cable brands like HBO. Among the earliest network broadcasts in high-definition were many live sporting events, such as college and professional football, Triple Crown horse racing, U.S. Open tennis, and the Olympic Games. ESPN was an early innovator in offering a substantial array of HD programming, and all of the networks' sports divisions were deeply invested in HD by mid-decade. The order in which programming genres went HD signals their cultural valuation. Prime time programming was available in HD in many instances several years before daytime programming, evening dramas preceded sitcoms, and network content came before local content. High-definition repeats of *The West Wing* could be seen on Bravo HD+ at a time when network and cable alike were rapidly moving to high-def, but little in the way of network daytime programming or local news had yet switched.[81] When local stations eventually adopted HD broadcasts for their news programs, they sold the upgrade aggressively as a branding strategy for attracting upscale viewers with high-def sets seeking content to best show off the image capabilities of the new technology, in some instances adding "HD" after the call letters in station identification.

As with the sale of HD sets, the rollout of HD programming was often linked quite closely with sports. "Sports is considered the ultimate driver wooing consumers to HD," claimed *Broadcasting & Cable* in 2006.[82] Among the earliest network HD broadcasts were professional sporting events, which served to promote not just network programming in HD but also flat-panel hardware. ABC's venerable *Monday Night Football* began the first season of regularly scheduled HD sports broadcasts in 1999 as a separate feed available in approximately 25 markets.[83] In the early 2000s, well before HD sets had gone mainstream, network sports divisions produced many live broadcasts in HD, including games in the various major and college leagues and special programs such as the Kentucky Derby.[84] NBC aired select events of the 2002 Salt Lake City and 2004 Athens Olympics in HD, but by the 2006 games in Torino the network was offering all events in high-definition, a huge undertaking for which it attracted welcome publicity.[85] In the mid-2000s, local and regional sports broadcasters switched to HD for baseball broadcasts in many parts of the U.S.[86] Fox Sports was the most resistant of the network divisions to HD in the early 2000s, but it began to roll out high-def broadcasts of NFL and Major League Baseball games and NASCAR races in 2004, at which time approximately five million consumers were ready to receive high-definition signals.[87] ESPN debuted its HD service in 2003 and, as the decade progressed, multiple new channels were introduced such as ESPN HD, ESPN 2 HD, ESPN News HD, and ESPNU HD, broadcasting more than 1,100 events in HD in 2008 alone.[88]

Aside from sports, with their masculinized cultural status and their appeal to male early adopters, the other main genre of programming to go HD early was the scripted prime time drama appealing to affluent demographics—shows such as *The Sopranos* and *The West Wing*.[89] *Crossing Jordan* was NBC's first regularly scheduled show in prime time to air in HD in 2002, while ABC did the same that year with *The Practice*.[90] By the spring of 2004, before flat-panel sets had fully penetrated the mainstream of American consumer culture, much of the networks' original prime time programming was in high-def, including all of ABC's and CBS's comedies and dramas, all of NBC's dramas and some of its comedies, and many of The WB's dramas such as *Gilmore Girls* and *One Tree Hill*.[91] In order to access the high-definition broadcast, viewers needed to have an HD receiver, so the majority of the audience still watched these programs in standard definition, though network promotionals touted the HD broadcasts in appealing to viewers. At this point in the mainstreaming of TV in high-def, the availability of network content to justify the acquisition of a new set was significant to both the media and consumer electronics industries, as viewers—mainly affluent early adopters— using the new sets would seek out HD content.[92] Cable and satellite providers adding HD channels to their offerings could sell these subscription upgrades as an added charge to customers. The channels programming in HD would thus be eager to reach this early adopter audience and to encourage the further saturation of HD in the market for television sets.

The priorities of the networks in establishing their most prestigious programming as the first HD offerings speak to the cultural valuation of the HD-ready audience. In the shift to high-def, reality TV shows lagged behind scripted shows, news lagged behind sports, and daytime lagged behind prime time.[93] When Scripps Networks launched HGTV-HD and Food Network-HD in 2006, it was greeted as a gesture opening up high-def programming to new audiences, taking aim at the "male-pattern viewing" afflicting the new format. Confirming the logic guiding its adoption, *Broadcasting & Cable* announced, "High-Def Isn't Just for Guys."[94] The 70 percent female audience for HGTV might be just as likely as the male audience for sporting events to value the new HD sets, but as aesthetic objects to improve their home décor. By the end of the century's first decade, HD content offered by cable and satellite providers was substantial and enormously varied, no longer appealing centrally to the masculine and upscale early adopter. In 2010, Wikipedia listed 11 broadcast networks, 80 basic cable networks, 19 national sports networks, 13 regional sports networks, 12 religious services, and 9 premium services such as HBO offering high-definition television channels in the United States.[95]

At the same time as the flat-panel set became ubiquitous in the United States, an additional source of valued content became available to consumers of HDTV. High-definition movies could be seen before 2006 on cable channels such as HBO and HDNet, but with the introduction of HD DVD and Blu-ray discs that year Hollywood movies could also be viewed in high-definition in a home video format for sale or rental to consumers, further prompting the public's adoption of the new technology. Late in 2006, Sony's PlayStation 3 emerged with a built-in Blu-ray playback capability (to be matched soon thereafter by Microsoft's Xbox). The multi-tasking functionality of the video game console further pushes the convergence of movies, television, and games on terms that affirm the newly upgraded status of TV. The first movies released on high-definition video discs included *The Last Samurai*, *Million Dollar Baby*, and *Serenity*, well-regarded films by male *auteurs* in genres with historically masculine cultural identities.[96] Along with the availability of major sports events and the impending transition to digital broadcasting, the emergence of HD films on home video was regarded as a central factor pushing the switch to flat-panel televisions and the resulting obsolescence of the 4:3 CRT set.[97]

Formats of programming shot on film, such as prime time dramas and movies, would find an easier path to HD availability in part because of technical factors that make conversion of film images to high-definition more feasible than standard-definition video images. Beginning in 2006 and 2007, genres shot on video, such as news and game shows, began to follow the lead of sports and prime time scripted programs. The conversion to HD for local news ventures and shows shot "live" to tape, such as *Jeopardy!* and *Oprah*, required often massive upgrades in all kinds of technology and equipment.[98] Everything from cameras and sets to graphics generators and editing suites needed to be replaced at considerable expense. Local newsroom staffs needed hours of training on new equipment.[99] Sports, movies, and prime time programming in HD had given some audiences an experience of a new format of television picture, and viewers using the new sets were seeking out HD content. Local television stations were eager to satisfy this preference, and to avoid being passed over for HD programming. By March 2007, at least three dozen stations were broadcasting local news and programming other than sports in high-def.[100] But these were largely in major markets such as Los Angeles, Atlanta, Washington, Cleveland, Chicago, Dallas, and New York. Many stations had still not upgraded in 2008, when a deep economic recession pushed many plans for conversion to HD onto the backburner.[101] Throughout the process of conversion from standard- to high-definition television content, divisions structure the adoption of the new format into more and less privileged technological haves and have-nots. This occurs not only in forms of programming available in HD and in the relative affordability of consumer technologies necessary to enjoy the newly improved image, but in terms of geographical regions of the country where one might find or not find high-def broadcasts, with viewers in big cities privileged ahead of those in rural areas and smaller cities.

Forms of programming that occupy lower levels of the cultural hierarchy would be later to move to high-definition and, when they did, the move was typically framed as a form of newfound distinction. Reality TV, the most culturally degraded programming of the 2000s, was unsurprisingly slower than any other format of popular TV to be shot and aired in HD. *American Idol* and *Dancing with the Stars*, both reliable Nielsen ratings hits, began in standard definition and awaited substantial ratings success before converting to HD. *Survivor*, a perennial hit since 2000, did not air in high-definition until 2008.[102] When it did, the conversion was hailed as a long-due improvement, making possible a finer appreciation of the natural beauty and splendor of the show's exotic locations. Reality TV appeals to producers and networks as inexpensive programming which can be made in quantity, and its inartistic reputation as pandering, hyper-commercialized trash would not help the case of reality show producers eager to follow scripted shows into high-def. When the showbiz infotainment stalwart *Entertainment Tonight* began its HD era in 2008, it made the transition into an opportunity to refine its image as a site of "Hollywood events." A newly built set came with its own red carpet and multiple large plasma monitors, two of them 103 inches. Segments shot on location in Europe and Africa showed off a picture "literally jumping off the screen."[103] Many daytime soap operas were also making the switch at this time, and, as with other forms of devalued programming, the coming of high-definition was taken to promise a kind of aesthetic redemption. *General Hospital*, which began to air in HD in 2009, aimed for a "filmic, prime-time look" which the lower lighting of HD cameras makes possible. Like other "live" shows, *General Hospital* used the transition as an opportunity to update its sets and inaugurate a new visual appeal, which the president of daytime for Disney-ABC, Brian Frons, hailed for its newfound realism.[104] Even if realistic or cinematic imagery would not be the selling point, a newly HD show could still offer itself as improved, as was the case with *The Price Is Right*, which updated its sets upon converting to HD in 2008 to make its visuals brighter and more extravagantly colorful to suit the capabilities of the new hardware.

In many of the less culturally valued programs to go HD, among them daytime talk shows like *Live with Regis and Kelly* and soft news programs like *Today* and *Entertainment Tonight*, as well as in some more serious current affairs shows like CNN's *Situation Room with Wolf Blitzer* and masculinized fare such as *SportsCenter*, one feature of the upgrade stands out for its special rhetorical power. A standard element in the *mise-en-scène* of television shows remade for HD is often multiple and very large flat-panel screens. For example, *The Early Show*, CBS's weekday morning news program, moved to HD in 2008 with a new set featuring dozens of LCD and plasma displays, including two 103-inch plasma sets often seen behind the anchors as the show's main backdrop.[105] The screens within the screen serve multiple functions, including the integration of different forms of imagery into the frame. But as a feature of a newly updated aesthetic, perhaps their most profound significance is to establish the ideal image of the television as large, flat, bright, vivid, and 16:9; as cinematic and culturally distinguished; and as markedly different from the outmoded conception of a bulky, boxy, boob tube. At once these representations promote their own high-definition and the audience's acquisition of new hardware to better appreciate the HD image. In the instance of shows of lesser status like *E.T.* they also signify a striving for legitimacy. By privileging the new conception of television, the old TV, along with its modes of representation and experience, becomes the bad object left behind by technological and cultural progress. The routine imagery of the new TV on television signals that the transition to high-definition is significant not merely as a change in picture resolution, but more importantly in television's place in the popular imagination. Thus the form and meaning of the new, improved TV become the content of the programming made over to suit it.

In its importance for gaming and especially cinema, and in its hyperreal promise of overcoming the mere mediation of reality, the new television stands in contrast to the old one. The new TV is a powerful magnet for consumer attention and desire, an object of beauty and fascination in its own right, and the means by which images of distinction are conveyed into the home. With its widescreen, high-def picture, television is understood to become a more fully visual medium, no longer impoverished by comparison to movies. Its ideal user is not the proverbial couch potato or distracted housewife, and not the audience for a previous era's least objectionable programming. The quality of the content offered to maximize the potential of the new technology distinguishes television by seeming to improve on the possibilities and achievements of earlier times, opening TV up well beyond traditional forms of broadcasting into deeper convergence with movies and video games. Future developments in 3D and TV–internet convergence—such as televisions or peripheral devices bringing web apps and streaming video to living room sets—might nudge the image of the television further into a new identity intensifying and going beyond the developments we have seen so far. The flat-panel HDTV conspicuously delivers on a longstanding promise of TV to progress technologically, undoing the bad reputation that had stigmatized it as a medium for 50 years, and casting aside the old television, its image and culture.

7

TECHNOLOGIES OF AGENCY

A TV that receives its signal digitally is no longer just a dumb box passively displaying pictures and sound. Digital televisions, properly equipped, can be powerful, interactive computers, hardly different from desktop PCs. With those capabilities, suddenly television comes alive.

Joel Brinkley[1]

From its earliest years of mainstream adoption, television has often been seen as a technologically deficient medium. Max Dawson describes this ideology as *TV repair*: the enduring notion that television's myriad inadequacies require innovative improvements.[2] To the extent that cycles of technological renewal have defined the whole history of television, we can think of TV as a perpetually new medium, regularly refreshing its identity. Since the 1950s, when remote control devices (RCDs) solved problems of unstable tuning and obnoxious and intrusive commercials, many new television technologies have emerged to redeem the console and the socially compromised experience of watching television.[3] As we have seen, the improvement of the television image in the form of flat-panel HDTV sets fits within this logic.

Prominent in the history of television technologies are a number of analog fixes—attempts at overcoming perceived inadequacies—anticipating the interactive digital devices that most evidently signify television's technological convergence. Cable and satellite transmission and videocassette recorders (VCRs) emerged during the 1970s as mainstream options for expanding the range of programming choices and managing the time of viewing. During the 1980s, along with the rise in usage of RCDs (itself a product of the expansion of cable and VCRs), these fixes marked a significant departure from the network era, nudging television toward interactivity. Watching a TV receiving cable service with a remote control in hand and a VCR at the ready to record programs for later viewing or to tape one show while watching another, the viewer of the 1980s and 1990s had some advantages missing from earlier modes of watching the small screen. These technologies afforded viewers easy muting and zapping during commercials and "time-shifting" programs for watching at their convenience. As a mode of experience of television, convergence thus predates the marriage of computers and TV.

Two new technologies that came to market in the late 1990s together have altered our idea of the experience of television viewing more than any in the convergence era. Commercially available TV shows on DVD and digital video recorders (DVRs) are two of the most transformative devices in TV history. Both are understood as digital improvements on videotape as a medium for recording, preserving, circulating, and accessing audiovisual texts. They promise the audience for television (and other media) a newfound empowerment, promoting the ideal of the individual who programs his or her own media experience. In the process, along with other convergence TV technologies, they continue the VCR's transformation of the television text from a live flow of programs, advertisements, and promotions to a durable, collectible good, capable of being separated from its presentation by broadcasters and the advertisers who support their programming. For instance, with media of digital convergence widely available, a television viewer can reasonably be expected to watch every episode of a series from the beginning, in order, making the experience of TV less casual and more intense. As a consequence of this transformation, the television text is frequently aestheticized and more highly valued.

The discourse surrounding the adoption of these new ways of watching is often ecstatic and religious, invoking liberation and redemption. A 2005 article in *Slate* proposed that "watching the tube on our schedule, not the broadcasters' . . . is our destiny."[4] In celebrations of the new technologies, we read of television viewers freed from their former status as "slaves to the schedule."[5] Nowhere in the recent history of television is this more apparent than in the case of TiVo, which was introduced in 2000 by a commercial CBS refused to air in which a TV network programmer is literally thrown out the window.[6] In such discourse, digital convergence means that TV is revolutionized. Freed from the temporal constraints of traditional broadcasting, TV viewers can avoid commercials and watch anything, anytime. Now that they are in control of their viewing, watching television is rehabilitated as a productive and respectable way to spend leisure time, and television programs are seen to improve to match the newly legitimated ways of viewing. Having a DVR changes not only the way you watch, it changes your life, full stop. TiVo is "how God watches television."[7]

Other digital ways of watching TV shows have arisen along with DVDs and DVRs. Video on Demand (VOD), streaming web video, and downloads of television shows through online retailers like iTunes and through peer networks like BitTorrent offer many of the same kinds of television experience. Mobile viewing on handheld devices allows for "place-shifting" as a complement to time-shifting. All of these promise to make the viewer into the programmer.[8] The potential customers for mobile TV service are promised, "You're in control now that TV goes where you go."[9] Such technologies extract the television text from the context of the broadcast schedule, disrupting the textual and economic logic of flow that defined television viewing during the network era.[10] VCRs and RCDs were being used to do this very same work in the decades before digital convergence, but with new digital tools the typical uses of anti-flow technologies for advertising-avoidance and time-shifting become more central practices, especially for upscale TV culture.

From VCRs to Interactive Television

The digital devices that have been replacing VCRs are positioned as overcoming the inadequacies of a flawed, analog medium. The VHS format was visually impoverished compared with DVD, digital cable, or high-definition signals, and the typical VCR programming interface was supposedly too challenging for most people to use (the VCR was generally deployed mostly for playing prerecorded tapes of feature films, though many viewers used it to record, as well). Tapes degraded and would need to be rewound and cued up. A VCR could never pause live TV, and lacked the "smart" features of DVR units, such as the ability to program the automatic recording of a whole series as a "season pass," and the recommendations feature which records shows for the DVR viewer based on established patterns of use. The digital improvements on videotape offer navigational interfaces such as more easily managed menus, metadata such as episode titles and summaries, search features, elapsed-time indicators scroll-bar graphics, and program grids, making possible the viewer's organization of television experience in newly individualized and active ways. DVDs, having the same physical form as music CDs, are more sleek and compact than cassettes and take up much less shelf space. Packaged in season box sets, TV shows on DVD become objects of intense consumer fascination and desire. The eagerness and alacrity with which television viewers have replaced VCRs with DVD players, DVRs, and other digital devices attest to the revolutionary character of the technological shift underway in the late 1990s and 2000s.

According to the more fervid, revolution-minded discourses of technological empowerment, changes would come not just for individual viewers but also for the institutions of television. Viewers' newfound freedom to avoid commercial pods and defy the official scheduling of programming meant that serious changes awaited the television and advertising industries. Techno-futurist writers at the moment of the technologies' emergence saw digital TV as a force for demolishing the mass audience by individualizing media experience.[11] Interactive television was thus to augur an end to the broadcasting model of the network era and the negative connotations of TV as lowest-common-denominator mass culture that it sustained. In its place, a new model of highly personalized media was supposedly soon to become the norm, with each viewer addressed as an audience of one presented with a televisual "Daily Me."[12] This would include advertising chosen to match the interests and preferences of the individual as measured by the very technologies that granted such freedom and interactivity.

The utopian promise of authentically personalized television, of the viewer as autonomous programmer, and of a new interactive mode of viewing, is to shift power from the media industries to the consumer-citizen, the newly empowered user who previously had been figured as practically a victim of media. Press coverage of the introduction of the DVR, Boddy observes, frequently opposes "the active, in-command viewer of new interactive TV with that fabled and disreputable figure of the previous era of network broadcasting, the barely sentient, lump like couch potato."[13] Hence the rhetoric of liberation and redemption.

The idea that viewers are empowered by these interactive technologies prompts questions about the extent to which newfound modes of experience are legitimated at the expense of historical ones. As in so many instances of TV's legitimation, the celebration of a new form or meaning is predicated on the systematic degradation of old television practices. To the extent that the new ways of experiencing TV are a minority practice available to early adopters and upscale, elite consumers, the rest of the television audience still experiencing the medium through its traditional technological ensembles is slighted by the progress narrative inherent in this iteration of TV repair.

The virtually sacred, new ways of watching television require a profane, old other against which to constitute an identity as advanced and liberated media experience. This is to a large extent television itself in its residual conception as a broadcasting receiver unsupported by convergence technologies. Watching in a mode of improved agency is the newly culturally sanctioned way to experience audiovisual media, and along with the class-tinged implications of the superiority of cutting-edge technology comes a masculinization of television as a newly active experience of mediated leisure employing high-tech gadgets rather than stodgy domestic appliances. The negative, feminized connotations of watching the old way are thus reinforced. DVDs and DVRs, along with myriad digital devices and interfaces that transform television viewing in the convergence era, are crucial for television's legitimation. They prompt a revision of our conception of the experience of television, one much in evidence in many forms of media during this time period. With interactive technologies we see a shift from centering our notion of TV experience from *viewers* or *audiences* to *users*. For instance, Derek Kompare proposes that when viewed streaming online or in some other digital format, old TV shows are no longer *reruns*, "a time-bound word tracing a linear chronology"; now they are *files*, "material arranged spatially and available at any time." This, he argues, adds a dimension of "user control" to the experience of television.[14] We can see this shift toward users in the choice of words used to describe the way the technologies are employed: personalization, customization, navigation, interactivity, choice, and empowerment.[15]

By the terms of this new logic, a passive recipient of TV programming is replaced in the popular imagination by an active agent managing media time. The shift from mass audience reception to individualized agency marks a major upgrade in the status of the TV experience, one newly articulated to technological progress, intelligence, and masculinity. Boddy notes that DVRs are seen as objects of such significant value as to "reconceptualize the medium as a valued domestic resource rather than an unwanted invasion."[16] Left behind is the low status of traditional (non-interactive) television technology and reception, ever figured as passive and feminine. The rhetoric of improved viewer agency implies a progress narrative that naturalizes gendered hierarchies with their assumption that moving forward technologically means moving away from the feminized past and toward a masculinized future. This assumes ways of thinking about the cultural status of media consumption in various modes, and of various genres and forms. Technologies of agency, as constructed through convergence-era discourses, transform television viewing into a more worthwhile and artistic endeavor, effectively ameliorating many of the medium's most enduring and disparaged flaws. These include the debased commercial functions of the television text, its ephemerality and lack of enduring value, and the domestic setting of its consumption.

De-Commercializing Television

As Raymond Williams argues in *Television: Technology and Cultural Form*, the distinctive characteristic of U.S. commercial television is ultimately economically determined. The ideology of consumer capitalism produces a cultural form integrating program, promotion, and advertising into one perpetual unfolding experience rather than a set of discrete texts. We see in the convergence era that new technologies and new social needs and desires have the power to disrupt this flow, but only partially and without necessarily disrupting the underlying ideology. The establishment of television as a broadcasting medium supported by commercial sponsors whose spots are integrated in a "magazine" style answered to economic needs of the networks and stations during the formative years of the American TV industry. By freeing the network from reliance on a single program sponsor, it concentrated power in the television industry, which could raise ad rates on hit shows and thus extract more value from them. Despite the emergence of various new business models and disruptive technologies, the industry has found no better way of making broadcast (and cable) television profitable. After years of techno-futuristic predictions of the old business model's imminent obsolescence, there are few reliable signs that the television industry's basic structure of selling the most sizable and desirable audiences to advertisers is fading away. Yet discourses of legitimation propose that viewers are empowered by their DVRs and other technologies of agency to resist the traditional commercial programming format, seizing control over their time and supplanting the networks as programmers. This is always given a positive moral valence, implying that advertising is somehow extraneous and damaging to television and a problem to be overcome, that television has the potential to be better when decoupled from advertising. This perspective is expressed in a 1999 *New York Times* article celebrating *The Sopranos* as a "megamovie," in which Vincent Canby compares it with network programming:

> More and more people are apparently realizing that so-called free television demands too high a price: that we surrender an ever-increasing proportion of our attention to the contemplation of commercials . . .There are ways to avoid commercials, of course—riding the remote, going to the fridge— but in the long run commercials win: it's just too much trouble to run away.[17]

Good television, by this logic, escapes from advertising and by extension from American television's most typical structure and form.

The long-standing debasement of television as a medium has been a product of its commercialism, of the function of broadcasts as an opportunity for commercial messages to reach mass audiences. According to the new rhetoric of distinction, television's technological convergence might be effectively purifying the television text by purging it of the hucksterish and crass appeals of advertisements, which are supposed to be a nuisance to viewers insofar as they interrupt the authentic content of TV. This purification has a strong component of gendered valuation and cultural hierarchy, which has long roots in broadcast history. As Michele Hilmes has shown, the designation of daytime programming as women's programming was the product of a confluence of forces in the early days of network radio. Because the networks were reluctant to be perceived as being baldly commercial entities amidst the public service expectations of federal regulators, they chose to "hide" their most overtly commercial fare—the serial dramas produced as pitch vehicles for household goods manufacturers—during the day, when the primary target, women, were assumed to be at home, tending the domestic sphere, while the male critics of radio's commercialism would be busy in their public workplaces, unlikely to be listening to radio. The criticisms of daytime soap opera that nonetheless ensued linked the soaps' commercialism with their feminized narrative characteristics and their female audience, making the soap genre "a new touchstone of discredited, feminized, commercialized mass culture."[18] This programming strategy and the cultural logic that undergirds it have continued in the ongoing association between less legitimated program-ming formats, genres, and day parts and more overt commercialism. Thus the feminized genres of soap opera, daytime talk show, and reality TV are heavily commercialized, while more masculinized genres such as prime time scripted narrative are more readily extracted from flow. In western societies, consumerism has long been feminized, so the economic agenda of television advertising functions within wider gendered ideologies of consumption and cultural legitimacy.

Contemporary discourses seek to disarticulate some forms of TV from the commercialism that has so long tainted broadcasting. We see a distinction between gendered TV forms in particular in discourses of television's aesthetic improvement. These often invoke a rhetoric of dichotomy between art and commerce, as when critics and creative workers insist (usually plaintively) that the function of network programs is not to be art but rather to sell soap. Of course the choice of soap as the emblematic consumer good feminizes TV advertising and by extension broadcast television in general. In such discourses there is never any value assumed in the selling of soap, and never any problem implicit in thinking of television art as potentially free from economic needs. Fantasies of artistic autonomy so central to discourses of aesthetics depend on the disparagement of television's more commercialized formats as a way of promoting the superiority of aestheticized shows, genres, and channels. Art finds hospitable environments, according to this logic, where television's commercial mandate is perceived to be weakest.

As we have seen, discourses of TV's newfound aesthetic legitimacy often center on the original premium cable series. In addition to constructing these as products of *auteur* visions, legitimation discourses prize the freedom of HBO from network and cable television's constraints. In one sense, HBO, Showtime, and other premium cable outlets are literally commercial-free. They do not segment their programming as network and cable channels do for the insertion of spots and promos. (When seen in other countries and in syndicated repeats, however, HBO shows like *Sex and the City* and *Six Feet Under* might be seen with commercials and sanitized of potentially offensive language and imagery.) Supported by subscription revenue, premium cable outlets avoid some of the most enduring negative associations of broadcast television, and the predictability with which HBO programs include taboo words and nude scenes attests to their eagerness to distinguish the "freedom" of the ad-free format from the kinds of constraint faced by their less culturally legitimate competitors. Much of what makes *The Sopranos* and other HBO shows seem cinematic is their lack of commercial interruption, and thus their lack of the kinds of dramatic segmentation into acts culminating in suspenseful act-outs familiar from network fare. This follows the identity of these premium cable channels as venues for watching movies ("home box office") that are relatively recently released (compared with the ones on basic cable), unedited for television, and without breaks for commercials. The idea of an original series on a movie channel already carries some of the cachet associated with cinema but not television.

It is thus highly significant that when TV on DVD box sets emerged around 2003 as a significant cultural phenomenon and source of revenue for the media industries, it was premium cable shows like *The Sopranos* that were among the most coveted and high-profile titles for sale, titles which frequently appeared in press coverage of the new format. TV on DVD was also essential for the promotion of HBO programming and of HBO subscription, functioning as a new kind of rerun for non-subscribers who had missed the first season or two of *The Sopranos* and wanted to catch up in time for subsequent installments. In this sense, the commercial-free experience of TV on DVD was central to its positioning in the cultural marketplace—its commercial appeal. As with iTunes and BitTorrent downloads, television on DVD is always commercial-free because it is supported by different economic and technological infrastructures. The commercial model of DVD is selling media as a consumer good rather than selling audiences to advertisers, but from the perspective of the audience the lack of advertising messages makes the experience non-commercial and legitimate. The non-commercial connotations of DVD viewing are another way in which movies and television shows are made to converge experientially, as the uninterrupted unfolding of television narrative when experienced via DVD comes closer to the experience of films in the theater. The modes of access of TV on DVD also cinematize television. When TV shows are shelved alongside films in a retailer or a video rental shop, when "television" is a category alongside genres of cinema at Amazon.com and Best Buy, when the Netflix mail rental service delivers discs of films and shows in the same red envelopes (or streams them online in the same browser window), the distinctions viewers make between film and television as media become thinner and thinner. A medium is more than a technology; as Henry Jenkins argues (following Lisa Gitelman), a medium includes cultural protocols for use. Media convergence is thus as much the convergence of uses as of technologies.[19] In its old conception as a strictly broadcast medium, the cultural protocols of television viewing did not include renting shows by mail or choosing episodes from a menu of entertainment options or extracting the program from its broadcast flow. Now the protocols of film and television viewing are, in some instances and with some formats of TV, converging into a single set of practices, and this has consequences for our cultural conception of television and of its worth.

A commercial-free, cinematized experience grants some forms of television a new cultural power, which comes with a more cinematic identity for TV. Thus, the general manager of cable channel AMC touts the commercial-free airing of *Mad Men*'s first season finale as being central to the channel's effort to make "cinematic television."[20] Netflix executive Ted Sarandos asserts, "Television on DVD is becoming part of the movie-viewing experience."[21] And viewers regularly conflate watching TV on DVD with watching feature films. As theologian blogger Dave Belcher introduced a post about his TV on DVD favorites, "Most theologian-types with blogs will let you know what books they are currently reading, or which ones they just read . . . not me. Let's talk cinema . . . well, at least TV on DVD."[22] Belcher thus equates books, cinema, and TV on DVD, acknowledging a cultural distinction between books and the latter two media, but listing television series viewed on DVD as basically interchangeable with film (only his "well" indicates his acknowledgement that TV on DVD may be a slight step downward from cinema, though it is not as set apart as is cinema from books).

Derek Kompare has argued that TV on DVD takes television away from the flow model with which it has long been associated and moves it to a publishing model, the economic system upon which film distribution (particularly on home video) is premised.[23] Indeed, recent market research has found that consumer spending has overtaken advertising as the primary revenue source for the American media industries.[24] This shift alters not only the economics of TV production and distribution; it alters television's cultural value, or at least the cultural value of that television deemed worthy of DVD distribution. As Matt Hills notes, some TV genres, especially those that air daily such as soaps, news, and game shows, are unlikely to be released on DVD.[25] In Kompare's terms, they are unlikely to be removed from television's flow, to be presented "without the 'noise' and limitations of the institution of television."[26]

The fact that this "other" kind of television exists, unable to distance itself from the medium's commercialized flow, testifies to the cultural hierarchies implicit in the imagined non-commercial spaces of media convergence. Not all forms of TV are typically extracted from flow using technologies of agency, though increasingly the presence of streaming content online makes more and more television available on demand. However, the streaming versions of daytime soaps or of news stories on the web maintain both the commercial taint—one must sit through advertiser messages to view the episode or story—and some of the space restrictions of television flow (in that streaming content must be viewed via a high-speed internet connection, although that connection need not be in the home). It also lacks the permanence and archival potential of downloadable content or DVD, significant given the designation of value inherent in the archival act.

Perhaps most overt in the discourses of convergent television's removal from the commercial are the ways that the rejection of conventional television, watched on a daily or weekly schedule, in the home, advertiser interruptions intact, is positioned as an act of liberation for the active viewer. In such discourse, the rejection of conventional television in favor of the new, convergent TV is also a rejection of passivity. The embrace of the active is most closely tied to the rejection of the commercial that so many convergent technologies are imagined to provide. DVR viewing, like VCR and RCD use in pre-convergence days, fulfills a fantasy of audience empowerment not only by liberating viewers from the broadcast schedule but by eliminating the need to view commercials. TV on DVD offers a similar appeal. Australian journalist Brigid Stapleton writes that TV on DVD enables "watching what we want, when we want, and shunning the unreliable, ad-laden land of network TV," allowing us "more control and choice to the way we watch our TV programs."[27] And media financing executive James Rutherford contends that

> Time is (the consumer's) most precious commodity and people are not
> tolerating as much ad-supported media in their daily lives. Consumers are
> voting with their pocketbooks and one of the things they seem to want to
> do is avoid or minimize advertising.[28]

Everyday viewers make similar assertions, touting the active nature of viewing
via convergent technologies. As "avid DVD collector" Daniel Malcomb explained
of his habits in a newspaper article entitled "DVDs Offer Viewer Freedom,"

> Buy it on DVD and it's commercial free. That's the biggest thing to me.
> For what little free time I have, I hate commercials . . . With a DVD I can
> watch it without commercials; I can pause and get up.[29]

The freedom of action available through convergent technologies, a freedom
voiced by everyone from the home viewer to the media industry executive, has
become a dominant discourse in television's legitimation.

Because the feminized trait of passivity has long characterized television
viewership (only with DVD can Malcomb "get up"), this discursive shift is crucial
not only to television's legitimation but also to the masculinization and class
privilege at its center. Such discourse implies an acceptance of the gendered
hierarchies that have long positioned television as a denigrated medium,
characterizing it as less significant, less prestigious, and less worthy of serious
consideration than those cultural products that escape the binds of the domestic,
the commercial, and the feminine. With convergent technologies taking an
increasingly prominent place in the media landscape, television itself is seen as
escaping those binds—as long as one possesses the economic means to access
television in such ways. What is not shed are the gendered values that have made
television something to break free of in the first place. If anything, such gendering
is further reinforced in narratives of ad-free activity (available to those with the
resources to access it) over commercialized and consumerist passivity.

From Ephemeral to Collectible: Aestheticizing the Television Text

The digital technologies that have engendered the shift from flow to post-flow
television have ramifications for the experience of viewing TV. They also affect
the value assigned to television programs and the medium of television more
broadly. As a result, conceptions of the television text change as new forms of
programming and storytelling arise in adaptation to convergence-era viewing
circumstances. New trends in television narrative form and aesthetics are seen to
emerge as a consequence of these new technologies. These trends are crucial to
the formation of a nexus of production practices, new technologies, and modes
of consumption within discourses of legitimation. We would hardly deny that

programming has been shaped by convergence as technology and experience. But our concern in considering the changes in television's textual forms is with the interpretive strategies that invest new conceptions of the television text with high cultural value. We are not content to describe and celebrate the effects of technologies of agency on television storytelling when the ideological work of these aesthetic discourses promotes inequitable class and gender distinctions.

One of the most pervasive ideas in legitimation discourses is that the TV of recent years is a marked advance past the TV of previous times. As we have seen, such discourse asserts that now the shows are just better, and television has taken a giant leap forward. *Variety*'s television critic wrote in 2006, "As extreme makeovers go, it's hard to top the one television has engineered over the last several years—a quantum leap from 'boob tube' to 'brain teaser.'" He asserted, moreover, that "technology . . . has altered the TV equation, providing viewers more opportunities to tangibly demonstrate their love and largesse by directly paying for programs through buying or downloading."[30] This suggests that one putative cause of this improvement is the new possibility of preserving the television text, capturing and holding onto it, saving and savoring it. In Raymond Williams's day the television text was like time itself, constantly moving on from moment to moment, leaving itself behind forever in the past. It's harder to make a case for art in a medium that makes it difficult or impossible for the work to be preserved, displayed, archived, and valued as a classic to be revisited and appreciated over time. The drama and music critic Terry Teachout made just this point in an essay called "The Myth of 'Classic' TV," arguing that television could never be genuine art because it cannot be re-experienced over time as a book or musical composition can.[31] But with technologies of agency, the television audience potentially becomes archivists of television. DVDs are acquired to be watched again and again, and stored and displayed on shelves like books. No longer ephemeral, the television text becomes collectible like works of plastic arts, like literary works, and like movies. As with VCRs before them, DVRs and DVDs allow for the television text to be arrested and repeated, to be saved for later, and most of all to be appreciated as an object of intricacy, richness, complexity, and beauty.

One influential example of this thinking is Steven Johnson's 2005 book *Everything Bad is Good for You*, which attacks the conventional wisdom that popular culture is harmful to intellectual maturity and argues that recent and contemporary forms of gaming, cinema, and television are actually "making us smarter," as the book's subtitle puts it. Television is no longer the idiot box of network-era thinking; now watching TV amounts to a program for cognitive fitness. During the pre-convergence days, television networks preferred to air the "least objectionable programming" or LOP to best maximize the value of a mass audience. Such history asserts that plots were simplistic and creators had no ambition of making something of lasting value. Technology, Johnson says, changed all of that. The release of television shows on DVD and the use of TiVo are supposedly to be credited for "narrative complexity," what Johnson calls the "most repeatable programming" or MRP, of which he gives examples such as *Seinfeld*, *The West Wing*, *ER*, *The Simpsons*, and *The Sopranos*. *Hill Street Blues* is an important precursor. These are shows made to be seen multiple times and studied carefully using convergence technologies.[32] Johnson writes: "The MRP model cultivates nuance and depth; it welcomes 'tricks' like backwards episodes and dense allusions."[33] "You don't want instant gratification; you want something that rewards greater scrutiny."[34] Against this new standard of sophistication, Johnson offers examples of the old linear and simple way of telling stories from the network era: *Dragnet*, *Joanie Loves Chachi*, *Starsky and Hutch*.

Time's critic, James Poniewozik, makes a similar point in assessing the impact of TV on DVD on the television industry: "Traditional TV, which depends on ad and syndication sales, rewards breadth of appeal: the ability to keep millions from changing the channel. DVDs reward depth of appeal: the ability to get thousands to pay to watch something again."[35] In a *Newsweek* article trumpeting the superiority of television over Hollywood movies, TV shows on DVD are credited for introducing new possibilities for storytelling. Making a clear connection between niche audiences and distinguished programming, the *Newsweek* critic promotes the narrative and aesthetic superiority of contemporary shows:

> The roster of channels has ballooned into the hundreds, creating a niche universe where shows don't need to be dumbed down in order to survive (because the dummies have their own channels). DVDs, meanwhile, have upended how we watch television, transforming shows from disposable weekly units into 8-, 12-, sometimes 22-hour movies.[36]

Television is not alone in having adapted to the repeat viewing made possible by home video technologies. Films of the same period are also supposed to have gained in complexity as a product of new technologies, and this development is further evidence of convergence thinking. David Bordwell, Barbara Klinger, and Jason Mittell all have argued that DVDs have encouraged film and television producers to make content that rewards repeat viewing.[37] Klinger identifies a "replay culture" of fandom surrounding favorite cult films such as *The Big Lebowski*, often viewed on cable television as well as DVD.[38] Repetition is central to cult and fan experiences, but it is also a way of extending the modes of appreciation of traditional art worlds to television. It leads toward the consecration of classics, whether cult or not, experienced in the formalist mode of aesthetic appreciation which Bourdieu notes is a hallmark of bourgeois culture.

The aesthetic appreciation of TV prizes precisely the forms that are associated with technologies of agency, which allow for the television text to be "slowed down" for analysis, and which package television texts as objects with coherence and unity, as evidenced by DVDs released as seasons and series. As one critic explains:

> Now instead of shuffling your schedule to catch the next heart pounding
> adventure of Jack Bauer, you can simply wait until the season comes out
> on DVD and watch it at your own pace, even pausing and rewatching
> intricate scenes or to catch dialogue that might have been missed.[39]

Matt Hills argues that, on DVD, TV shows are selected and isolated from
television's flow and converted into symbolically bounded objects that function
within discourses of value.[40] Steven Johnson, again, articulates the virtues of this
new conception of the television text: "Viewers now curate their own private
collections of classic shows, their DVD cases lining living room shelves like so
many triple-decker novels."[41] Thus, when publishing replaces flow, the artistic
potential of television is better realized because the TV show finds a new mode
of textuality. But the forms of television that are appreciated are those which
appeal to viewers of high cultural status, and which are masculinized as well.

This process of legitimation works by negation—of forms and technologies
that are positioned either as feminine or as low in class status or as both. Thus
watching TV the old-fashioned way, as flow, is the background against which
the better, newer way is constructed. "What typically gets left out in the cold,"
Matt Hills argues of DVD's consecration of Quality TV classics, "is . . . 'ordinary
television.'"[42]

The rise of the DVD box set as an object signifying aesthetic value is the
product of a confluence of forces. The function of the DVD format to legitimate
is most notable in the case of more heavily serialized forms of television text, and
the intensification of serial storytelling in Quality TV is significant in this regard.
Serialized dramas (and comedies) aimed at upscale demographics sell well on
DVD and at the iTunes store and get the most ratings boost from the inclusion
of DVR viewers. They are also among the most downloaded shows on peer-to-
peer networks. Shows like *Lost*, *Grey's Anatomy*, *True Blood*, *24*, and *The Office*
repeatedly appear in these lists.[43] "Novelistic" cable dramas are seen as particularly good fits for DVD. A thirteen-episode cable season lends itself to effective
and affordable packaging on DVD. A season of serialized TV on DVD, when
thought of as a single long story, also might have a unity and coherence which
seasons of more episodic shows or longer seasons of network programs likely
lack. A season-long narrative on a show like *Mad Men* can have exposition and
denouement parceled out over several episodes, recurring motifs and themes, and
patterns of rising and complicating action that stretch over hours of storytelling.
These qualities of formal coherence and unity are made to justify judgments of
television's artistic merit. They underwrite literary analogies and align the cable
drama with an already legitimated art form.

Many observers have noted that consuming episodes all at once—on a "binge"
—changes the experience of television, and that the intensity of uninterrupted
viewing makes the experience of a TV show more like that a book or film.[44] In
describing serialized television shows like *The Sopranos* as "megamovies," Vincent

Canby was not only cinematizing television texts as a way of distinguishing good from bad TV, but also aestheticizing the experience of television viewing by proposing that it commands the same kind of attention and interest as films watched in a theater. The prominent blogger Jason Kottke elaborated on this in a 2008 post riffing on Canby's idea:

> Episodes of these megamovies, Canby argued presciently, are best watched in bunches, so that the parts more easily make the whole in the viewer's mind. For many, bingeing on entire seasons on DVD or downloaded via iTunes has become the preferred way to watch these shows. If stamina and non-televisual responsibilities weren't an issue, it would be preferable to watch these shows in one sitting, as one does with a movie.[45]

Kottke offers examples beyond *The Sopranos* of megamovies best experienced in this mode of aesthetic appreciation: *The West Wing*, *Lost*, *Deadwood*, *Mad Men*, *Six Feet Under*, and *The Wire*.

In her brief for television's artistic upgrade, Emily Nussbaum contends that technologies of agency have had a causal role in making television storytelling more adventurous and rewarding:

> A series like *The Wire* might not have found that audience were it not for galloping advances in technology: DVDs that allowed viewers to watch a whole season in a gulp and, later, DVRs that let viewers curate, pause, and reflect. By opening up TV to deeper analysis, these technologies emboldened a community of TV-philes, fans and academics who defended the medium as worthy of critical respect. Online, writers were forced to reckon with their most passionate viewers (and some loopy new critical forms: the recap, fan fiction, "filk"). A show like *Lost*, with its recursive symbol-games, couldn't exist without the Internet's mob-think. But this was true as well for *The Sopranos* and *Mad Men*, allusive dramas that rewarded rumination, causing nationwide waves of appreciation and backlash for months after each new episode.[46]

As terms like "curate" and "ruminate" indicate, the function of technologies of agency in such accounts is to give television creators a justification for making shows, for telling stories that the audience will find worthy of intensive appreciation. This is the exact opposite of the traditional conception of the television audience as passive victims of commercialized, mind-numbing "entertainment." And this newly active audience, as Nussbaum notes, is more likely to engage with television in a mode not only of aesthetic contemplation but of passionate, committed fandom.

Technologies of agency have thus been central to the rise of cult TV and to the flowering of television fan communities online. Annalee Newitz, editor of the science-fiction and technology blog *io9*, asserts that technologies of agency have given communities of fans new opportunities to engage with their objects of fascination:

> DVRs are the perfect tools for the television obsessive, which is what sci-fi fans tend to be. I can't tell you how many times I paused for intense debate with friends (often with rewinding and rewatching) in the middle of watching *Battlestar Galactica* or *Dollhouse*. Honestly, how is anybody supposed to watch *Lost* without a DVR?[47]

This observation resonates with experiences of earlier waves of television fans of shows such as *The X-Files* and, before it, *Twin Peaks*, whose intense engagement was aided by home video technologies (as we saw in Chapter 2).[48] It is significant that, with rare exceptions such as *Star Trek* and *Doctor Who*, there were relatively few and rather circumscribed fan communities centered on television programs before video cassettes and then DVDs made possible the preservation of the television text. Cult TV, like cult media more generally, is most essentially a phenomenon of repetitive communal experiences. The repetition of the television text at the will of the cult fan requires a medium of television experience that the cult community can own and manipulate to return to at will, to study and worship. The internet is also a technology of agency, offering the TV audience opportunities to congregate and exchange knowledge about favorite shows.

Cult TV also functions to make subcultures, and subcultures always distinguish themselves against a perceived mainstream culture. As such, cult TV fandom is positioned in relation to "ordinary" TV as a more engaged and passionate form of cultural experience. The object of cult affection is held to be superior to the typical television fare. Like legitimated television more broadly, cult texts are the fetish objects of a narrow segment of the larger television audience. They are constituted in relation to a different kind of television unworthy of the same degrees of passion and devotion. Fan cultures are aesthetic cultures, prizing the textual object, and submitting the text to the scrutiny and worship that is central to artistic traditions. To some extent the media industries have taken to courting fans. They do so by making the kinds of media products that demand fans' modes of engagement, a business strategy that helps them exploit their conglomerate corporate structure through techniques of franchise branding and transmedia storytelling. TV networks and producers have adopted legitimation as an expedient business practice in an age of narrowcasting, a way of cultivating passionate consumers.[49] They recognize that technologies of agency encourage television viewing that is serious, intense, and intellectually stimulating, which subverts the traditional idea of television viewing as distracted and unfocused. Thus John Miller, chief marketing officer of NBC Universal Television Group, told the *New York Times* in 2007 that DVDs have the "power to turn casual viewers into loyal ones."[50] Loyal viewers do not merely tune in regularly; as Henry Jenkins argues in

Convergence Culture, they are more likely to become active participants. But this activity is necessarily comparative, constructing the casual and traditional television audience in a passive and unsophisticated way that conforms to the low-class and feminine characteristics long associated with pre-convergence television. The audience conceived as "mass" during the network era is newly liberated by the cult television text, the object of intense fandom, which is itself in part a product of interactive new technologies.

Technological convergence is an ongoing process, and DVDs and DVRs might well be obsolete by the time you are reading this. The media industry dream of a "celestial jukebox" offering every media product ever created, online, and on demand for a price, might come closer to being realized. A *Scientific American* story asserted in 2009, "it should be possible to sit on one's couch, push a button or two, and call up to your television any form of video-related entertainment you desire."[51] DVDs and DVRs might not bring us to this utopian destination, but in the very late 1990s, the 2000s, and the early 2010s, they have been crucial to television's newly legitimate status. They have brought about a new conception of the television text as an aesthetic object of lasting value demanding close and careful and even repeated viewing by an active user. Not all television texts are seen this way, however. The aestheticized formats of television are those aligning with dominant class and gender identities. Television was once a medium addressed at the largest possible audience. When its address splinters into so many niches, upscale and sophisticated audiences—the ones most likely to be employing technologies of agency—are addressed with programming that flatters their sensibilities. The new conception of television textuality arising out of the use of digital technologies of agency promotes traditional aesthetic virtues such as unity, coherence, complexity, and personal vision. But it constructs this new ideal of artistic television only by invoking ideological distinctions between textual forms and audiences of greater and lesser worth.

Space-Shifting TV: New Screens and the Undomesticated Medium

The technologies of agency we have discussed so far are generally digital improvements on the VCR, facilitating new interactions with the television set but still ideally in the same home environment in which television has been situated for many decades. A complementary cluster of new technologies has emerged in the same period, allowing for users to access television content away from the television set—whether in public or private—on computer monitors and handheld mobile devices. Just as the DVD and DVR promise to free the television audience from the commercial formats of broadcasting, these new technologies offer a kind of liberation from traditional television viewing. A 2006 *New York Times* article about TV for small screens proposes, "Mobile video is starting to make the very definition of television, as a place where people watch 'shows' on 'channels,' sound pleasantly anachronistic, like a description from an old issue of *Popular Mechanics*."[52] By establishing new sites and protocols for television consumption, these new screens and services remap the geography of media consumption, establishing an alternative to the domestic setting that has been so central to television's cultural status since the medium's earliest years. If the VCR and DVR are devices for time-shifting, mobile viewing as well as web streaming and downloads can be considered space-shifting technologies. In a literal sense, the experience of watching television programs on a cell phone or laptop screen potentially brings TV into new and varied sites, such as corporate office cubicles, buses and trains, and libraries. A *Wired* review of a mobile TV service exclaims, "*The Daily Show* on the toilet? W00t!"[53] Television has long had a presence in public places, as Anna McCarthy discusses in *Ambient Television*.[54] As Stephen Groening describes, the experience of watching on cellular phones offers a personalization of television viewing in public environments.[55] One trade press commentator declares that the personalization offered to the mobile TV user is "anathema to mass media—to broadcasting as we have known it for a century."[56]

The public spaces in which such viewing occurs, such as airport departure lounges, waiting rooms, and fitness centers, might already have televisions for common use. But no matter where mobile devices are used, new technologies for viewing TV content away from the television set revise popular understandings of television's cultural status. These technologies of agency disarticulate TV from the gendered space of the private family home, undoing long-standing associations between TV viewing and feminized domesticity. One mobile television service offered by the cable company Comcast is called "TV Everywhere," and this idea of ubiquitous screen entertainment is meant to evoke powerful commercial and emotional responses. While undoubtedly a product of media companies eager to extract revenue from new platforms and formats, building their brand at every conceivable opportunity and site, "TV Everywhere" and numerous similar ventures are also products of changes in television's identity, and efforts to mold that identity to fit the technologies and industrial strategies of convergence.[57] A first-person report on Fox News represents this new conception of television as a space-shifting medium by tying mobility to other technologies of agency:

> Just as my daughter can't conceive of a time when we couldn't record a TV show, or a day when we had to go to a theater to see a movie, in a few years time it may be difficult to remember what it was like when we couldn't watch whatever we wanted, whenever we wanted—and wherever we wanted.[58]

The historical identity of television, as Lynn Spigel and Cecelia Tichi have shown, was a product of its emergence in the post-war years as a domestic appliance to be integrated into feminized, private, domestic environments. The location of the television is the space of the surburban family home, at least in the popular ideal of television cultivated in advertising and other discourses of the post-war period. Feminized by this spatial identity, television viewing came to be seen as pacifying and emasculating, and as commercial mass culture rather than legitimate art. The private, home-bound context of TV viewing led to the creation of many conventions of television programming such as the day parting of the broadcast schedule according to which family members were likely to be home at various times, "tailoring low-visual-involvement, highly segmented program styles to hours when the housewife was the presumed primary audience," as Boddy writes.[59] By being made to fit domestic routines, the commercial medium of American television became the primary leisure-time activity to service an ideology of advanced consumer capitalism. The consumption promoted by TV is thoroughly feminized, as we have seen. The place of the medium itself in the domestic sphere feminizes and delegitimates it, so the disruption of associations between television and domestic space can thus serve to legitimate and enhance the cultural value of TV. The technologies of agency allowing for space-shifting are undoing the deep associations, for instance, between television viewing during weekday hours and women in the home. Outside of the home, the television shifts from one set of values to another: now it may be public rather than private, active rather than passive, productive rather than just passing time, and masculine rather than feminine. As Max Dawson argues, the discourse of mobile television suggests that it is "*placeless*, and unburdened by television's attachments to domesticity and a stifling and sedentary suburban way of life."[60] Representations of mobile TV picture the experience of taking television out in public as a "journey of escape from domestic routine, particularly as it materializes in the contours of the television timetable and the conventions of domestic television reception."[61]

Television away from home is not particularly new. Lynn Spigel has explored the emergence of portable and compact sets in the 1960s in terms of their promise to mobilize and masculinize the private experience of television viewing, so central to establishing popular understandings of the medium in the previous decade.[62] A portable TV set, however, is still a television receiver in the traditional sense, a cathode-ray tube monitor receiving an over-the-air signal from local transmitters. The space-shifting television technologies of agency emerging in the convergence era are different in a number of ways. Downloaded programming from an online retailer or peer-to-peer network makes for an experience of users accessing files rather than of audiences for televised flow, and storing and accessing this content on a laptop or iPod is literally a way of keeping television shows in your purse or pocket. DVDs are space-shifting in this sense as well, allowing for television texts—rather than television as a signal—to be taken on trips and played while flying or commuting. Even if the cubicle or home office desk is stationary, making the workplace into a site of entertainment consumption means a new fluidity of space and activity as work and leisure blend together. The smartphone is a gadget marked by this same spatiotemporal fluidity, merging work and leisure uses and affording its user the perpetual monitoring of social and public streams of information, in addition to a potentially vast menu of games and other amusements, productivity applications, and entertainment.[63] Even if many uses of services like Hulu's and Netflix's streaming on-demand content are in the home rather than out in public, the personalization and portability of television texts in domestic settings mark a significant break from the spatial and ideological configurations of the suburban "family circle" or "electronic hearth."

Other new technologies like Slingbox and mobile TV services offering live (as well as on-demand) programming are in some ways even more radically space defying. The Slingbox allows the user to access a home DVR's programming— even live programming—from any web-connected device, making possible a simultaneous experience of home and away. While its users largely may be frequent business travelers and other elite adult consumers, its potential suggests a kind of untethering of the home set from its physical location, allowing the Sling subscriber the opportunity to maintain the routines of home from anywhere with an internet connection. Mobile TV services provide users of certain smartphone devices a cluster of channels with a combination of live and on-demand programming, and require both a specific model of phone capable of receiving the service (to date most are not capable) and a monthly fee, usually around $10. While popular in some parts of Asia and Europe, these have had a slow start in the U.S. and by 2010 were commonly considered a failure.[64] The most desired content for mobile viewing, according to industry professionals, is live programming, especially sports but also media events like Michael Jackson's funeral that are magnets for massive attention. Scheduled pre-recorded shows, on the other hand, find little demand.[65] Digital mobile TV might eventually return us to the conditions of portable television considered by Spigel if digital devices like smartphones eventually receive a free digital signal over the air.[66] Of course the context of convergence will layer on new connotations and technological possibilities if this comes to pass, fitting the mobile digital receiver into the omnipresent discourses of improved agency, usage rather than spectatorship, and television's cultural legitimation.

As has also been true of flat-panel HDTV sets, mobile television services have been marketed extensively at the early-adopter demographic of 18- to 34-year-old, affluent, adult males, and often by selling the mobile service as a new and improved way of watching sports. Such services are typically marketed at this group by appealing to its sense of gender difference. "To consume mobile television," Max Dawson observes of efforts to reach these consumers, "is to escape the social and spatial constraints of the home—as well as the feminine connotations of domestic viewing—for more interactive (and appropriately masculine) forms of perambulatory public leisure and consumption."[67] One of the most important forms of programming used to promote mobile TV is live broadcasts of events such as World Cup soccer games and *Monday Night Football*, looking for an audience eager not to miss big games when they are unable to be at home or at a fixed public viewing location such as a sports bar. For example, ESPN claimed to have streamed more than 100 million minutes of World Cup soccer in 2010 to American mobile phones.[68] Forms of new technology are routinely masculinized through the rhetoric of high-tech gadgetry. But by associating mobile viewing with sports, the electronics and media industries have forged powerful associations between media mobility and an ideal of heterosexual adult masculinity constituted in distinction to feminized realms and practices. Such realms and practices include not only the home as a private domestic sphere but also activities and concerns, like shopping and heterosexual romance, that are extensions of the gender relations typical of heteronormative constructions of home and family.

A standard trope of the television advertising for sports programming through mobile services is the defense of masculinity in the face of demands on male leisure time. As Dawson argues, mobile television advertising often relies on narratives of "gendered conflicts over space, leisure, and consumption."[69] Even in public spaces away from the home, the heterosexual male sports fan cannot avoid the need to be present and available to women and children, despite his preference for watching football games. This marks the use of the mobile TV service as an escape from the routines and practices associated with normative gender roles, relations, and family life, wherein feminine influences are taken to threaten male autonomy and to emasculate the man. The availability of sports programming "on the go" makes possible an assertion of male liberation from feminized spheres of influence and a recuperation of male authority in resistance to female encroachment. The mobile television service offers the man an escape route out of the demands made on him by women and by feminized social spheres, allowing for him to shift his attention and time back to masculinized spectatorship, for instance, by slipping away from the table at a restaurant to sneak a look at the baseball game he can watch using his mobile device and his Slingbox.

A television spot for Verizon NFL Mobile Redzone seen during football games in 2010 pictures a couple in their twenties lounging by a glassy resort pool (Figure 7.1). The woman, clad in a black bikini, announces that she is "going to take a quick dip," rising to wade into the water with her conventionally attractive body displayed to the man, offered up to his visual contemplation and pleasure. But instead of gazing at the form of his romantic partner, he reaches for his mobile as a baritone voice-over admonishes, "Keep your head in the game!" The image counterposes the curvy female form of the girl in the black bikini, pictured from behind but out of focus in the background, with the high-tech black rectangle of the phone in the foreground, football game in the man's hands. The phone screen is in crisp focus to indicate his attention on the sportscast rather than the woman and his relationship with her. The voice-over continues: "Never miss a touchdown with NFL *Redzone* every Sunday afternoon." This ad jokes that mobile football broadcasting might have the power to distract the heterosexual man from his desire for an alluring woman, but it is undergirded by the masculine rejection of the feminine as well as the need for the male viewer to reclaim his leisure time for appropriately manly interests and activities.

FIGURE 7.1 A television spot for Verizon's mobile TV service

A FLO TV ad seen during Super Bowl XLIV in 2010 depicts another young, straight couple, shopping in a department store where the man is pressed into service as the woman's abject helper, carrying her shopping bags and even keeping a brassiere for her draped over his shoulder. CBS play-by-play announcer Jim Nantz reports from this scene as though it were the broadcast of a sporting event, offering an "injury report" on the man, whose "girlfriend has removed his spine, rendering him incapable of watching the game" he attempts to catch on the flat-panel screens of the electronics department. The solution is to carry mobile TV in your pocket so that "live sports goes where you go." Nantz ends the ad with the line, "Change out of that skirt, Jason!" As Dawson writes, this spot "races over a cursory description of FLO TV's technical features, and makes no mention of the types of content available to the service's subscribers, focusing instead on the decidedly masculine pleasures mobile television delivers to its audiences."[70] In this instance, the female demands on male time and attention are portrayed as much more threatening than in the Verizon ad, and the solution thus comes as much more of a defense of masculinity under siege by tyrannical femininity, but the underlying gender roles and implications are not all that different.

Print advertising often sells the mobile video functionality of cell phones as an occasion for wonder and amazement in typical hyperbolic tones, offering less overt gendering of the technology and more of a rhetoric of spatiotemporal revolution. (All of the examples in this paragraph come from September and October 2010 issues of *ESPN: The Magazine*.) An ad for the ESPN Mobile TV service asserts, "There's a flat screen TV in your pocket," while a Verizon print ad pictures the mobile device framing an image of an NFL player over the tagline, "Add Buffalo wings, and you pretty much have a mobile sports bar" (Figure 7.2). In these instances, the mobile television experience allows for a virtually miraculous subversion of the strictures of space and time, allowing you to carry a television set on your person and to create your own ideal viewing environment wherever you happen to be. In some instances, the mediated representation accessed through the mobile devices is depicted in a direct encounter with the body of the user who carries the screen on his person. For instance, a Samsung ad pictures an elaborate battle scene with armored soldiers wielding swords and shields staged in the glowing palm of a man's outstretched hand, accompanied by copy touting "cinema quality entertainment" on a "screen that is brighter and more vivid than anything you've seen before" (Figure 7.3).

Here cinema is equated with the masculine genres of action-adventure or historical epic, with violent spectacle and high-tech visual effects, and of course cinema is—compared with television—public and legitimate. In advertising for mobile screen technologies, categories of personal and communal, outside and inside, public and private, home and away are confounded and superseded by the new technology's ability to create spatiotemporal and physical realities. The stability and routine of traditional television viewing on the living room set are most certainly the antithesis of this form of mobile media.

As with television's de-commercialization and aestheticization, the extraction of TV from domesticity has as much to do with ideas about the medium as with its actual uses. The technologies affording this extraction are part of a larger ensemble of innovations in media consumption that are transforming notions of work, family, leisure, and identity. To the extent that they are transforming notions of television, they do so by encouraging viewing in a mode of newfound agency—and by promoting this agency as the key improvement promised by the digital technological revolution. The television viewer's rebirth as the television user is one outcome of the convergence of TV with computers. To become users, the television audience must leave behind the popular conception of TV as a

FIGURES 7.2 AND 7.3 Print advertising for mobile TV in *ESPN: The Magazine* presents new technology transcending limits of place and time, promising new freedom and agency for the mobile viewer

passive, feminine medium. Television is thus legitimated not only by better content, whether considered as narrative representations or images and sounds, but also by better, more masculine, means of accessing that content. But the new means have not replaced the old ones, and, as is generally true of new media, old technologies won't just go away when new ones come along. Old and new co-exist and continue to develop in relation to one another, giving the new ample opportunities to be defined in contrast to the old. Even with a DVR, one can still watch "live TV" with commercials, the old-fashioned way. Indeed, reports indicate that many DVR users often prefer *not* to fast-forward, perhaps because long-standing habits of use are not so easily disrupted, or because exercising agency is not always the first priority of the audience for entertainment.[71]

William Uricchio notes that when Raymond Williams wrote his account of watching American television, which is to say when flow was identified as television's distinctive cultural form, he had available approximately six channels, no cable, no RCD, and no VCR.[72] The most common image of television in this earlier era, according to William Boddy, was "quotidian, advertising dominated, audio driven, visually impoverished, female centered, and passively consumed."[73] Williams' mode of viewing and its set of cultural assumptions form the background against which we must understand the contemporary upscaling of TV. The new modes of television experience accrue value by revealing the inadequacies of the previous era's television. Thus the phenomenon of people who claim that they don't watch TV or that they even have a TV, but who binge on TV on DVD or iTunes or BitTorrent downloads. They don't think of what they do as watching TV, and this idea of "watching TV" is instrumental in creating a new conception of what television can be—watching TV meaning watching what's on when it's on, watching at home on the communal family set, and watching commercials and promotions and whichever show comes on when the last one ends. In other words, TV minus technologies of agency.

8

TELEVISION SCHOLARSHIP AND/AS LEGITIMATION

> The segmentation of the media is closely aligned to social segmentation, so that the legitimated media are aimed at the high status social groups . . . So those of us who are in media education have a responsibility to our students and to our society to first of all try and destroy this hierarchy of legitimation.
>
> John Fiske[1]

The multiple sites that contribute to the legitimation of television in the convergence era indicate the reach of this discursive formation. Even while the denigration of (certain kinds of) television persists in many quarters, legitimation is increasingly pervasive. Thus far, however, we have avoided exploration of an additional, key site for the legitimation of television in the convergence era. Television scholarship is an important space for the legitimation of the medium, but it can be particularly challenging to document, and to critique. While in many ways the discourses of academics exist in a marginalized space, well removed from the television industry and the popular and trade presses, some scholars are regular sources of expertise for journalists and scholarly, popular, and trade discourses can and do influence one another. Besides, most television scholars help to shape public understandings of media in their interactions with students, if nowhere else. Study in institutions of higher education has historically marked the ascent of cultural forms such as theater and film to high status, as intellectualization promotes the serious contemplation of meaning and value and aligns new forms with old conceptions of cultural legitimacy.[2] As a means of concluding our analysis and raising questions about the future, then, we investigate the role of scholarship itself in processes of television's legitimation. Assessing the role of television scholarship in the medium's revaluation requires us to be self-reflexive, given our own participation in the scholarly realm and this very book's status as a work of

TV scholarship. If television scholars contribute to the legitimation of the medium in the convergence era, and if these processes of legitimation perpetuate hierarchies of taste, value, and cultural and social worth, then we are—wittingly or not—complicit in the very discursive formation we intend to critique.

We hope it is no secret that we love television. We both identify as scholars of TV (among other media), we publish works of television history, theory, and criticism, we teach courses with titles such as "Television and Radio in American Society." And we are equally passionate about television in our personal lives; indeed, it is nearly impossible for us to separate our professional and personal engagements with the medium. We spend much of our (minimal) leisure time watching TV, for pleasure, yes, but also for scholarly purposes, so as to reference current TV to our students, to participate in scholarly conversation, to generate our own research agendas. We watch that TV through a multitude of convergence-era technologies—a flat-panel HD set assisted by satellite service and an HD DVR, a DVD player, laptops, tablets, and handheld mobile devices. We almost never watch commercials. We subscribe, intermittently, to premium channels. We fill a bookcase in our living room with DVD titles, many of them TV series box sets. We watch a wide range of programs, but current favorites include *Mad Men*, *Terriers*, *In Treatment*, and *Friday Night Lights*. We blog and tweet about our TV passions.[3] Educated professionals on the young end of middle age, straight, white, married, homeowners, Amazon.com patrons, Costco shoppers, parents to young children, we are the quality demographic the television industry and its advertisers crave. Personally and professionally, we *are* the legitimation of television.

While we recognize our participation in—and even our enabling of—some of the very discourses we challenge, we also assert that television scholars can and should strive for awareness and transparency in the ways their tastes shape their practices, including their practices of teaching and scholarship. At the same time, we advocate for a cultural studies-influenced television studies, one that understands television and all popular culture as a site of struggle over taste and value, a site wherein the inequalities and hierarchies that shape society sometimes are resisted but more frequently are reinforced. While we hope that this book contributes to that kind of television studies, we are mindful of the ways in which our work is possible only as a result of the growing legitimation of television as a cultural object, worthy of serious attention. Just as we enjoy the fruits of television's legitimation even as we are critical of it, our efforts question legitimation practices even as they are an outgrowth of them. Our precarious positioning leads us to wonder how we can love and value TV, not to mention how we can function as television scholars, without engaging in discourses of legitimation and replicating their cultural hierarchies. More than the foregoing self-reflexivity, we hope that our effort to historicize, contextualize, and criticize the scholarly contribution to the convergence-era revaluation of television moves in that very direction.

The Institutionalization of Television Studies

When Kenneth, the TV network page slavishly devoted to his employer on the NBC sitcom *30 Rock*, was asked about his major at Kentucky Mountain Bible College, he proudly answered, "Television studies with a minor in Bible sexuality!"[4] In an earlier era, the joke could have stopped at "television studies"; the absurdity of someone majoring in our culture's most lowbrow medium would have been apparent. Indeed, in campus novels of the 1980s and 1990s, a professor of popular culture, or one who obsessively studied sitcoms, functioned as a parodic archetype, an egghead proving his ivory tower isolation by making the mass and the trivial into objects of importance.[5] Even in television programming itself, the study of television was ridiculed.[6] But in *30 Rock*'s 2010 incarnation, the punchline falls equally on the "Bible sexuality" part of Kenneth's answer; after all, a television devotee like Kenneth could have no other major, especially within a series that rewards rather than mocks its viewers' encyclopedic knowledge of television. Because Kenneth is such an over-the-top caricature, however, the program also invites us to laugh at the fact that such a mismatched course of study was available, especially at this fictionalized backwater. Although the TV-obsessed Kenneth could have had no other major, there is still a decided absurdity to the choice, one bested only by the even more outrageous "Bible sexuality" minor. The construction of the joke depends dually upon the growing recognition that the field of television studies exists and the realization that the (fictional) field of Bible sexuality is even more laughable.

In both acknowledging and ridiculing the growing legitimation of television, this joke demonstrates that institutionalizing television studies as an academic field has been a gradual process, one that is far from wholly accomplished. Today there are academic job lines, conferences, (partial) department names, book series, and a Library of Congress subject heading for the study of television. This is a significant, and relatively recent, set of developments that has contributed to—and been enabled by—the convergence-era legitimation of the medium. As Charlotte Brunsdon remarked in the late 1990s, at that point it was possible to take university-level courses in television studies "in a way which was inconceivable in as recent a past as the 1970s." As a result, she could see "television studies" as a "relatively recent, aspirationally disciplinary name."[7]

Academic disciplines are constructed by differentiation of the discipline's work from that of others, a means of practitioners recognizing "just who they are and what they do."[8] Dana Polan lists a number of developments that indicate such a "concretization of a discipline":

> The rise of professional societies, the legitimation of some critical practices (and a concomitant delegitimation of others, deemed to be less scholarly, rigorous, or scientific), the regularization of practices of credentialization (the granting of degrees and diplomas, for instance), the garnering of academic

respect through the publication of books that become standard points of reference, the crystallization of networks of dialogue and interchange among credentialed practitioners through such venues as conferences, [and] the perfection of channels for the dissemination of disciplinary research in the form of scholarly journals.[9]

All of the above have been an increasingly prominent part of television studies in recent years, suggesting that Brunsdon's "aspirational" disciplinarity may have become less aspirational and more fully realized since the late 1990s. Just as the 1960s were the period in which film studies took on "disciplinary solidity and regularity," perhaps the 2000s have done the same for television studies.[10]

Much of the early academic study of the medium was undertaken within the largely American field of mass communication, which typically relied upon social-scientific methods in considering television's effects upon its viewers and the larger populace. As condemnatory of mass media as this sort of research could be, it often existed within academic departments teaching students "the crafts of reporting, advertising and public relations," and so television scholarship often pursued "questions of more or less direct utility to the communications industry."[11] Less common was the study of television programming as texts, as works of art or even generators of meaning, though some more humanistic television inquiry was underway as early as 1962.[12]

By the 1970s, academic interest in a "literary analysis"-style approach to a wide range of popular cultural forms was growing. Yet, "Television was among the last [popular cultural] topics for which legitimacy was sought," which testifies to its low cultural status.[13] In 1975, Richard Adler lamented that "the critical study of television has no place at all in the academic world."[14] It was around this time, however, that scholarship engaging with television texts in the "serious" way Adler desired began to appear. In the volumes Adler edited but also in Horace Newcomb's *TV: The Most Popular Art* (1974), scholars began to engage with the medium's output as text.[15] As Hal Himmelstein characterized this turn, "In the early 1970s . . . a group of young scholars, most of whom had done their graduate work within English departments, began to take television seriously as an art form with unique aesthetic properties and cultural meanings."[16]

From here, the field continued to grow. In 1979, the U.S. Library of Congress added a subject heading for Television—Study and Teaching, indicating a sedimentation of the medium as an object of study.[17] This development further progressed in the 1980s when scholars such as John Fiske helped bring British cultural studies and its attention to popular culture—television included—as a site of struggle over meaning to the U.S. Fiske's work joined Newcomb's ongoing scholarship and gradually helped to build a field that took television seriously, rather than treating it dismissively, and that combined theoretical and methodological approaches from mass communication, sociology, film studies, and English to grapple with television both as a textual and a social force. The growth of the field from the 1980s on has been steady, proceeding alongside the increasing segmentation of television distribution and audience targeting and the labeling of certain instances of television as Quality.

A number of markers help to identify the growing legitimation of the field since the 1980s. In this time, the practice of studying television as a branch of the humanities has become increasingly institutionalized. Take the career of television scholar Horace Newcomb as one telling trajectory. Newcomb earned a Ph.D. in English in 1969, and held faculty positions in that field, as well as American Studies, into the early 1980s. He began to publish his foundational work on television in the mid-1970s. He was hired to the Department of English at the University of Texas at Austin in 1978, adding a joint appointment in the Department of Radio-Television-Film in 1981. Beginning in 1982, his appointment was wholly located in the Radio-TV-Film department, where he would stay until 2001. In his tenure at Texas, Newcomb mentored the next generation of television scholars while also working to improve television's public standing, as in his mid-1990s role as curator for the Museum of Broadcast Communications and editor of the Museum's *Encyclopedia of Television*. In 2001, Newcomb furthered his participation in the legitimation of television when he took a faculty position at the University of Georgia, a move that brought him the title of Director of the George Foster Peabody Awards.[18] The Peabody Awards, "often cited as the most selective and prestigious in electronic media," model themselves after the Pulitzer Prize and have sought to "recognize distinguished achievement and meritorious service" in the radio and television industries since 1941.[19] Over the course of his career, then, Newcomb has been central to the rise of television studies as an academic discipline as well as the elevation of the medium's public profile. That Newcomb became Director of the Peabody Awards in the early 2000s, succeeding a history of directors with academic qualifications in more conventional fields such as journalism or mass communication, even further illustrates the role of a humanistic and critical television studies in the popular legitimation of television since the new millennium.

Many other developments also illustrate the concretization of television studies as a discipline and as a legitimate scholarly enterprise. In 1989, a group of feminist television scholars joined together to form the Console-ing Passions collective, a group that organized the first in a regular series of feminist television studies conferences in 1992.[20] In 1995, Console-ing Passions co-founder Lynn Spigel began to edit the Console-ing Passions book series for Duke University Press, the first title of which, Jane Feuer's *Seeing Through the Eighties*, marked the continuing shift of a scholar originally trained in film studies into the television studies realm.[21] Indeed, a number of scholars trained in film studies during the 1970s and 1980s began to study and publish on television during this time, among them Robert C. Allen, Henry Jenkins, William Boddy, and Michele Hilmes.[22] Our own experience follows this established pattern, as one of us (Newman) was trained as a film scholar before turning to the study of TV.

The growth of television studies out of cinema studies is also clear in the history of both fields' central professional organization. The Society for Cinema Studies (SCS), begun in 1959 as the Society for Cinematologists, had incorporated television into the organization's mandate by the mid-1980s, albeit with some controversy.[23] In the mid-1980s, SCS debated the "place" of television within film studies, and the Society's scholarly publication, *Cinema Journal*, had to formally institute a new policy to allow for the publication of work on television.[24] By the turn of the millennium, however, television became increasingly prominent within the organization. In the late 1990s, SCS members formed a Television Studies Interest Group and in 2002 the organization changed its name to the Society for Cinema and Media Studies to better encompass not only work on television, but also on a range of rapidly converging media.

Alongside this incorporation of television has been an increase in the tenure-track jobs advertised through the organization that specifically seek a candidate with a specialization in TV studies. As illustration, consider that in the fall of 1999, the SCS job list of 55 tenure-track jobs featured just two jobs in television studies. In October 2000, a list of 67 tenure-track jobs featured just six that listed television as one of multiple possible research specializations. In contrast, in December 2010, the SCMS online listings for tenure-track positions mentioned television in 11 of 31 positions listed, a leap of over 20 percent in 10 years.[25]

Scholarly publishing has also witnessed a notable increase in attention to television. Along with the Console-ing Passions book series and individual works published by a range of other university presses are a number of book series that focus on particular television programs. Duke University Press' *Spin Offs* series and Wayne State University Press' *TV Milestones* series are two notable examples. Open Court Publishing's *Popular Culture and Philosophy* series has featured a number of television programs in its volumes, while I.B. Tauris publishes scholarly work on television in several different series: *Investigating Cult TV Series*, *Popular TV Genres*, and *Reading Contemporary Television*. In 2000, Sage Publications began to publish the peer-reviewed journal *Television and New Media*, while, in 2003, Routledge began publishing *New Review in Film and Television Studies* and, in 2006, Manchester University Press began publishing *Critical Studies in Television*.

Undergraduate and graduate coursework in television studies has become more prominent alongside these other developments. Departments of telecommunication, broadcasting, and mass communication had been preparing students to work in the television business since the medium began, but in the late 1980s and early 1990s, a number of courses began to take a more critical and humanistic approach. Indeed, we have experienced such developments first hand. As an undergraduate major in telecommunications and English in the late 1980s and early 1990s, I (Levine) encountered a field in transition. My coursework included studio and field-based TV production, but also included an introduction to a critical and cultural approach to TV scholarship. One course, The Broadcast Program, taught by a new assistant professor, Christopher Anderson, introduced me to television studies as I know it today, largely through the work of Newcomb's *Television: The Critical View*. Given the course's title, it had clearly taken a different form before Anderson began teaching it. Excited by this course, I eagerly registered for TV Aesthetics and Criticism the following semester, only to be confronted with a course that focused on television broadcasts of the arts—opera, theater, classical music—as if the question of aesthetics could only be paired with television when true art forms were involved. Anderson took over teaching TV Aesthetics and Criticism in subsequent semesters, reworking it in the vein of the "new" television studies.

In 1988, the Department of Communication Arts at the University of Wisconsin-Madison hired John Fiske, author of *Reading Television* and *Television Culture*, to help spearhead undergraduate and graduate programs in "telecommunications." Fiske brought his cultural studies approach to television studies to the program, shaping a new generation of scholars in the process. In the late 1990s, the graduate program in telecommunications changed its name to Media and Cultural Studies in an effort to better characterize the changes in the field that the program had long embraced. In this instance and many others, television studies became institutionalized only after the field could be characterized more broadly as *media* studies. Indeed, as Michele Hilmes notes of the change in name at the Society for Cinema Studies, "Certainly, SCMS could have added 'media' to its name at any time in the last twenty years but chose to do so only under the seductive influence of the emerging new media paradigm."[26] Thus, while television itself has become increasingly legitimated, it has done so in part through its convergence with other media.

Since the early 2000s, the institutionalization of television studies courses and concurrent legitimation of television have been perhaps most evident in the spread of attention to television beyond radio–TV–film and communication studies curricula. This arguably has been most apparent in college-level courses focusing on HBO's series *The Wire*. While some of these have been taught by professors of television and other media, a number of faculty in other disciplines, such as history and sociology, have also constructed courses around the series.[27] This happens on occasion with other select instances of television, as well, for example a spring 2011 course in the Department of History at the University of Wisconsin-Madison, Gender Through *Mad Men*, or the English/Art History course Smart TV: Television as Art and Literature, at the University of Utah.[28] There is no doubt that faculty and administrators recognize the appeal of television as a draw for students; however, it is significant that these kinds of television courses are oriented around specific or individual series (as series, more than genres or media, are most often legitimated) and that the series so chosen are among the most lauded of contemporary TV.

In her assessment of the state of the field, Brunsdon points out that a prerequisite for conceiving of TV studies as a discipline is the notion that TV itself is worthy of study. She claims that "academic and popular writing about the medium is haunted by anxiety about the cultural legitimacy of watching television."[29] If the premise of our argument is correct, and watching television has increased in cultural legitimacy in recent years, then the hesitancy Brunsdon offered in the 1990s about the establishment of the field may have since achieved some degree of resolution, allowing for a more secure position for TV studies as an academic discipline. Yet television studies remains far from an entirely secure and institutionally respected discipline. In part, this reflects the deliberately interdisciplinary nature of TV scholarship. At the same time, it is significant that the study of television has achieved its greatest degree of institutionalization thus far in the convergence era, when technological and experiential shifts have allowed for the use of "media studies" rather than "television studies" as a label for the field. Clearly, the status of television as bad object has not wholly disappeared. As Hilmes has pointed out, the most prestigious of U.S. universities have neither departments nor interdisciplinary programs on the study of television or other media, typically allowing only the study of (some kinds of) film in an arts context, a situation she characterizes as scholars "[skipping] . . . over television and radio and [forming] a film/new media 'high-art' alliance." As she tellingly predicts, "Most Ivy League students will be studying 'new media' before television is ever allowed to darken the doorsteps of their institutions."[30] Nonetheless, we are witnessing an increasingly secure institutionalization of the study of television in other quarters, whether in the very *Cinema Journal* fora to which Hilmes is contributing or in the course on *The Wire* taught by Harvard sociologist William Julius Wilson. Television scholarship has been both participant in and beneficiary of broader processes of legitimation. As with all such processes, however, what gets ignored, unnamed, and *de*legitimated can be especially significant. In the institutionalization of media studies, only certain kinds of television scholarship, and certain kinds of television, reap the benefits of legitimation.

Legitimation in Television Scholarship

In the convergence era, television scholarship has flourished, finding a range of homes both conventional and innovative. A number of university and commercial scholarly presses regularly publish academic work on TV, peer-reviewed journals dedicated to television and other media circulate article-length studies, and a cluster of blogs and online journals edited by participants in graduate film, television, and media studies programs offer shorter, more informal insights on a frequent basis.[31] As participants in the scholarly communities that generate this work, we benefit from this dimension of television's legitimation, adding publications to our curriculum vitae and achieving the kind of recognition that leads to significant material rewards—secure employment, cultural status, the respect of peers. We also have a deep affective investment in this dimension of television's legitimation. To be able to study, write about, and teach TV—to think about television and other media for a living, with the bulk of one's working hours—

is to us a great gift, one that enhances the quality of our lives in infinite ways. It is a product of our deep material, intellectual, and emotional investment in the field that leads us to question some developments in contemporary television studies, to ask how recent TV scholarship participates in legitimation, and to worry about the effect of that participation not only on the social and cultural positioning of television, but on television studies, as well. How might certain developments in convergence-era television studies reproduce the hierarchies and inequalities that are bound up with legitimation?

Some convergence-era TV scholarship has embraced the "Golden Age" rhetoric perpetuated in popular and TV industry discourse, constructing the television of the scholars' present as a marked improvement over what came before. In popular discourse, such statements typically are made baldly and boldly, with little or no attention to historical precedent. Scholarly accounts are often more subtle, with nods to history. Yet the perpetuation of Golden Age rhetoric in TV scholarship nonetheless voices some of the ahistorical progress narratives that mark other discourses of legitimation. Robert J. Thompson's book *Television's Second Golden Age* is one such instance, although the title, more than the content, perpetuates a narrative of television's natural progression over time.[32] Thompson more explicitly declares television's chronological path of improvement in other work, such as his co-authored essay (with David Lavery) on David Chase and television creativity. Lavery and Thompson construct Chase's work on *The Sopranos* as the teleological end point of a TV storytelling path years in the making. They write of *Hill Street Blues* in the 1980s: "The creative and commercial success of the show inspired two decades of programming that was more sophisticated, more complex—indeed *better* than what had gone before," and discuss *The Sopranos* as the inevitable outgrowth of this progression.[33] Constructing Chase as the (somewhat tortured) artist struggling to release a vision both personally and culturally resonant, Lavery and Thompson contribute to the discourse of the showrunner *auteur* so prominent in convergence-era popular culture.

Lavery's work as editor or co-editor of a number of volumes of TV scholarship focused on single series is also a primary indicator of the legitimation of the present as an improvement on the past. Not only are the series that receive such treatment examples of the most legitimated programming of the convergence era (*The X-Files, Twin Peaks, Buffy the Vampire Slayer, Deadwood, The Sopranos*); the trend of centering books on individual series is a clear outgrowth of legitimation—in an earlier era, neither academic publishers, nor scholars, regularly identified single series as worthy of such concentrated attention. Amelie Hastie writes of these volumes, focused on individual, Quality series, that they suggest a "hierarchical understanding of television." Because the contributors to such collections often come from fields such as English, their attention to these kinds of series suggest "a lack of understanding of television as a medium that is *generally* appropriate as an object of academic scholarship."[34] Instead, certain series are awarded attention because they seem exceptional, works of art worthy of critical study.

Paul Levinson makes this case in a piece on *The Sopranos* in which he contrasts that series with Quality dramas of the 1980s: "Even at their most complex, these night-time serials were usually paper-thin compared to *The Sopranos* . . . The result is an intensity and intricacy seldom attained even in motion pictures."[35] At the heart of the distinction, Levinson notes, is the elimination of commercials in premium cable fare: "Undriven, unriven by commercials, *The Sopranos* is able to soar."[36] Much work on *The Sopranos* and premium cable in general makes similar claims. For example, Trisha Dunleavy describes the series as "the most innovative American drama serial in a creatively eventful decade" and cites the "freedoms" of premium cable as a root cause: "Its cable domicile freed the emerging drama not only from anxieties about FCC content rules, but also from the other constraints on a TV drama's design, content, and style that can be attributed to the context of an advertising-funded broadcast network."[37] Brian G. Rose praises HBO's *The Wire* by differentiating it from the cop shows of the broadcast networks:

> Instead of offering a dramatic alternative to the program formats of its commercial broadcast rivals, *The Wire* was a direct assault against that most venerable of TV genres, the cop show, with the goal quite literally to explode the creaky, hidebound world of prime time crime and law enforcement from within.[38]

Throughout such scholarly work, select instances of convergence-era television are celebrated for their difference from network-era and/or advertiser-supported TV, for their literal escape from the (gendered and classed) constraints of TV proper. Because such a narrow category of programs receives such inordinate attention, and because that attention so heavily distinguishes these programs from "television" (while affiliating them with cinema) this sort of scholarship perpetuates the hierarchization and exclusion that accompany legitimation.

The characterization of a select group of convergence-era programs as evidence that television has entered a new Golden Age too often presupposes an ahistorical conception of television. For example, Jason Jacobs writes in the *International Journal of Cultural Studies* that:

> The historical development of television's dramatic efforts has reached a point where issues of excellence are pressing to an extent that has not been before . . . I doubt whether many previous shows could compete . . . to the extent of [contemporary series'] popular and critical success, or whether we would discover excellence in the terms that they make available to us.[39]

Not only does Jacobs invest in a progress narrative of television quality here, he also openly admits to not doing the historical analysis that would better allow him to support his claims. Apparently, the "excellence" of contemporary television in comparison to the past is self-evident. Other scholars have made similar claims. In the online journal *Flow*, Craig Jacobsen points to the fact that even "unremarkable" television (he cites *How I Met Your Mother*, CBS, 2005–) draws on "atypical narrative strategies" (such as voice-overs and a flashback structure) as evidence that "Television may be ready to fulfill its potential as a sophisticated narrative medium."[40] Jacobsen here implies a natural progression through the metaphor of maturation—now that television is "growing up," it can achieve "sophistication." The assumption herein is that television, like the human organism, has matured naturally over time, that history inevitably moves forward progressively, and that television can thereby leave its less admirable reputation in the past.

Jason Mittell's essay on "narrative complexity" in contemporary American television is a widely cited analysis of storytelling trends in some forms of prime time programming of recent years. While it makes a persuasive case that certain distinctive kinds of television narrative form emerge in this context, Mittell's work is also invested in discourses of progress similar to those discussed above, although he is more nuanced in crafting his argument. Mittell details a number of developments that he identifies as contributing to the complexity of convergence-era television: the multiplication of distribution outlets and the fragmentation of audiences, the technologies of viewer "control" such as DVDs and DVRs, and the movement of creative personnel from other media (namely film) into TV production, all of which he understands not as "straightforward causes" of narrative complexity but instead as "enabling the creative strategies to flourish."[41] He states that he is not making an "explicitly evaluative" claim about the worth of narrative complexity over "conventional programming." Still, one suspects that Mittell wants to assert that "the pleasures potentially offered by complex narratives are richer and more multifaceted than conventional programming" but refrains from doing so overtly in this context.[42]

These underlying claims do become clear in other instances of Mittell's work. In *Flow*, Mittell has written of his agenda of cultivating his students' tastes for "television that [he thinks] is great," which unsurprisingly includes many of the series he classifies as "complex."[43] In such discourses, Mittell does not address the ways in which his privileged position might perpetuate hierarchies of value that reinforce inequalities of gender, age, or class, among other markers. In still other contexts, Mittell has championed such distinctions. In a "Meet the Faculty" video interview—entitled "Television's New Golden Age"—for Middlebury College, Mittell declares:

> We're in a real Golden Age of television that aims for something higher. And I really think that ... is going to continue because the quality demographics and people who are willing to invest their money and time into television [are] really focused on these programs that are thinking highly of their audience and really aiming up rather than aiming down.[44]

In public discourses like this, television scholars are able to point out television's worth, to intervene in long-standing discourses that disparage television and assert the value of the medium. This is an understandable impulse, and one with which we wholly sympathize. But we question the ramifications of praising television within discourses of legitimation, discourses that imply or overtly state a chronological historical progression in which the "good," "complex," "sophisticated" television of the present is an improvement upon the television of the past, in which terms like "Golden Age," with all of their associations of exclusion and elitism, get authoritatively applied, and in which the tastes of academics dictate the parameters of the television that is worthy of serious attention. In his interview, Mittell praises the fact that "Golden Age," convergence-era television is made to please elite audiences, and suggests that this state is preferable to television that "aims down," presumably at less valued demographics. That such a claim dismisses the television before this moment, as well as the television of the present that does not pass muster with elites, participates—intentionally or not—in discourses of legitimation.

As Mittell's claims about television narrative indicate, some of the key distinctions drawn in the television scholarship that engages in discourses of legitimation grapple with aesthetic questions. The comparisons made in popular and media industry discourse between multiple- and single-camera sitcoms and between soap operas and prime time serialized drama appear in TV scholarship, as well. Such analyses thus perpetuate some of the very aesthetic hierarchies upon which legitimation depends. Television scholars have discussed single-camera comedies in terms more or less identical to those of critics in the popular press, praising these shows for "reinvigorating the sitcom format" and for "resurrecting" the genre through their "stylistic innovation."[45] In such scholarship, the style of these programs is positioned as an upgrade on a lowly and exhausted formula, denigrating some television in order to celebrate other television, depending upon the same kinds of progress narratives that pervade Golden Age discourses. The idea that single-camera comedies are an improvement on the traditional sitcom rests on problematic assumptions about television history and aesthetics, and denies the cultural functions of aesthetic discourses.

Jeremy Butler's impressively detailed and thorough analysis of sitcom style is a case in point. In *Television Style*, Butler explores the ways that TV style has become more prominent and aggressive in recent years, a conception that meshes in some respects with John Caldwell's notion of "televisuality" as a description of the "excess" and "exhibitionism" in TV style noticeable since the 1980s.[46] Butler follows Caldwell's use of the term "zero-degree" style—an absence of style—to describe the multi-cam sitcom, contrasting it with the single-cam, televisual sitcom, which he celebrates for bringing him "pure aesthetic pleasure."[47] In this characterization, Butler (and Caldwell before him) adopts a film-centered conception of television style, one that emphasizes features such as camerawork and editing. This conception of style has origins in classical film theory, which was often concerned above all with defending the status of cinema as an art form and, thus, with finding those aspects of cinema that are essentially cinematic. Literary or theatrical values, such as dialogue and acting, both of which have centrally important roles in TV comedy, are hard to defend as "cinematic" style, and have a limited place in the history of film theory and stylistics. The conception of style from which Butler works is one premised in the medium essentialism of cinema, a conception that was itself an effort at legitimation. As a result, this kind of stylistic analysis fails to recognize the style of a theatrical genre like the traditional, multi-cam sitcom in a positive sense. However, an aesthetic analysis of television that is sensitive to history rather than invested in a narrative of aestheticized (and cinematized) value would not find the multi-cam style deficient in its difference. Rather, it would recognize that television style changes over time, fulfills specific purposes, and need not rise or fall on the basis of its similarity to another, more culturally respected medium.

Scholarly analyses of the increasing presence of serialized narration in prime time drama also employ aesthetic judgments, replicating the distinctions that elevate certain prime time series above the feminized soap operas that share their narrative structure. Often, serialized prime time drama is distinguished from soaps in scholarly work when scholars unquestioningly quote industry workers who insist upon this distinction. Thus, when Lavery and Thompson quote David Chase on his disdain for television and his refusal to let *The Sopranos* fall into the soap opera traps of *Twin Peaks*, they let this comparison stand as fact.[48] When scholars fail to interrogate the discourses of the media industries, including those of creative personnel, they lend that discourse the authority of their own scholarly reputation. Serialized prime time drama is also distinguished from soap opera when scholars simply ignore the long history and ongoing presence of soap opera as television's foremost serialized form. Thus, when Roberta Pearson praises the creators of *Lost*, she highlights their ability to sustain a serialized narrative as if no other programming has accomplished this feat. She writes,

> In an act of creative bravado unequalled in any other contemporary medium, *Lost*'s creators had to devise a narrative premise and group of characters capable of sustaining audience involvement over tens of episodes until an ultimate resolution that probably, given the show's current success, lies years in the future.[49]

That soap opera creators face the same challenges, carrying their narratives over tens of thousands of episodes and multiple decades, is ignored.

The acceptance of "narrative complexity" as the descriptor of choice for convergence-era prime time serials but not daytime dramas implies a relative valuation of different modes of seriality. Mittell acknowledges that his conception of narrative complexity necessitates a comparison to soaps, but soaps are assumed to be something other, unnamed, not complex.[50] When he does address the relationship between daytime and prime time seriality, he insists that daytime and prime time dramas be categorized separately, and denies an abiding influence or affinity between them. While careful to avoid appraising their relative quality, he also makes clear that the prime time dramas he values are "much more influenced" by comic books and nineteenth-century novels than by soap opera.[51] Thus Mittell sidesteps explicit comparisons in terms of value while nonetheless perpetuating cultural hierarchies that distance the more aestheticized prime time serials from the feminized mass culture space of daytime.

It is understandable that scholars might engage in comparative analyses of TV aesthetics. Yet, in so doing, we should remember that, as Henry Jenkins has written, "Aesthetics is a discourse of power, claimed as the exclusive property of dominant classes as a club to use against the 'debased' tastes and preferences of the lower orders."[52] In this respect, attending to the aesthetics of a form as historically debased as television may be seen as "a way to fight back against the social awareness of television as a bad object," as Greg M. Smith declares.[53] Of course, celebrating television aesthetics in and of themselves does not necessarily accomplish this sort of "fighting back;" indeed it might replicate more cultural hierarchies than it displaces. For example, when the "zero degree style" of the multi-cam sitcom is used as a means of appreciating the "sophistication" of the single-cam comedy, scholarly accounts can reinscribe class distinctions.[54] Thus, even an effort like Smith's (to appreciate the aesthetics of *Ally McBeal*) can ring hollow when the text to be appreciated fits within a body of texts (Smith calls them "drop-dead gorgeous" and "an embarrassment of riches")[55] that are often distinguished from the medium's low Others, be they the reality series of the present or the comedies and dramas of television's past.

There is one additional way in which contemporary television scholarship too often engages in discourses of legitimation: by accepting and perpetuating the logic and interests of the media industries. This is especially problematic when the television in question is addressed at privileged fragments of the media audience. In such instances, legitimation is not only a cultural or ideological force, it is a savvy industrial strategy for matching products to markets. This kind of legitimating scholarship extends beyond the unquestioning iteration of the perspectives of creatives such as David Chase. Across various instances of television scholarship, the logics of the industry, those that endorse and further the commercial interests of massive, global conglomerates, get both repeated and supported in the voice of TV scholarship.

At times, scholars end up endorsing the perspectives of the media industries by quoting or paraphrasing creatives or executives without questioning what may be motivating their claims, much as we have seen in scholarship that accepts as truth the distinctions between prime time dramas and soap operas as articulated (or ignored or disavowed) by prime time showrunners.[56] Thus, Amanda D. Lotz, writing of *Sex and the City* creator Darren Star's choice to produce the series for HBO rather than for ABC, points out that:

> The premium cable channel was necessary in Star's mind in order to maintain elements of "eliteness" in writing and production, as well as a budget . . . on which he could afford independent directors and writers. The series' home on HBO also provided Star with considerable content freedom. This enabled the series to derive its humor from the sexual adventures of the four characters, rather than from the double entendres and hidden discussion about sex typical of broadcast sitcoms.[57]

It is not entirely clear how much of this claim is Star's and how much is Lotz's, but in any case Lotz leaves unquestioned several assumptions that serve the interests of Star and HBO. She notes the cultural baggage of Star's claims of eliteness by placing the term in quotes, but she does not challenge the links between budget, the "independence" of behind-the-scenes talent, and "eliteness." The passage also arguably mischaracterizes the humor of the series in a way that elevates its position in a cultural hierarchy of comedy, as it is pretty indisputable that *Sex and the City* made liberal use of double entendres regardless of the "content freedom" afforded by the premium channel. This passage makes no active endorsement of the interests of the media industries, but neither does it unpack the ways that cultural hierarchies shape Star's perspective on his work and on the industry more generally. By reporting on claims like Star's without considering them critically, Lotz's generally timely and comprehensive book misses an opportunity to challenge industrial tactics of legitimation, and thereby accords them further authority.

Scholarship on premium cable is particularly guilty of accepting industry discourse without question. Even while some of its chapters explicitly critique the motives and strategies of HBO, for example, *It's Not TV: Watching HBO in the Post-Television Era* has the appearance of endorsing the channel's promotional effort at distinction through its well-known slogan simply by repeating that slogan as the book's title.[58] Like many of the edited collections on single series, those books focusing on a single premium cable channel (typically HBO) are also a clear product of the growing legitimation of television. A cable channel becomes worthy of (multiple) instances of scholarly investigation once it, and television more generally, achieve a certain degree of cultural status. For example, the detailed attention to each of HBO's original series in *The Essential HBO Reader* suggests that every instance of the channel's output demands concentrated study.[59] On this HBO-centered scholarship, we share the concerns of Dana Polan, who has argued that it works to HBO's benefit to have "independent" academic critics praise their product: "The patina of purity that comes with the academic critics' declarations of independence makes it appear as if academia has discovered the deep virtues of HBO on its own and has gravitated naturally to its cultural riches."[60] Endorsing HBO's claims to "not TV" status not only serves Time Warner's corporate interests, it also helps to reproduce class-based hierarchies of cultural value.

Scholarship considering the media industries' employment of new technologies can also end up reinforcing the interests of the industries, at times in the name of "the people" as fans. Henry Jenkins's work on convergence culture has quite usefully pointed to the tension that exists between "top-down, corporate-driven" and "bottom-up, consumer-driven" interests in this new cultural and techno- logical context.[61] Often, however, Jenkins emphasizes the ways in which these interests collude rather than conflict, and ends up championing practices that may sometimes serve the interests of some viewers—and particularly young, active, and affluent fans—but definitely serve the interests of the media industries. These implications emerge in quite subtle ways in Jenkins's work, but together with the larger discourse of legitimation, they contribute to a climate in which the media industries' interests come to be equated with the interests of all. As Jenkins writes regarding the media industries' increasing awareness of and desire to cater to fan practices and preferences:

> We should certainly avoid celebrating a process that commodifies fan cultural production and sells it back to us with a considerable markup. Yet, these same trends can also be understood in terms of making companies more responsive to their most committed consumers, as extending the influence that fans exert over the media they love, and fans as creating a context in which more people create and circulate media that more perfectly reflects their own world views.[62]

Jenkins's opening qualifier is important, yet what ends up getting emphasized is the ways that fan practices benefit from the efforts of the media industries. Instead of attending to fan activities for how they might challenge hierarchies of domination and subordination, the ways that fan interests gel with media industry interests become paramount. Such a perspective is possible because of discourses of legitimation; when television gets legitimated, the industries that create TV can more readily be seen as helping rather than harming public interests.

When Jenkins' perspective is picked up in other scholarship, some of the same tendencies are repeated. Thus, Jonathan Gray seeks to distinguish between "successful" and "unsuccessful" paratexts—those texts that supplement a central media text through transmedia storytelling—by assessing how well incorporated they are with the central text, a distinction that presumably serves the interests of fans who want coherence and narrative unity across textual sites.[63] He deems less significant the fact that many of the paratexts circulating in the convergence era are primarily meant to serve a promotional function, to drive traffic back to the central text and/or to generate new revenues and thereby serve the interests of the media industries first and foremost. Indeed, he ends his book-length exploration of paratexts with a consideration of "the practical issue of how film and television creators can more meaningfully integrate paratexts into the storytelling and production process."[64] In other words, he sees one ultimate purpose of his scholarship as helping the media industries to better make and sell their wares. The logic of legitimation is at work here. For if TV is as high Quality as discourses of legitimation would have us believe, then helping the TV business to do its job more effectively can only be a good thing. Only in an era of legitimation, one in which instances of television and other media valued by privileged audiences are championed, is it reasonable for purportedly critical scholarship to suggest that helping the media industries make a product that better meets their promotional and profit-centered goals is a service to the people.

This advisory, applied function of media research is especially evident in the work of the MIT Convergence Culture Consortium ("C3"), with which a number of the scholars cited above are affiliated. C3 has been supported financially by major media companies and has produced scholarly reports for its clients, advising them how to engage audiences and harness new technologies, among other things, to best achieve their corporate agendas. Jenkins's *Convergence Culture* is prominently featured in official C3 literature and functions as the "impetus" for the founding of the consortium as well as the source of its "underpinning principles."[65] The role of media scholars as consultants to major media companies, predicting future trends and forecasting best practices to maximize revenue, strikes us as symptomatic of a kind of media scholarship that too easily takes the perspective and shares the interest of the media industries. This is not to imply that C3 researchers *necessarily* adopt the prevailing logics of the industries they advise, or that they cannot challenge these logics, only that the agenda of independent analysis and critique may sometimes be incompatible with those of industry consulting. Moreover, we are not arguing that the only appropriate perspective to take on convergence-era media is one of outright, negative criticism; rather we are hoping to see media scholarship that recognizes, speaks to, and grapples with the tensions between corporate interests and the fragmented interests of citizens in an era of convergence and legitimation. It would be particularly welcome to see more work seizing on the role of legitimation in the media industries' strategies of niche marketing at upscale and masculine consumers and in the industries' cultivation of the supposedly more active and engaged, "participatory" audiences that they (and C3 researchers) so highly, and so problematically, value.

Positive Directions for the Future

The participation of convergence-era television scholarship in the discourses of legitimation does not mean that this is the sole perspective contemporary scholars offer. In fact, a number of scholars have engaged in critiques of legitimation as a whole and have overtly challenged the scholarship that perpetuates it. Christopher Anderson identifies HBO's role in constructing "an aristocracy of culture," complete with classed tiers of television: "The ability to think of one television series as a work of art exists alongside a belief that others are nothing more than noisy diversions clattering along the conveyor belt of commercial culture."[66] Other scholars have analyzed the premium channel's strategies of distinction, as well, understanding such efforts as part of a broader discourse of legitimation to different extents.[67] As early as 1996, Lynne Joyrich warned of the dangers of this sort of reach for cultural distinction, including its gendered implications:

> Some viewers and/or critics have attempted to rescue television from its place of low self esteem by arguing that television can and does meet . . . aesthetic standards, pointing, for example, to possible instances of television auteurs even where they might be least expected. . . . In this way, one might try to indicate an elevating vision and coherent aesthetic behind the television text and so salvage a sense of "masculine" authority lying just beneath the amorphous surface of what is then only ostensibly a "feminine" form.[68]

While Joyrich's study attends more to the ongoing feminization and denigration of television, she offers a critique of the kind of legitimation that would only escalate in subsequent years.

Even when TV scholarship does not directly take on the discourse of legitimation it can play a part in resisting and challenging it. For example, when David Thorburn analyzes *The Sopranos*, he refuses attempts made by David Chase, as well as many popular and some scholarly critics, to see the series as repudiating or transcending television. Instead, he insists:

> *The Sopranos* is not a film. It is a television series. It uses the strategies perfected over decades in daytime soaps and prime-time series. It draws on a tradition of visual mastery developed equally in the interior spaces and tight, compelling close-ups of soaps, sitcoms, and family melodramas *and* in the fluid editing and skill at framing action and exterior spaces for TV's small screen of the cop and private-eye shows.[69]

He is admiring of the series and engaged with aesthetic questions, to be sure, but he does not deny its status as television or its indebtedness to television history.[70]

Work on *The Sopranos* and premium cable is perhaps the most obvious site within which to identify legitimation at work and to notice those rarer moments when it is challenged. But other contemporary scholarship also manages to examine convergence-era television without echoing broader discourses of legitimation. We have cited much of this work throughout our own analysis. Some exemplary cases include Derek Kompare's exploration of the rise of television series on DVD, William Boddy's dissections of popular discourses surrounding new media such as DVRs, Dana Polan's examination of *The Sopranos*, Matt Hills' inquiries into fandom and cultural value, and Glen Creeber's analyses of contemporary serialized drama.[71] Barbara Klinger's study of discourses around home theaters and Lynn Spigel's deconstruction of "smart home" technologies also work in this vein, even if they are not focused on television exclusively.[72] We are also encouraged by the recent scholarship that analyzes the representations and address of convergence-era television in the contexts of contemporary social inequalities, work that continues television studies' impressive history as a politically engaged field in the tradition of cultural studies. Despite the lines we may seem to be drawing, we have no single prescription for television scholarship; we want to read and support a wide range of perspectives on television present and past, including considerations of television texts and genres, industrial strategies, new technologies, and qualities of media experience in the context of everyday life. We simply hope to encourage more self-reflexivity and caution as scholars take on the changes of television's present, when discourses of legitimation run so rampantly throughout conversations about the medium.

The discourse of legitimation is a powerful one. Having observed its power so closely, we find ourselves more resigned to its continued prevalence than optimistic about its downfall. The legitimation of television is well on its way to becoming a new, hegemonic common sense. But a hegemonic victory is always a product of negotiation; a position of dominance is always precarious. It requires continual reassertion, and involves continual trade-offs. Television achieves a new level of cultural respectability as long as the focus remains on certain *kinds* of television. And TV technologies can be seen as new tools of empowerment and control as long as they can be constructed as rejecting the denigrated devices of years past, as well as the people associated with their use. Because of such trade-offs, there are always small spaces, slight openings, for resistance and challenge to these logics. *Legitimating Television* is an attempt to step into those openings before they become so slight as to be nearly imperceptible.

There is no hiding the fact that we benefit professionally and personally when the object of our scholarship and much of our leisure time pleasure is considered a site of cultural value and worth. But our aim has been to encourage an awareness of the ideological dangers residing within these discourses of cultural uplift. Celebrating the television that appeals to elite tastes over that associated with the "masses," championing the masculinization of TV technology, praising the television industry for finding new ways to monetize our attachment to TV characters and worlds—these are not developments to endorse. We love television. But legitimizing that love at such a cost? Paying for the legitimation of the medium through a perpetuation of hierarchies of taste and cultural value and inequalities of class and gender? No.

NOTES

1 Legitimating Television

1 Pierre Bourdieu, *Distinction: A Social Critique of the Judgment of Taste*, trans. Richard Nice (Cambridge, MA: Harvard University Press, 1987), 6.

2 "Could *Heroes* Move Away from Serialization?" *IGN*, November 17, 2008, http://tv.ign.com/articles/931/931067p1.html.

3 James Poniewozik, "*Heroes*: Serial Killer?" *Time*, November 20, 2008, http://tunedin.blogs.time.com/2008/11/20/heroes-serial-killer/. Poniewozik's column and the comments on it exemplify this sort of response. Here and throughout we use capital-Q Quality TV in reference to those programs that target a narrow, upscale audience and that are widely viewed as high quality by these viewers as well as by many critics and scholars. We do not use the term as our own designation of value. In this respect, our use follows that of Jane Feuer, Paul Kerr, and Tise Vahimagi, eds., *MTM: Quality Television* (London: British Film Institute, 1984).

4 Josef Adalian, "'Black Thursday' Hits ABC Dramas Hard," *TV Week*, November 2008, http://www.tvweek.com/news/2008/11/adalian_column_black_thursday.php.

5 Ibid. A similar perspective emerges in Michael Hirschorn, "The Future is Cheese: Why the Networks are Surrendering Prime Time to Jay Leno and the Lord of the Dance," *The Atlantic*, March 2009, http://www.theatlantic.com/magazine/archive/2009/03/the-future-is-cheese/7277/.

6 Linda Holmes, "10 Reasons This Was TV's Decade," *NPR*, Dec. 26, 2009, http://www.npr.org/templates/story/story.php?storyId=121843993.

7 For examples of the early buzz around *Heroes* that places the series amidst a turn toward "smarter" TV, see Robert Bianco, "TV Smartens Up for Fall Season; Viewers Get Something to Think about Thanks to Brainy Hits Like *Lost*, *24*," *USA Today*, September 1, 2006, 1E; Mike McDaniel, "TV's Fall Season Turning Golden; Five Best New Shows Easy to Pick; Five Worst Aren't All That Bad," *Houston Chronicle*, August 1, 2006, 1.

8 Christopher Lisotta, "Hyping *Heroes*," *Television Week*, July 31, 2006, 4. Jonathan Gray, *Show Sold Separately: Promos, Spoilers, and Other Media Paratexts* (New York: New York University Press, 2010), 211–213, 217–218.

9 Ibid., 217. Christopher Hagenah, "Day 3 Society for Cinema and Media Studies Conference LA 2010," *HASTAC*, April 1, 2010, http://www.hastac.org/blogs/

chagenah/day-3-society-cinema-and-media-studies-conference-la-2010. Jason Mittell, "Rethinking *Heroes* and *Mea Culpas*," *Just TV*, November 16, 2007, http://justtv. wordpress.com/2007/11/16/rethinking-heroes-and-mea-culpas/. *Heroes* producers also participated in the Futures of Entertainment conference held at MIT in 2007. "NBC's *Heroes*: 'Appointment TV' to 'Engagement TV'?" Futures of Entertainment: MIT Communications Forum, November 15, 2007, http://web.mit.edu/comm-forum/forums/heroes.html.

10 Ben Vershbow, "The Novelodeon," *if:book*, November 26, 2007, http://www. futureofthebook.org/blog/archives/2007/11/the_novelodeon.html.

11 Devin Gordon, "Why TV Is Better than the Movies," *Newsweek*, February 26, 2007, http://www.newsweek.com/id/68462/output/print.

12 John Seabrook, *Nobrow: The Culture of Marketing, the Marketing of Culture* (New York: Vintage, 2001).

13 Bethany Bryson, "'Anything But Heavy Metal': Symbolic Exclusion and Musical Dislikes," *American Sociological Review* 61, no. 5 (October 1996): 884–889; Richard A. Peterson, "Understanding Audience Segmentation: From Elite and Mass to Omnivore and Univore," *Poetics* 21 (1992): 243–258; Richard A. Peterson and Roger M. Kern, "Changing Highbrow Taste: From Snob to Omnivore," *American Sociological Review* 61, no. 5 (October 1996): 900–907.

14 Michael Z. Newman, *Indie: An American Film Culture* (New York: Columbia University Press, 2011).

15 Ryan Hibbett, "What is Indie Rock?" *Popular Music and Society* 28, no. 1 (February 2005): 55–77.

16 Bourdieu, 470.

17 Ibid., 174.

18 Ibid., 2.

19 Ibid., 6.

20 Ibid., 56.

21 Lawrence W. Levine, *Highbrow/Lowbrow: The Emergence of Cultural Hierarchy in America* (Cambridge, MA: Harvard University Press, 1988), 8.

22 Paul DiMaggio, "Cultural Boundaries and Structural Change: The Extension of the High Culture Model to Theater, Opera, and the Dance, 1900–1940," in *Cultivating Differences: Symbolic Boundaries and the Making of Inequality*, ed. Michèle Lamond and Marcel Fournier (Chicago: University of Chicago Press, 1992), 21–57.

23 Bourdieu, 16.

24 Richard W. Christopherson, "From Folk Art to Fine Art: A Transformation in the Meaning of Photographic Work," *Urban Life and Culture* 3, no. 2 (July 1974): 123–157; Paul Lopes, *The Rise of a Jazz Art World* (Cambridge: Cambridge University Press, 2002).

25 Howard S. Becker, *Art Worlds* (Berkeley: University of California Press, 1982).

26 Daniel J. Czitrom, *Media and the American Mind: From Morse to McLuhan* (Raleigh: University of North Carolina Press, 1982), 30–59; Robert Sklar, *Movie-Made America: A Cultural History of American Movies*, rev. ed. (New York: Vintage, 1994).

27 Douglas Gomery, *Shared Pleasures: A History of Movie Presentation in the United States* (Madison: University of Wisconsin Press, 1992).

28 Shyon Baumann, *Hollywood Highbrow: From Entertainment to Art* (Princeton, NJ: Princeton University Press, 2007); Greg Taylor, *Artists in the Audience: Cults, Camp and American Film Criticism* (Princeton, NJ: Princeton University Press, 1999).

29 Baumann.

30 Levine, 234.

31 Andreas Huyssen, *After the Great Divide: Modernism, Mass Culture, Postmodernism* (Bloomington: Indiana University Press, 1986).

32 Among others, see Lynne Joyrich, *Re-viewing Reception: Television, Gender, and Postmodern Culture* (Bloomington: Indiana University Press, 1996); Patrice Petro, "Mass Culture and the Feminine: The 'Place' of Television in Film Studies," *Cinema Journal* 25, no. 3 (Spring 1986): 5–21; and Michele Hilmes, "Desired and Feared: Women's Voices in Radio History," in Mary Beth Haralovich and Lauren Rabinovitz, eds., *Television, History, and American Culture: Feminist Critical Essays* (Durham: Duke University Press, 1999), 17–35.

33 Lynn Spigel, *Make Room for TV: Television and the Family Ideal in Postwar America* (Chicago: University of Chicago Press, 1992).

34 Joyrich, 40.

35 Ibid., 17.

36 In so doing, this work follows the paths laid by earlier television and new media scholarship. Spigel, *Make Room for TV*; William Boddy, *New Media and Popular Imagination: Launching Radio, Television, and Digital Media in the United States* (Oxford: Oxford University Press, 2004).

37 Christine Geraghty, "Exhausted and Exhausting: Television Studies and British Soap Opera," *Critical Studies in Television* 5, no. 1 (Spring 2010): 82–96.

38 Quoted in Geraghty, 83.

39 Foucault explores the concept of genealogy throughout a number of his writings. For two useful insights, see Michel Foucault, "Two Lectures," in *Power/Knowledge*, ed. Colin Gordon (New York: Pantheon Books, 1980), 83–85, and Michel Foucault, "The Discourse on Language," in *The Archeology of Knowledge* (New York: Pantheon Books, 1971), 233–234.

40 Virginia Heffernan, "On the Field and Off, Losing Isn't an Option," *New York Times*, October 3, 2006.

2 Another Golden Age?

1 Heather Havrilesky, "TV's Golden Age," *Salon*, August 21, 2006, http://www.salon.com/entertainment/feature/2006/08/21/golden_age/.

2 Richard Burgheim, "Television Reviewing," *Harper's Magazine*, August 1969, 101. William Boddy has cited Burgheim's ideas as evidence of an earlier attitude toward television. William Boddy, "Loving a Nineteen-Inch Motorola: American Writing on Television," in *Regarding Television*, ed. E. Ann Kaplan (Los Angeles: The American Film Institute, 1983), 2.

3 Jaime Weinman, "A Golden Age of Taking TV Seriously," *Macleans.ca*, September 7, 2010, http://www2.macleans.ca/2010/09/07/a-golden-age-of-taking-tv-seriously/.

4 Alessandra Stanley, "You Are What You Watch," *New York Times*, September 23, 2007.

5 Patrick Brantlinger, *Bread and Circuses: Theories of Mass Culture as Social Decay* (Ithaca, NY: Cornell University Press, 1983), 18.

6 Ibid., 251.

7 Rose K. Goldsen, *The Show and Tell Machine: How Television Works and Works You Over* (New York: Dial, 1975), 145.

8 Joyrich, 22.

9 "Three-Ring Circus" is a phrase used in Jerry Mander, *Four Arguments for the Elimination of Television* (New York: William Morrow and Co., 1978), 26; "blaring, glaring midway" is from Goldsen, *The Show and Tell Machine*, xiv.

10 David Foster Wallace, *A Supposedly Fun Thing I'll Never Do Again* (Boston: Little Brown, 1997), 50.

11 Mark Crispin Miller, *Boxed In: The Culture of TV* (Chicago: Northwestern University Press, 1988), 11, 24.

12   George W.S. Trow, *Within the Context of No Context* (New York: Atlantic Monthly Press, 1997), 45. Trow's essay was originally published in *The New Yorker* in 1981.

13   Jason Mittell analyzes this stream of anti-television discourse in depth in "The Cultural Power of an Anti-Television Metaphor: Questioning the 'Plug-In Drug' and a TV-Free America," *Television and New Media* 1, no. 2 (May 2000): 215–238.

14   Center for SCREEN-TIME Awareness website, http://www.screentimeinstitute.org/.

15   Daniel J. Boorstin, *The Image: A Guide to Pseudo-events in America* (New York: Atheneum, 1961), 13.

16   Mander, 111.

17   Neil Postman, *Amusing Ourselves to Death* (New York: Penguin, 1985).

18   Robert Putnam, *Bowling Alone: The Collapse and Revival of American Community* (New York: Simon and Schuster, 2000).

19   Goldsen, xi.

20   Marie Winn, *The Plug-In Drug*, rev. ed. (New York: Viking, 1985), 3.

21   Mander, 348, 351.

22   Michele Hilmes, *Radio Voices: American Broadcasting, 1922–1952* (Minneapolis: University of Minnesota Press, 1997), 17.

23   Shawn Vancour, "Popularizing the Classics: Radio's Role in the American Music Appreciation Movement, 1922–34," *Media, Culture and Society* 31, no. 2 (2009): 290.

24   Ibid., 292.

25   Ross Melnick, "Station R-O-X-Y: Roxy and the Radio," *Film History* 17 (2005): 218.

26   Hilmes, *Radio Voices*, 62–63.

27   Roland Marchand, *Advertising the American Dream: Making Way for Modernity, 1920–1940* (Berkeley: University of California Press, 1985), 90.

28   Ibid., 93.

29   Marchand, 69, makes these points about ad agencies' conception of consumers; Hilmes connects the idea to radio; Hilmes, *Radio Voices*, 152.

30   A number of scholars have documented this response to daytime radio and its serials, including Hilmes, *Radio Voices*; Robert C. Allen, *Speaking of Soap Operas* (Chapel Hill: University of North Carolina Press, 1985); and Jennifer Hyland Wang, "Convenient Fictions: The Construction of the Daytime Broadcast Audience, 1927–1960" (Ph.D. diss., University of Wisconsin-Madison, 2006).

31   William Boddy, *Fifties Television: The Industry and Its Critics* (Urbana: University of Illinois Press, 1990), 16–17.

32   Ibid., 80.

33   Ibid., 81.

34   Ibid., 87.

35   Elana Levine, "Distinguishing Television: The Changing Meanings of Television Liveness," *Media, Culture and Society* 30, no. 3 (2008): 394–395.

36   Michael Curtin, "*Redeeming the Wasteland: Television Documentary and Cold War Politics* (New Brunswick, NJ: Rutgers University Press, 1995), 24.

37   Aniko Bodroghkozy, *Groove Tube: Sixties Television and the Youth Rebellion* (Durham, NC: Duke University Press, 2001).

38   Mark Alvey points out that the TV industry was increasingly interested in narrower demographic segments during the 1960s but that it took until the 1970s for academics to recognize any television as Quality. Mark Alvey, "'Too Many Kids and Old Ladies': Quality Demographics and 1960s US Television," in *Television: The Critical View*, 7th ed., ed. Horace Newcomb (New York: Oxford University Press, 2007), 15–36.

39   See Todd Gitlin, *Inside Prime Time* (New York: Pantheon Books, 1983), as one of several scholars and journalists who have documented this shift.

40 Jane Feuer, "MTM Enterprises: An Overview," in *MTM: Quality Television*, ed. Jane Feuer, Kerr, and Vahimagi, 3–4.

41 Kirsten Marthe Lentz examines the ways that "quality" and "relevance" were in fact two separate discourses applied to this new wave of programming, the former more typically articulated to *The Mary Tyler Moore Show* and considerations of gender; the latter to *All in the Family* and concerns about race. Kirsten Marthe Lentz, "Quality Versus Relevance: Feminism, Race, and the Politics of the Sign in 1970s Television," *Camera Obscura* 15, no. 1 (2000): 45–93.

42 Gary Deeb, "MTM & Co.: Alive and Doing Well, Though Bruised," *Chicago Tribune* June 11, 1979, A10.

43 Elana Levine, *Wallowing in Sex: The New Sexual Culture of 1970s American Television* (Durham, NC: Duke University Press, 2007).

44 David Shaw, "What Happened, Pussycat?" *TV Guide*, September 23, 1978, 28–29; Deeb.

45 Deeb.

46 Feuer, "MTM Enterprises," 12–13.

47 Ibid., 24.

48 Michael Pollan, "Can *Hill Street Blues* Rescue NBC?" *Channels* (March/April 1983), 30–34.

49 Tom Shales, "*Hill Street Blues*: TV's Embattled Precinct," *Washington Post* March 8, 1981, M1.

50 Ibid.

51 Joyce Carol Oates, "The Best of Television: For Its Audacity, Its Defiantly Bad Taste and Its Superb Character Studies," *TV Guide*, June 1, 1985, 4–7.

52 Philip W. Sewell, "From Discourse to Discord: Quality and Dramedy at the End of the Classic Network System," *Television and New Media* 11, no. 4 (2010): 235–259.

53 Denise Worrell, "Like Nothing on Earth," *Time*, April 9, 1990, http://www.time.com/time/magazine/article/0,9171,969786–1,00.html.

54 Howard A. Rodman, "The Series That Will Change TV," *The Connoisseur* 219 (September 1989): 139.

55 Amy Taubin, "*Cheers* It Ain't," *Village Voice*, April 10, 1990, 33. The identification of "quality" series in opposition to more populist fare was a common trope throughout the 1980s. See Sewell, 242.

56 Rodman, 143.

57 See, for example, "The Triumph of *Twin Peaks*," *Entertainment Weekly*, April 6, 1990, http://www.lynchnet.com/tp/articles/ew1990.html.

58 Mark Harris, "Why TV Had to Make *Peaks*," *Entertainment Weekly*, April 6, 1990, http://www.lynchnet.com/tp/articles/ew1990b.html.

59 Quoted in Matt Roush, "High Hopes for *Twin Peaks*," *USA Today*, April 6, 1990.

60 Taubin, 34.

61 Harris.

62 Richard Goldstein, "Rad TV," *Village Voice*, April 10, 1990, 32.

63 Henry Jenkins, "'Do You Enjoy Making the Rest of Us Feel Stupid?' alt.tv.twinpeaks, the Trickster Author, and Viewer Mastery," in *Full of Secrets: Critical Approaches to "Twin Peaks*," ed. David Lavery (Detroit: Wayne State University Press, 1995), 54, 55.

64 Ibid., 55.

65 Ibid., 65–66.

66 Jimmie L. Reeves, Marc C. Rodgers, and Michael Epstein, "Rewriting Popularity: The Cult *Files*," in *Deny All Knowledge: Reading "The X-Files*," ed. David Lavery, Angela Hague, and Marla Cartwright (Syracuse, NY: Syracuse University Press, 1996). Henry Jenkins, *Textual Poachers: Television Fans and Participatory Culture* (New York: Routledge, 1992).

67   Catherine Johnson, "Quality/Cult Television: *The X-Files* and Television History," in *The Contemporary Television Series*, ed. Michael Hammond and Lucy Mazdon (Edinburgh: Edinburgh University Press, 2005), 60.

68   Sara Gwenllian-Jones and Roberta Pearson, "Introduction," in *Cult Television*, ed. Sara Gwenllian-Jones and Roberta Pearson (Minneapolis: University of Minnesota Press, 2004), xv.

69   Matt Hills, "Defining Cult TV: Texts, Inter-Texts and Fan Audiences," in *The Television Studies Book*, ed. Robert C. Allen and Annette Hill (New York: Routledge, 2004), 516.

70   Ibid.

71   Stacey Abbott designates *Lost* as a "cult blockbuster." She says:

> *Lost* is a series that is cult to the core in terms of its content and narrative structure and yet it has been carefully marketed and strategically structured so as to appeal to as wide an audience as possible while also encouraging a level of engagement with the show previously associated with cult audiences. *Lost* demonstrates that with the changes to programming strategies, viewing habits and broadcast/playback technologies that characterize contemporary television, the cult programme is no longer simply the purview of the discerning viewer distinguishing one show from the mass of mainstream material. Rather, cult has been appropriated for the mainstream.
>
> (Abbott, 2009, 23)

72   Charles McGrath, "The Triumph of the Prime-Time Novel," *New York Times*, October 22, 1995, SM52–56.

73   Richard Turner, "The Highbrow Ghetto," *New York*, November 6, 1995, 22–23.

74   Thompson, 159.

75   Horace Newcomb, "'This Is Not *Al Dente*': *The Sopranos* and the New Meaning of 'Television'," in *Television: The Critical View*, 7th ed., ed. Horace Newcomb (New York: Oxford University Press, 2007), 574.

76   Avi Santo, "Para-Television and Discourses of Distinction: The Culture of Production at HBO," in *It's Not TV: Watching HBO in the Post-Television Era*, ed. Marc Leverette, Brian L. Ott, and Cara Louis Buckley (New York: Routledge, 2008), 20.

77   Janet McCabe and Kim Akass, "It's Not TV, It's HBO's Original Programming: Producing Quality TV," in *It's Not TV: Watching HBO in the Post-Television Era*, ed. Leverette, Ott, and Buckley, 88.

78   Christopher Anderson, "Producing an Aristocracy of Culture in American Television," in *The Essential HBO Reader*, ed. Gary R. Edgerton and Jeffrey P. Jones (Lexington: University Press of Kentucky, 2008), 38.

79   David Chase, "Introduction," in "The Sopranos" *Scriptbook* (London: Channel 4 Books, 2001), 10.

80   Vincent Canby, "From the Humble Mini-Series Comes the Magnificent Megamovie," in *The New York Times on* "The Sopranos" (New York: ibooks, 2000), 79.

81   *The New York Times on* "The Sopranos" (New York: ibooks, 2000).

82   Kendall Hamilton and Corrie Brown, "They're Havin' A Heat Wave," *Newsweek*, June 21, 1999, 68.

83   David Goetzl, "The Biz: Taking Cue from Cable, Gingerly," *Advertising Age*, March 18, 2002, 63.

84   Jim McConville, "FX Cops an Attitude with Risqué New Series *Shield*," *Hollywood Reporter*, March 7, 2002.

85   Ibid.

86   "Monkey See," *All Things Considered*, National Public Radio, September 21, 2010, npr.org.

87 Neal Gabler, "Different Mind-sets," *Los Angeles Times*, April 4, 2010, D1.
88 Ibid.
89 Landon Palmer, "Culture Warrior: The 3rd Golden Age of Television," *Film School Rejects*, January 12, 2010, http://www.filmschoolrejects.com/features/culture-warrior-the-3rd-golden-age-of-television-lpalm.php.
90 Emily Nussbaum, "When TV Became Art," *New York*, December 4, 2009, http://nymag.com/arts/all/aughts/62513/.
91 Stanley.
92 Nussbaum.
93 Alex Zalben, "The Revenge of the Three-Camera Sitcom," *UGO Entertainment*, September 23, 2010, http://www.ugo.com/tv/the-revenge-of-the-three-camera-sitcom.
94 Caroline Stanley, "An Open Letter to James Franco: *General Hospital*? Really?" *Flavorpill: Flavorwire*, October 1, 2009, http://flavorwire.com/41344/an-open-letter-to-james-franco-general-hospital-really.
95 For example, see James Franco, "A Star, a Soap and the Meaning of Art," *Wall Street Journal*, December 4, 2009, http://online.wsj.com/article/SB10001424052748704107 10457457031337287 8136.html; Cathy Yan, "Conceptual Artist Carter on James Franco's *General Hospital* Appearance: 'It Was My Idea'," *Wall Street Journal*, December 3, 2009, http://blogs.wsj.com/speakeasy/2009/12/03/conceptual-artist-carter-on-james-francos-general-hospital-appearance-it-was-my-idea/. Sam Anderson, "The James Franco Project," *New York*, July 25, 2010, http://nymag.com/movies/profiles/67284/.

3 The Showrunner as *Auteur*

1 Quoted in Roberta Pearson, "The Writer/Producer in American Television," in *The Contemporary Television Series*, ed. Hammond and Mazdon, 18.
2 Shyon Baumann, *Hollywood Highbrow: From Entertainment to Art* (Princeton, NJ: Princeton University Press, 2007), 83.
3 Andy Meisler, "The Man Who Keeps *E.R.*'s Heart Beating," *New York Times*, February 26, 1995.
4 Lisa de Moraes, "From Start to Finish Line, Show Runners Lead the Way," *Washington Post*, November 14, 2004.
5 James Hibberd, "Showrunners Enjoy Bigger Profile," *Hollywood Reporter*, October 28, 2008.
6 Cynthia Littleton and Stuart Levine, "TV Creators Ace Face Time," *Variety*, April 2, 2010.
7 "Slanguage Dictionary," *Variety*, http://www.variety.com/static-pages/slanguage-dictionary/#s.
8 Ben Grossman, "Showrunner 101" *Broadcasting and Cable*, April 3, 2006, 10–11.
9 Scott Collins, "Show Runner Runs the Show," *Los Angeles Times*, November 23, 2007.
10 Nikki Finke, "Action Comedy TV: Showrunner Matt Nix," *Deadline Hollywood Daily*, March 14, 2010, http://www.deadline.com/2010/03/action-comedy-tv-showrunner-matt-nix/.
11 Alex Witchel, "*Mad Men* Has Its Moment" *New York Times*, June 22, 2008.
12 Derek Kompare, "What Is a Showrunner?: Considering Post-Network Television Authorship," paper presented at the Console-ing Passions conference, Santa Barbara, CA, April 25, 2008; Derek Kompare, "More 'Moments of Television': Online Cult Television Authorship," in *Flow TV: Television in the Age of Media Convergence*, ed. Michael Kackman et al. (New York: Routledge, 2011), 100. See also Matt Hills,

Fan Cultures (London: Routledge, 2002), which Kompare cites in relation to conspicuous authorship.

13   On the norm of freelance writing in the network era, see Muriel G. Cantor and Joel M. Cantor, *Prime-Time Television: Content and Control*, 2nd ed. (Newbury Park, CA: Sage, 1992), 77–78; on shooting out of order, see David Jacobs, "Confessions of a Story Editor," in *TV Book*, ed. Judy Fireman (New York: Workman, 1977), 57–60.

14   Pearson, "The Writer/Producer in American Television," 17.

15   David Wild, *The Showrunners: A Season Inside the Billion-Dollar, Death-Defying, Madcap World of Television's Real Stars* (New York: HarperCollins, 1999).

16   On the commercial function of *auteurism* in cinema, see Timothy Corrigan, *A Cinema Without Walls: Movies and Culture After Vietnam* (New Brunswick, NJ: Rutgers University Press, 1991), 103.

17   Tom Carson, "Hip to the Squares," *American Film* 15 (September 1990), 16.

18   Randall Rothenberg, "Yesterday's Boob Tube Is Today's High Art," *New York Times*, October 7, 1990.

19   Pearson, "The Writer/Producer in American Television," 17.

20   Littleton and Levine.

21   Henry Jenkins, "'Infinite Diversity in Infinite Combinations': Genre and Authorship in *Star Trek*," in *Science Fiction Audiences: Watching "Doctor Who" and "Star Trek,"* ed. John Tulloch and Henry Jenkins, 188.

22   Hills, *Fan Cultures* (New York: Routledge, 2002), 132–133.

23   Jenkins, "'Do You Enjoy Making the Rest of Us Feel Stupid?': alt.tv.twinpeaks, the Trickster Author, and Viewer Mastery."

24   Christine Scodari, "Possession, Attraction, and the Thrill of the Chase: Gendered Myth-making in Film and Television Comedy of the Sexes," *Critical Studies in Mass Communication* 12 (1995): 23–39.

25   Jenkins, "'Do You Enjoy. . .,'" 65.

26   Andrew Sarris, *The American Cinema: Directors and Directions, 1929–1968* (New York: Da Capo, 1968), 3.

27   John Thornton Caldwell, *Televisuality: Style, Crisis and Authority in American Television* (New Brunswick, NJ: Rutgers University Press, 1995), 105–106.

28   Dana Polan, *The Sopranos* (Durham, NC: Duke University Press, 2009), 86–89, discusses a number of instances of Chase disparaging television, with rare exceptions, and revering cinema, in particular, art cinema.

29   Virginia Heffernan, "The Real Boss of *The Sopranos*," *New York Times*, February 29, 2004.

30   Peter Biskind, "An American Family," *Vanity Fair*, April 2007.

31   Jonathan Storm, "*Sopranos*: A Symphony of Television Done Right," *Philadelphia Inquirer* March 4, 2001.

32   Bill Carter, "'West Wing' to West Coast: TV's Auteur Portrays TV," *New York Times*, September 11, 2006.

33   Lisa de Moraes, "Aaron Sorkin's Crack about Television," *Washington Post*, July 22, 2006.

34   Nussbaum, "When TV Became Art."

35   Carter, "*West Wing* to West Coast."

36   Biskind, "An American Family."

37   Andrew Sarris, "Notes on the *Auteur* Theory in 1962," in *Film Theory and Criticism: Introductory Readings*, 6th ed., ed. Gerald Mast, Marshall Cohen, and Leo Braudy (New York: Oxford University Press, 2004), 562.

38   David Marc and Robert J. Thompson, *Prime Time, Prime Movers: From "I Love Lucy" to "L.A. Law"—America's Greatest TV Shows and the People Who Created Them* (Syracuse: Syracuse University Press, 1995).

39   Denise Worrell, "Video: Like Nothing Else on Earth," *Time*, April 9, 1990.

40 Richard B. Woodward, "A Dark Lens on America," *New York Times*, January 14,1990.

41 Taubin, "*Cheers* it Ain't.

42 Emily Nussbaum, "Must-See Metaphysics," *New York Times Magazine*, September 22, 2002.

43 See, for instance, Heather Havrilesky, "Trapped in the Dollhouse," *Salon*, February 12, 2009; Josef Adalian, "The Auteur," *Television Week*, February 2, 2009.

44 Sarris, *The American Cinema*, 24.

45 Daisy Whitney, "Sci Fi Podcasts for Promotion," *Television Week*, April 4, 2005.

46 Kompare, "More 'Moments of Television,'" 106–110.

47 Allison McCracken, "'Say Goodnight, Mrs. Ron': Ronald D. Moore and the Gender Politics of the *Battlestar Galactica* Podcast," paper presented at Console-ing Passions conference, Santa Barbara, CA, April 2008.

48 Wyatt Mason, "The HBO Auteur," *New York Times Magazine*, March 15, 2010.

49 Denise Mann, "It's Not TV, It's Brand Management TV: The Collective Author(s) of the *Lost* Franchise," in *Production Studies: Cultural Studies of Media Industries*, ed. Vicki Mayer, Miranda J. Banks, and John Thornton Caldwell (New York: Routledge, 2009).

50 Ibid.

51 Scott Collins, "*Sons of Anarchy*'s Kurt Sutter Lives Up to His 'Wild One' Reputation," *Los Angeles Times* September 5, 2010.

52 Ibid.

53 Littleton and Levine.

54 Stuart D. Hobbs, *The End of the American Avant-Garde* (New York: New York University Press, 2000), 153.

55 Robert Hughes, "Man for the Machine," *Time*, May 17, 1971.

56 Margaret Talbot, "Stealing Life: The Crusader Behind *The Wire*," *The New Yorker*, October 22, 2007.

57 John Metcalfe, "The Celebrity Twitter Ecosystem," *New York Times*, March 27, 2009.

58 Nick Muntean and Anne Helen Petersen, "Celebrity Twitter: Strategies of Intrusion and Disclosure in the Age of Technoculture," *m/c journal* 12, no. 5 (December 2009), http://journal.media-culture.org.au/index.php/mcjournal/article/viewArticle/194.

59 Myles McNutt, "Tweets of Anarchy: Showrunners on Twitter," *Antenna*, September 17, 2010, http://blog.commarts.wisc.edu/2010/09/17/tweets-of-anarchy-showrunners-on-twitter/.

60 Gray, *Show Sold Separately: Promos, Spoilers, and Other Media Paratexts*, 107–113.

4 Upgrading the Situation Comedy

1 Ross Simonini, "The Sitcom Digresses," *New York Times*, November 21, 2008.

2 For instance, of *My Big Fat Greek Wedding*, David Denby wrote, "I enjoyed parts of [it], and I'm not about to tell people that they should not have enjoyed it. I'm just afraid that Hollywood will respond to its success by making many more sitcoms in the guise of movies." *The New Yorker*, September 23, 2002, 98. Of *Little Miss Sunshine*, J.R. Jones wrote, "This isn't much more than a glorified sitcom, but it deftly dramatizes our conflicting desires for individuality and an audience to applaud it." *Chicago Reader*, August 3, 2006.

3 Bernard Weintraub, "The *Malcolm* Sensibility: New Sitcom's Early Success May Spawn Host of Imitators," *New York Times*, January 24, 2000.

4 Christopher Lisotta, "NBC's *Earl* Opens Door for Sitcoms; Single-Camera Format Looking Like a Winner Again," *Television Week*, November 28, 2005.

5 James Poniewozik, "No Laugh Track Required: The Comeback of the Sitcom," *Time*, October 12, 2009.

6 Joe Hagan, "Is NBC's *The Office* Too Prickly for Primetime?" *New York Observer*, January 7, 2007.

7 Jeremy Butler, *Television Style* (New York: Routledge, 2010), 62.

8 Hagan.

9 Brett Mills, "Comedy Verite: Contemporary Sitcom Form," *Screen* 45, no. 1 (Spring 2004): 63–78; Ethan Thompson, "Comedy Verité? The Observational Documentary Meets the Televisual Sitcom," *The Velvet Light Trap* 60 (Fall 2007): 63–72.

10 Stephen Battaglio, "Networks Rediscover the Single-Camera Comedy," *New York Times*, July 8, 2001.

11 Quotations of Greg Garcia and Jason Lee are from the special features of the season one DVD box set of *My Name is Earl*.

12 *Breaking Ground: Behind-the-Scenes of Arrested Development*, included with the season one DVD box set of *Arrested Development*.

13 Quotations of Jason Bateman and Ron Howard from Ibid.

14 Deborah Eckerling, "The Small Screen: *My Name Is Earl*," *Scr(i)pt* (January/February 2007): 76–81.

15 Battaglio.

16 For an example, listen to the DVD commentary track on the pilot episode of *Malcolm in the Middle*.

17 Brian Ford Sullivan, "On the Futon With . . . *My Name Is Earl* Creator Greg Garcia," *The Futon Critic*, October 30, 2006, http://www.thefutoncritic.com/rant.aspx?id= 20061030.

18 Mills, 75.

19 Simonini.

20 Nicole Laporte, "Why Don't Smart Comedies Build Big Audiences?" *Variety*, June 12, 2007.

21 Jon Silberg, "Making Sitcoms 'Sexy,'" *American Cinematographer* 89 (March 2008): 58–65.

22 Virginia Heffernan, "Put on Your Best Gimme Hat: It's the Upscale Redneck Show," *New York Times*, September 11, 2005.

23 Bill Keveney, "The Critics Know *Earl* by Name," *USA Today*, August 26, 2005.

24 James Poniewozik, "CBS Upfront: Selling Boring in Too-Interesting Times," *Tuned In* (*Time* blog), May 21, 2009, http://tunedin.blogs.time.com/2009/05/21/cbs-upfront-selling-boring-in-too-interesting-times/.

25 Alan Sepinwall, "Interview: Lizzy Caplan on the *Party Down* Cancellation," *What's Alan Watching? Sepinwall on TV*, July 2, 2010, http://www.hitfix.com/blogs/whats-alan-watching/posts/interview-lizzy-caplan-on-the-party-down-cancellation.

26 Tom Bissell, "A Simple Medium: Chuck Lorre and the Rules of the Network Sitcom," *The New Yorker*, December 6, 2010.

27 H. Cheadle, "Who Chuck Lorre Is and Why He Sucks," *Essays on Sucking*, December 3, 2010, http://cheadlesucks.blogspot.com/2010/12/who-chuck-lorre-is-and-why-he-sucks.html.

28 Nancy Franklin, "Boys in the Hood," *The New Yorker*, November 7, 2005.

29 Steven Kurutz, "Chuck Klosterman, out with a New Essay Collection, Talks Seriously about Laugh Tracks" *The Wall Street Journal* Speakeasy blog, October 19, 2009, http://blogs.wsj.com/speakeasy/2009/10/17/chuck-klosterman-out-with-a-new-essay-collection-talks-seriously-about-laugh-tracks/.

30 Ser Greguh, comment #10, http://asoiaf.westeros.org/index.php/topic/37148-single-cam-v-multi-cam/.

31 Jacob Smith, "The Frenzy of the Audible: Pleasure, Authenticity and Recorded Laughter," *Television and New Media* 6, no. 1 (February 2005): 23–47.

32 Brett Mills, *Television Sitcom* (London: BFI, 2005), 38.

33 Amelie Gilette, "Parker Posey Gets the Laugh Track She Never Wanted," *The Onion A.V. Club*, August 7, 2007, http://www.avclub.com/articles/parker-posey-gets-the-laugh-track-she-never-wanted,14576/.

34 Jace at Televisionary, "Pilot Inspektor: FOX's *The Return of Jezebel James*," film.com, June 21, 2007, http://www.film.com/features/story/pilot-inspektor-foxs-return-jezebel/15150663.

35 Buzzsugar, "Pilot Watch: *The Return of Jezebel James*," *Buzzsugar*, June 6, 2007, http://www.buzzsugar.com/Pilot-Watch-Return-Jezebel-James-289522; Alan Sepinwall, "Sepinwall on TV, *Jezebel James* Review," *nj.com*, March 14, 2008, http://blog.nj.com/alltv/2008/03/sepinwall_on_tv_jezebel_james.html; Ginia Bellefante, "You're Having My Baby: Two Bickering Sisters, United by Pregnancy," *New York Times*, March 14, 2008.

36 Jennifer Armstrong, "Life Goes on," *ew.com*, March 17, 2007, http://www.ew.com/ew/article/0,,20039476,00.html.

37 internettoday, "Big Bang Theory Minus Laughter," YouTube, January 16, 2010, http://www.youtube.com/watch?v=q_iEY9pSHT0. On June 22, 2010 this video had 684,891 views. It was later taken down from the site following a complaint of copyright infringement.

38 Lindsay Robertson, "*The Big Bang Theory* Minus the Laugh Track," *Vulture*, January 17, 2010, http://nymag.com/daily/entertainment/2010/01/the_big_bang_theory_minus_the.html.

39 This comment, posted in May 2010, is by YouTube user rb6elite.

40 This comment, posted in February 2010, is by YouTube user MrShatera.

41 Will and Grace, comment on "*Big Bang Theory* Without the Laugh Track," *Geekologie*, February 2, 2010, http://www.geekologie.com/2010/02/big_bang_theory_without_the_la.php#comment-198958.

42 Cynthia Littleton, "Comedy in Cable Push," *Variety* January 6, 2011.

5 Not a Soap Opera

1 Tania Modleski, *Loving with a Vengeance: Mass Produced Fantasies for Women*, 2nd ed. (New York: Routledge, 2008), 78.

2 Jeff Jensen, "This Was The Year That TV's Second Golden Age Ended," *Entertainment Weekly* December 19, 2008, http://www.ew.com/ew/article/0,,20247685,00.html.

3 Richard Beck, "Treasure Island: How TV Serials Achieved the Status of Art," *n+1* May 20, 2010.

4 Lacey Rose, "Shawn Ryan's '*The Chicago Code*': A Love Letter to His City," *Moneywood Forbes* blog, February 2, 2011, http://blogs.forbes.com/laceyrose/2011/02/02/shawn-ryans-the-chicago-code-a-love-letter-to-his-city/, makes a distinction between mass audience procedurals and serials addressed at passionate, engaged fans.

5 Quoted in Maureen Ryan, "Has TV Lost Its Nerve When it Comes to Complex Dramas?" *The Watcher* February 27, 2009, http://featuresblogs.chicagotribune.com/entertainment_tv/2009/02/has-tv-lost-its-nerve-when-it-comes-to-complex-dramas.html.

6 Daniel Mendelsohn, "The *Mad Men* Account," *New York Review of Books* February 24, 2011.

7 See, for example, Robert J. Thompson's characterization of this history in *Television's Second Golden Age*, 33–35.

8 Angela Ndalianis, "Television and the Neo-Baroque," in *The Contemporary Television Series*, ed. Hammond and Mazdon, 91–92.

9 Jim Cox, *The Daytime Serials of Television, 1946–1960* (Jefferson, NC: McFarland & Company, 2006), 26.

10 Ibid., 53–54.

11 Edgar J. Scherick to Paul Monash, May 13, 1964, Box 18, Cables and Tele. 1964, Paul Monash Collection, American Heritage Center, Laramie, WY.

12 Douglas Cramer to Paul Monash, May 21, 1963, Box 19, Correspondence—Letters 1963, Paul Monash Collection, AHC.
13 Caryn Murphy, "Selling the Continuing Story of *Peyton Place*," paper presented at Console-ing Passions International Conference on Television, Audio, Video, New Media and Feminism, Eugene, OR, April 24, 2010.
14 TV Sales Development, "*Peyton Place*," ABC '64–'65 Program Notes, Box 51, *Peyton Place* (Publicity), Paul Monash Collection, AHC; Murphy.
15 Vernon Scott, "The Surprise Television Success . . .," UPI, January 1, 1965, Box 18, Correspondence-Cables & Tele., 1965, Paul Monash Collection, AHC.
16 Bob Lawrence, "Soap Opera: A Slippery Term," *New York Sunday News*, April 11, 1965, 8, Box 8, Folder 14—Promotion & Publicity, 1958–74, Procter & Gamble collection, Wisconsin Historical Society, Madison, WI.
17 Alan Patureau, "*Peyton Place* to Spread Woe," *Newsday*, January 14, 1965, 5C.
18 Lawrence, "Soap Opera."
19 Glen Creeber, *Serial Television: Big Drama on the Small Screen* (London: BFI, 2004), 9.
20 Harry F. Waters, "Night at the Soap Opera," *Newsweek*, February 23, 1976, 63.
21 Elayne Rapping, *The Movie of the Week: Private Stories, Public Events* (Minneapolis: University of Minnesota Press, 1992), xi.
22 Jane Feuer, "The MTM Style," in *MTM Quality Television*, ed. Feuer, Kerr, and Vahimagi, 46.
23 David Jacobs, "Foreword," in Barbara A. Curran, "*Dallas*"*: The Complete Story of the World's Favorite Prime-Time Soap* (Nashville, TN: Cumberland House, 2004), xii.
24 Richard Corliss, "TV's *Dallas*: Whodunit?" *Time*, August 11, 1980, http://www.time.com/time/printout/0,8816,924376,00.html.
25 Jacobs, "Foreword," xi–xii.
26 These short-lived efforts at serialized storytelling in the 1970s include *Beacon Hill* (CBS, 1975), *Executive Suite* (CBS, 1976–1977), *Husbands, Wives & Lovers* (CBS, 1978), *Cliffhangers* (NBC, 1979), and *From Here to Eternity* (NBC, 1979–1980). Bruce B. Morris, *Prime Time Network Serials* (Jefferson, NC: McFarland & Co., 1997), 4.
27 Levine, *Wallowing in Sex: The New Sexual Culture of 1970s American Television*.
28 For example, see this cover story: "Sex and Suffering in the Afternoon," *Time* January 12, 1976, http://www.time.com/time/magazine/article/0,9171,913850-1,00.html.
29 Levine, *Wallowing in Sex*, 251.
30 "If the Eye Offend Thee," *Time*, September 26, 1977, 53; "Advertisers Feel Pressure on 'Soap'," *Broadcasting*, August 29, 1977, 22.
31 Jason Mittell, *Genre and Television: From Cop Shows to Cartoons in American Culture* (New York: Routledge, 2004), 160–178.
32 Ibid., 168.
33 Also controversial was the syndicated, serialized satire *Mary Hartman, Mary Hartman*, although this program's more marginalized place in the TV schedule kept it from reaching the heights of *Soap*'s controversy. Much like *Soap*, *MH, MH* drew upon soaps' narrative structure and concerns with personal and family life, but matched these with a satirical tone. See Levine, *Wallowing in Sex*, 200–207.
34 Jacobs, "Foreord," xi.
35 Information on failed prime time soaps from Morris.
36 Oates, "The Best of Television," 5.
37 Gitlin, *Inside Prime Time*, 273.
38 Pollan, "Can *Hill Street Blues* Rescue NBC?," 32.
39 Jane Feuer, "The Lack of Influence of *thirtysomething*," in *The Contemporary Television Series*, ed. Hammond and Mazdon, 27.
40 Peter J. Boyer, "Prime Time TV Serials Lose Edge," *New York Times* January 20, 1986, C29.

41 For example, see ibid. and Bruce Guthrie, "American Soapies All Washed Up," *The Advertiser*, May 30, 1986. The November 1986 run of *Fresno*, a mini-series parody of the prime time soaps, may also have signaled the increasing datedness of the form in the popular imagination.

42 "*Dallas* May Drop Serial Format," *Globe and Mail*, January 21, 1988 and Matt Roush, "*Falcon Crest* Will Try a New Recipe for Scandal," *USA Today*, July 18, 1989, 3D.

43 For example, see Matt Roush, "High Hopes for *Twin Peaks*," *USA Today*, April 6, 1990, Janis Froelich, "Soaps for the '90s," *St. Petersburg Times*, April 24, 1990, 1D.

44 John Fiske, *Television Culture* (London: Routledge, 1987), 183.

45 Stephen King, "*Lost*'s Soul," *Entertainment Weekly*, February 1, 2007, http://www.ew.com/ew/articles/0,,1100673,00.html.

46 Ivan Askwith, "'Do You Even Know Where This Is Going? *Lost*'s Viewers and Narrative Premeditation," in *Reading "Lost,"* ed. Pearson, 161.

47 Polan, *The Sopranos*, 2–7.

48 David Lynch, quoted in *Lynch on Lynch*, ed. Chris Rodley, 180.

49 Jennifer Hayward, *Consuming Pleasures: Active Audiences and Serial Fictions from Dickens to Soap Opera* (Lexington: University Press of Kentucky, 1997), 153.

50 Modleski; Charlotte Brunsdon, "*Crossroads*: Notes on Soap Opera," in *Regarding Television*, ed. Kaplan, 76–83.

51 Rodley, *Lynch on Lynch*, 180.

52 Mark Dolan, "The Peaks and Valleys of Serial Creativity: What Happened to/on *Twin Peaks*," in *Full of Secrets*, ed. Lavery, 37–41.

53 David Lavery, "*Buffy the Vampire Slayer*," in *Fifty Key Television Programmes*, ed. Glen Creeber (London: Arnold, 2004), 32.

54 Quoted in Abbott, "How *Lost* Found Its Audience: The Making of a Cult Blockbuster," ed. Roberta Pearson, 21.

55 Mark C. Rogers, Michael Epstein, and Jimmie L. Reeves, "*The Sopranos* as HBO Brand Equity: The Art of Commerce in the Age of Digital Reproduction," in *This Thing of Ours: Investigating "The Sopranos,"* ed. David Lavery (New York: Columbia University Press, 2002), 54.

56 Michael Z. Newman, "From Beats to Arcs: Toward a Poetics of Television Narrative," *The Velvet Light Trap* 58 (Fall 2006): 16–28.

57 This combination of narrative types has been labeled a number of different ways by scholars and critics, including "flexi-narrative" by Robin Nelson, *TV Drama in Transition: Forms, Values and Cultural Change* (New York: St. Martin's Press, 1997), 34, and "cumulative narrative" by Horace M. Newcomb, "*Magnum*: The Champagne of TV?" *Channels of Communications* 5, no. 1 (1985): 24. It is also discussed in Jeffery Sconce, "What If? Charting Television's New Textual Boundaries," in *Television After TV: Essays on a Medium in Transition*, ed. Lynn Spigel and Jan Olsson (Durham, NC: Duke University Press, 2004), 93–112.

58 Christine Scodari and Jenna L. Felder, "Creating a Pocket Universe: 'Shippers,' Fan Fiction, and *The X-Files* Online," *Communication Studies* 51, no. 3 (2000): 240, 245.

59 Jason Mittell, "*Lost* in a Great Story: Evaluation in Narrative Television (and Television Studies)," in *Reading Lost*, ed. Pearson, 125.

60 Matt Hills, "Defining Cult TV: Texts, Inter-Texts and Fan Audiences," in *The Television Studies Book*, eds. Allen and Hill, 513.

61 Quoted in Matt Hurwitz, "Hooked: Crafting the Serialized Storylines that Keep Audiences Begging and New Viewers Caught up," *Written By: The Journal of the Writers Guild of America* xix:6 (September 2006), 31.

62 David Lavery and Robert J. Thompson, "David Chase, *The Sopranos*, and Television Creativity," in *This Thing of Ours: Investigating "The Sopranos,"* ed. David Lavery (New York: Columbia University Press, 2002), 23.

63   Interview with David Chase, in Allen Rucker, "The Sopranos": *A Family History* (New York: New American Library, 2000), no page.

64   David Chase, "Introduction," in "The Sopranos" *Scriptbook* (London: Channel 4 Books, 2001), 8.

65   David Lavery and Robert J. Thompson, "David Chase, *The Sopranos*, and Television Creativity," in *This Thing of Ours*, ed. Lavery, 23.

66   Cindy Donatelli and Sharon Alward, "'I Dread You'? Married to the Mob in *The Godfather, Goodfellas*, and *The Sopranos*," in *This Thing of Ours*, ed. Lavery, 64.

67   Glen Creeber, "'TV Ruined the Movies': Television, Tarantino, and the Intimate World of *The Sopranos*," in *This Thing of Ours*, ed. Lavery, 125, 127. See also Creeber, *Serial Television*, 103.

68   Scodari and Felder, "Creating a Pocket Universe," 242–244.

69   Ibid., 249.

70   Ibid.

71   Christine Scodari, "Possession, Attraction, and the Thrill of the Chase: Gendered Myth-Making in Film and Television Comedy of the Sexes," *Critical Studies in Mass Communication* 12 (1995): 29.

72   Feuer, "The Lack Of Influence of *Thirtysomething*," 31.

73   Ibid., 31–34.

74   Mark Jancovich and Nathan Hunt, "The Mainstream, Distinction, and Cult TV," in *Cult Television*, ed. Gwenllian-Jones and Pearson, 32.

75   Joanne Hollows, "The Masculinity of Cult," in *Defining Cult Movies: The Cultural Politics of Oppositional Taste*, ed. Mark Jancovich, Antonio Lázaro Reboll, Julian Stringer, and Andy Willis (Manchester: Manchester University Press, 2003), 37.

76   Hills, "Defining Cult TV," 513.

77   Rachel Moseley, "The Teen Series," in *The Television Genre Book*, ed. Glen Creeber (London: BFI, 2001), 41–42.

78   Sharon Marie Ross and Louisa Ellen Stein, "Introduction: Watching Teen TV," in *Teen Television: Essays on Programming and Fandom*, ed. Sharon Marie Ross and Louisa Ellen Stein (Jefferson, NC: McFarland & Co., 2008), 7–8.

79   Ibid

80   Matt Hills, "*Dawson's Creek*. 'Quality Teen TV' and 'Mainstream Cult'?" in *Teen TV: Genre, Consumption and Identity*, ed. by Glyn Davis and Kay Dickinson (London: BFI, 2004), 63.

6 The Television Image and the Image of the Television

1   Mark Kermode, "So, Is There Really Life on Mars?" *Guardian*, September 23, 2007.

2   Eric McLuhan and Frank Zingrone, eds., *Essential McLuhan* (New York: Basic Books, 1995), 134.

3   Pete Engardio, "Flat Panel, Thin Margins," *BusinessWeek Online*, February 16, 2007, 18; David Goetzl, "HDTV Set Sales to Soar" *Broadcasting and Cable*, November 26, 2007, 11.

4   "Thin Screens, Fat Margins," *The Economist*, December 20, 2003, 97.

5   "LCD TVs Pass CRTs," *TWICE: This Week in Consumer Electronics*, February 25, 2008, 16.

6   David Chartier, "Nielsen Says HDTV Adoption in US Doubled since July 2007," *Ars Technica*, December 12, 2008, http://arstechnica.com/old/content/2008/12/neilsen-says-hdtv-adoption-in-us-doubled-this-past-year.ars.

7   "Across America, HDTV Rapidly Becoming the Standard," *Nielsenwire*, May 21, 2009, http://blog.nielsen.com/nielsenwire/consumer/across-america-hd-tv-rapidly-becoming-the-standard/.

8   Sam Grobart, "A Bonanza in TV Sales Fades Away," *New York Times*, January 6, 2011.

9   Goetzl.
10 Joel Brinkley, "They're Big. They're Expensive. They're the First High-Definition TV Sets," *New York Times*, January 12, 1998.
11 Joel Brinkley, "HDTV: High Definition, High in Price," *New York Times*, August 20, 1998.
12 Peter H. Lewis, "Thin and Stylish, Flat Panels Still Cost a Bundle," *New York Times*, August 27, 1998.
13 "Thin Screens, Fat Margins," *The Economist*, December 20, 2003, 97.
14 "HDTVs: The Price Is Right," *Consumer Reports*, December 2005, 22–29.
15 Barbara Klinger, *Beyond the Multiplex: Cinema, New Technologies and the Home* (Berkeley: University of California Press, 2006).
16 For example Maryanne Murray Buechner, "I Want My HDTV!" *Time*, December 16, 2002, writes:

> Wouldn't you like a TV so clear you could count the stitches on a baseball as it crossed the plate? Or watch individual snowflakes kiss the sidewalk? That's what we've been hearing ever since high-definition television (HDTV) arrived as a consumer product in 1998. And if you've ever seen it firsthand, you know it's true. HDTV really is that good, with a picture resolution six times as rich as ordinary analog TV—some 2 million pixels. Colors pop, and edges are crisp and distinct, revealing every hair and wrinkle.

Later in the same article she continues, "Even if you decide that you don't need to count the pores on President Bartlet's face, there are other reasons to trade in your analog TV."

17 Brinkley, "HDTV: High Definition, High in Price."
18 Ken Kerschbaumer, "High-Def Ticket: Fox Network Says Yes to HD Sports; DirecTV Could Benefit." *Broadcasting and Cable*, March 22, 2004, 18.
19 Frank Rose, "Prime Time for High Def," *Wired* 14, no. 6 (June 2006).
20 Jeanne McDowell, "For TV Stars, High Def is Dicey," *Time*, April 12, 2004.
21 Spigel, *Make Room for TV* (Chicago: University of Chicago Press, 1992), 133–135.
22 Judy Wajcman, *Feminism Confronts Technology* (Cambridge: Polity Press, 1991), 22.
23 Klinger, *Beyond the Multiplex*, 25.
24 William Boddy, "Archaeologies of Electronic Vision and the Gendered Spectator," *Screen* 35, no. 2 (Summer 1994): 121, 117.
25 Laura Heller, "Better Pricing, DVD Growth Keep HDTV Sales on the Rise," *DSN Retailing Today*, November 5, 2001, 35.
26 Yardena Arar, "Six Common HDTV Showroom Pitfalls," *PC World*, December 2008, 34.
27 "Samsung, Microsoft Ink HDTV Alliance for Next-gen X-box Console," *Electronic News*, May 2, 2005, N. Beth Snyder Bulik, "Stay-At-Home Trend Feathers Samsung Nest," *Advertising Age*, November 3, 2008, 18–19.
28 Ibid; Kenneth Hein, "Attack of the No-Name HDTV Brands," *Brandweek*, June 18, 2007, S30.
29 Grant Clauser, "HDTV HANDBOOK: A Retailer's Guide to Digital Television," *Dealerscope* (December 2007 supplement, *HDTV Handbook*).
30 Allison Romano, "The Pictures Are the Story," *Broadcasting and Cable*, November 24, 2008, 14–15.
31 Jeff Joseph, "The Year of HD," *Dealerscope* 48, no. 3 (March 2006).
32 Ibid.
33 Michel Dupagne, "Exploring the Characteristics of Potential High-Definition Television Adopters," *Journal of Media Economics* 12, no. 1 (1999): 47.
34 Hein; Bulik.

35 "HDTV Home Entertainment Guide: Products," *UGO: Lifestyle for Gamers*, http://www.ugo.com/programs/verizon/entertainmentguide/products.asp.

36 Bernadette Flynn, "Geography of the Digital Hearth," *Information, Communication and Society* 6, no. 4 (2003): 551–576.

37 Klinger.

38 Lynn Spigel, *TV by Design: Modern Art and the Rise of Network Television* (Chicago: University of Chicago Press, 2008), 1.

39 Leah Garchik, "Stand Up Tall and Pull That TV out of the Closet," *San Francisco Chronicle*, August 30, 1998, 2.

40 Christopher Muther, "The World Is Flat," *Boston Globe*, January 31, 2008, C3.

41 Spigel, *Make Room for TV*.

42 "Prime Time: Conceal or Reveal? Design Solutions for Working a TV into Your Condo," *House and Home: Condos: Lofts and Apartments* 8, no. 2 (Fall 2010): 20.

43 "Old World Design Meets Modern Living and Dining," originally aired July 31, 2010.

44 Michelle Gringeri-Brown, "Like a Virgin: Homeowners New to MCM Find a Meeting of the Minds in a Pristine Eichler," *Atomic Ranch* (Fall 2010): 14–23.

45 Lisa Cregan, "Modern and Easy: Spiffing up a 1950s Birmingham Cottage from So-So to Oh-So-Sleek," *House Beautiful* (October 2010): 122–131.

46 See, for example, "A TV Complicates the Mantelpiece: Tips on Trim Details and New Design Tools from a Big Project," *Tauton's Fine Homebuilding* 186 (2007): 86–91.

47 Amy Goldwasser, "Where to Put a TV So Big That It's on When It's off," *New York Times*, January 31, 2002, F1. Madeleine McDermott Hamm, "At Long Last, TV Can Show Its Face," *Houston Chronicle*, March 11, 2001, TM6.

48 Stephwebb, "Flat Screen TV over Fireplace—Ideas for Making it Look Nice?" thread, GardenWeb.com, February 25, 2006, http://ths.gardenweb.com/forums/load/homeentertain/msg0219112810437.html.

49 Glen Dickson, "Comcast's High-Def Art Gallery," *Broadcasting and Cable*, November 13, 2006, 23.

50 The Nielsen Company, *Affluence in America: America's Changing Wealth Landscape*, May 2008.

51 For instance, according to its description in catalog copy, the Dimplex Wall Mounted Gunmetal Sahara Plasma Fireplace has a "similar aspect ratio to plasma televisions." Electric Fireplace Source, http://www.electricfireplacesource.com/electric-fireplaces/wall-mounted-electric-fireplaces/dimplexsaharasandwallmountedelectricfireplace.cfm, accessed October 19, 2010.

52 "The Visit," originally aired November 16, 2000.

53 Bill Keveney, "*ER* Says Widescreen Format Is Here to Stay," *USA Today*, December 27, 2000, 4D.

54 Tom Shales, "Vital Signs: *ER* Still Full of Life," *Washington Post*, November 16, 2000, C01.

55 Bill Carter, "*X-Files* Tries to Keep Its Murky Promise," *New York Times*, November 7, 1998, B7.

56 MTV videos were often letterboxed in the 1990s. Ann Sherber, "Letterboxing Spreads Its Horizons: Studios Find Growing Acceptance of Format," *Billboard*, January 25, 1997.

57 Anthony Vagnoni, "Out of the Box," *Advertising Age*, November 8, 1999.

58 Geoff King and Tanya Krzywinska, *Screenplay: Cinema/videogames/interfaces* (London: Wallflower, 2002), 118.

59 John Belton, *Widescreen Cinema* (Cambridge, MA: Harvard University Press, 1992).

60 James Kendrick, "What is the Criterion? The Criterion Collection as an Archive of Film as Culture," *Journal of Film and Video* 53, no. 2/3 (Summer/Fall 2001): 124–139.

61 James Kendrick, "Aspect Ratios and Joe Six-Packs: Home Theater Enthusiasts' Battle to Legitimize the DVD Experience," *The Velvet Light Trap* 56 (Fall 2005): 58–70.

62 Seth Goldstein, "Picture This: New DVD Owners May Not Prefer Extra Features Now, But That Could Change," *Billboard*, December 5, 1998.

63 Kendrick, "What is the Criterion?"; Bradley Schauer, "The Criterion Collection in the New Home Video Market: An Interview with Susan Arosteguy," *The Velvet Light Trap* 56 (Fall 2005): 32–35.

64 Mark Landler, "Capitol Hill Fiat on HDTV Isn't the Last Word," *New York Times*, July 1, 1996.

65 David E. Sanger, "Advanced TV Makes Debut in Japan," *New York Times*, December 6, 1990.

66 *DTV: What Every Consumer Should Know*, Federal Communications Commission, Washington, DC (n.d.), page 8 available online: http://www.dtv.gov/DTV_booklet. pdf.

67 *Charting the Digital Broadcasting Future: Final Report of the Advisory Committee on Public Interest Obligations of Digital Television Broadcasters* (Washington, DC, February 18, 1998), 6.

68 Michael Zakula, "What Does the FCC Mean When It Says Digital Television is Here," *The Caucus* (Spring 1997), http://www.caucus.org/archives/97sum_digital.html accessed October 18, 2010; Mark Schubin, "Searching for the Perfect Aspect Ratio," *SMPTE Journal* (August 1996): 460–478; "HDTV Aspect Ratio," *Image Technology* 77 (March 1995): 70–76.

69 Schubin, "HDTV Aspect Ratio."

70 Zakula.

71 Stephanie Argy, "Big City Girl," *American Cinematographer* 80 (February 1999): 76–78; Jean Oppenheimer, "The Halls of Power," *American Cinematographer* 81 (October 2000): 74–83.

72 John Dempsey, "Letterboxing Format: A D.P.'S Delight," *Variety*, April 18, 2001.

73 Eric Rudolph, "Mob Psychology," *American Cinematographer* 80 (October 1999): 62–64.

74 Jean Oppenheimer, "Espionage 101," *American Cinematographer* 83 (November 2002): 84–89.

75 Argy, Oppenheimer, "The Halls of Power"; Dempsey.

76 Dempsey.

77 Ibid.

78 Eriq Gardner, "Open Wide: Why *The Sopranos* and *ER* Put Those Black Bands across Your Screen," *Slate* February 6, 2002, http://www.slate.com/id/2061664/.

79 Rudolph.

80 Liz Shannon Miller, "Another Potential iPad Dealbreaker: The Aspect Ratio," *NewTeeVee*, January 28, 2010, http://newteevee.com/2010/01/28/another-potential-ipad-dealbreaker-the-aspect-ratio/.

81 Alison Romano and Ken Kerschbaumer, "Brighter, Clearer, Wider," *Broadcasting and Cable*, January 26, 2004, 14–20.

82 Ken Kershbaumer, "If You Broadcast in HD, Fans Will Come," *Broadcasting and Cable*, April 10, 2006, 18.

83 "ABC's NFL *Monday Night Football*" Game on September 13th to Make Television History: Start of First Season of Weekly HDTV Sportscasts," *Business Wire*, September 10, 1999.

84 Ken Kerschbaumer, "Where to Go for HD," *Broadcasting and Cable*, May 6, 2002, 58.

85 Glen Dickson, "NBC Climbs the High-Def Mountain," *Broadcasting and Cable*, February 6, 2006, 7–8.

86 Kerschbaumer, "If You Broadcast. . ."

87 Ken Kerschbaumer, "High-Def Ticket," *Broadcasting and Cable*, March 22, 2004, 18.

88 Allison Romano, "The Pictures Are the Story," *Broadcasting and Cable*, November 24, 2008, 14.
89 James Hibberd, "Survivor Sharpens Up with HD," *Hollywood Reporter* April 3, 2008.
90 Buechner.
91 George Winslow, "Look Sharp: Channels Big and Small Make the Move to High-Def," *Broadcasting and Cable*, May 3, 2004.
92 Daisy Whitney, "Local Stations High on HD," *Television Week*, April 16, 2007, 28.
93 Winslow.
94 Joel Brown, "High-Def Isn't Just for Guys," *Broadcasting and Cable*, April 10, 2006.
95 "High-Definition Television in the United States," *Wikipedia*, http://en.wikipedia.org/wiki/High-definition_television_in_the_United_States updated October 2, 2010.
96 Wilson Rothman, "Let the Format Wars Begin," *Time*, April 17, 2006.
97 Joseph.
98 Glen Dickson, "What's High-Def, Alex?" *Broadcasting and Cable*, August 21, 2006.
99 Whitney.
100 Paige Albiniak, "Local News in HD Gains Momentum," *Broadcasting and Cable*, March 19, 2007.
101 Paige Albiniak, "HD Look for 'Live'," *Broadcasting and Cable*, November 24, 2008.
102 Hibberd.
103 Paige Albiniak, "Hooray for Hollywood in HD," *Broadcasting and Cable*, September 8, 2008.
104 Glen Dickson, "High Definition for *Hospital*," *Broadcasting and Cable*, April 6, 2009, 3, 6.
105 "CBS Relaunches *Early Show* with New HD Set," *Broadcast Engineering*, January 14, 2008.

7 Technologies of Agency

1 Joel Brinkley, *Defining Vision: The Battle for the Future of Television* (San Diego: Harcourt Brace, 1998), xi.
2 Max Dawson, "TV Repair: New Media 'Solutions' to Old Media Problems" (Ph.D. dissertation, Northwestern University, 2008).
3 Ibid.
4 Adam L. Penenberg, "The Death of Television: Will the Internet Replace the Boob Tube?" *Slate*, October 17, 2005, http://www.slate.com/id/2128201/.
5 Larry Magid, "TiVo: Endless Entertainment," cbsnews.com, http://www.cbsnews.com/stories/2003/07/17/scitech/pcanswer/main563830.shtml July 17, 2003; Jim Harris, "The Decline of TV as You Know It," *Backbone Magazine*, January 19, 2004, http://www.backbonemag.com/Magazine/Big_Ideas_07060611.asp.
6 "Smart Boxes," *The Economist*, October 7, 2000, discusses CBS's refusal to air this commercial.
7 William Boddy, *New Media and Popular Imagination*, 123, quotes Andy Ihnatko, "TiVo Revolutionizes TV," *Chicago Sun-Times*, May 8, 2001, 50: "At the end of your first day with TiVo, you will finally blink and shout, 'Holy cats, this must be how God watches television!'" On the increased control and empowerment promised by the DVR, see "Smart Boxes," *The Economist*; and David LaGesse and Janet Rae-Dupree, "TV Recorders Let Viewers Program Their Prime Time," *U.S. News and World Report*, December 11, 2000, 82.
8 Joe Saltzman, "Its Not TV! It's HBO, USA, FX . . ." *USA Today*, November 1, 2006.
9 This was the advertising tagline of FLO TV, which went out of business in 2011.
10 Raymond Williams, *Television: Technology and Cultural Form* (London: Routledge, 1974).

11 Boddy, *New Media and Popular Imagination*, 133–134; Michael Lewis, "Boom Box," *New York Times Magazine*, August 13, 2000.

12 Nicholas Negroponte, *Being Digital* (New York: Vintage, 1995), coined the term "daily me," and argued that digital media would individualize television in particular.

13 Ibid., 107.

14 Derek Kompare, "Reruns 2.0: Revising Repetition for Multiplatform Television Distribution," *Journal of Popular Film and Television* (2010): 79–83, 82.

15 Daniel Chamberlain, "Scripted Spaces: Television Interfaces and the Non-Places of Asynchronous Entertainment," in *Television as Digital Media*, ed. James Bennett and Niki Strange (Durham, NC: Duke University Press, 2011), 230–254.

16 Boddy, *New Media and Popular Imagination*, 129.

17 Vincent Canby, "From the Humble Mini-Series Comes the Magnificent Megamovie," *New York Times*, October 31, 1999.

18 Michele Hilmes, *Only Connect: A Cultural History of Broadcasting in the United States* (Belmont, CA: Thompson/Wadsworth, 2007), 105.

19 Henry Jenkins, *Convergence Culture: Where Old and New Media Collide* (New York: New York University Press, 2006), 13–16.

20 Claude Brodessar-akner, "*Mad Men* Gives Wide Berth to Madison Ave," *Advertising Age*, October 8, 2007.

21 Scott Collins, "Some Television Reruns Hit Their Prime on DVD," *Los Angeles Times*, November 13, 2005.

22 Dave Belcher, "Recently Viewed," *La Perruque*, April 13, 2008, http://laperruque. blogspot.com/2008/04/recently-viewed.html.

23 Derek Kompare, "Publishing Flow: DVD Box Sets and the Reconception of Television," *Television and New Media*, 7, no. 4 (November 2006): 335–360.

24 Jim Aitchison, "Consumers, Not Ads, Now Bankrolling US Media," *Media Asia*, September 24, 2004, 22.

25 Matt Hills, "From the Box in the Corner to the Box Set on the Shelf: TVIII and the Cultural/Textual Valorizations of DVD," *New Review of Film and Television Studies* 5, no. 1 (2007): 41–60.

26 Kompare, "Publishing Flow," 352.

27 Brigid Stapleton, "New Couch Communities," *The Age*, October 28, 2006, theage.com.au/news/tv—radio/new-couch-communities/2006/10/26/1161749 253583.html.

28 Aitchison.

29 Toni Ruberto, "DVDs Offer Viewer Freedom," *Buffalo News*, September 17, 2006, www.buffalonews.com/editorial/20060917/1023568.asp?PFVer=Story.

30 Brian Lowry, "TV Is Finally Giving Auds Some Respect," *Variety*, September 26, 2006.

31 Terry Teachout, "The Myth of 'Classic' TV," in *The Terry Teachout Reader* (New Haven, CT: Yale University Press, 2004), 174–177, originally published in the *New York Times* in 1991.

32 Steven Johnson, *Everything Bad is Good for You: How Today's Popular Culture is Actually Making Us Smarter* (New York: Riverhead, 2005), 157–179.

33 Ibid., 162.

34 Ibid., 162–163.

35 James Poniewozik, "Show Business: It's Not TV. It's TV on DVD," *Time*, April 19, 2004.

36 Devin Gordon, "Why TV is Better Than Movies," *Newsweek*, February 26, 2007.

37 David Bordwell, *The Way Hollywood Tells It: Story and Style in Modern Movies* (Berkeley: University of California Press, 2006), 74; Klinger, *Beyond the Multiplex: Cinema, New Technologies, and the Home*, 135–190; Jason Mittell, "Narrative Complexity in Contemporary American Television," *The Velvet Light Trap* 58 (Fall 2006): 29–40.

38   Barbara Klinger, "Becoming Cult: *The Big Lebowski*, Replay Culture and Male Fans," *Screen* 51 (2010): 1–20.

39   Mark R. Leffler, "The New Golden Age of TV Drama: How HBO and AMC Became the New NBC and CBS," *Review*, (n.d.), http://review-mag.com/archive/680-689/689/captain_video.htm.

40   Hills, "From the Box in the Corner."

41   Johnson, *Everything Bad is Good for You*, 168.

42   Hills, "From the Box in the Corner," 4. Hills cites Frances Bonner, *Ordinary Television: Analyzing Popular TV* (London: Sage, 2003).

43   In 2009, the top-selling DVD titles included *True Blood*, *The Office*, *Lost*, *Heroes*, *Grey's Anatomy*, and *24*. Robert Seidman, "Serialized Dramas Overwhelmingly Top TV Show DVD Sales in 2009," *TV By the Numbers*, February 1, 2010, http://tvbythenumbers.zap2it.com/2010/02/01/serialized-dramas-overwhelmingly-top-tv-show-dvd-sales/40666. Programs that show the greatest ratings gains after figuring in DVR "plus-7" viewing in Fall 2010 were mainly Quality dramas and comedies: *Modern Family*, *Grey's Anatomy*, *Parenthood*, *House*, *Glee*, and *The Office*, though *Hawaii 5–0* gains most percentage-wise. *TV by the Numbers*, http://tvbythenumbers.zap2it.com/category/weekly-tv-ratings-rankings/top-timeshifted. The most downloaded TV shows of 2008 according to the blog TorrentFreak were *Lost*, *Heroes*, *Prison Break*, *Terminator The Sarah Connor Chronicles*, *Desperate Housewives*, *Stargate Atlantis*, *Dexter*, *House*, *Grey's Anatomy*, and *Smallville*, http://torrentfreak.com/top-10-most-pirated-tv-shows-of-2008-081223/. The 2009 list included many of the same titles, as well as *True Blood* and *24*. http://torrentfreak.com/top-10-most-pirated-tv-shows-of-2009-091231/.

44   Mark Lawson, "Are You Sitting Comfortably?" *Guardian*, November 2, 2006; Michael Z. Newman, "TV Binge," *Flow*, January 23, 2009.

45   Jason Kottke, "Megamovies, TV Shows as Days-Long Movies," kottke.org, October 9, 2008, http://www.kottke.org/08/10/megamovies-tv-shows-as-dayslong-movies.

46   Nussbaum, "When TV Became Art."

47   "2000s: Decade of the PVR," Pvrblog.com, December 29, 2009, http://www.pvrblog.com/2009/12/decade-of-dvr.html.

48   Henry Jenkins, "'Do You Enjoy Making the Rest of Us Feel Stupid?'

49   On the television industry's efforts to "invite in" audiences as participants and producers, see Derek Johnson, "Inviting Audiences in: The Spatial Reorganization of Production and Consumption in 'TVIII,'" *New Review of Film and Television Studies* 5, no. 1 (April 2007): 61–80.

50   Claire Atkinson, "What to Watch? How About a *Simpsons* Episode from 1999?" *New York Times*, September 24, 2007.

51   Michael Moyer, "The Everything TV," *Scientific American* (November, 2009): 74–79.

52   Randy Kennedy, "The Shorter, Faster, Cruder, Tinier TV Show," *New York Times*, May 28, 2006.

53   "LG VX8400," *Wired*, October 2007.

54   Anna McCarthy, *Ambient Television: Visual Culture and Public Space* (Durham, NC: Duke University Press, 2001).

55   Stephen Groening, "From 'A Box in the Theater of the World' to 'The World as Your Living Room': Cellular Phones, Television and Mobile Privatization," *New Media and Society* 12, no. 8 (2010): 1331–1347.

56   Steve Smith, "And Another Thing: I'm Still Not Watching Mobile TV," *MediaPost*, November 23, 2010.

57   As an example of a media company using new television technologies to extend and monetize its branded content, see Frank Rose, "ESPN Thinks Outside the Box," *Wired* (September 2005).

58 Josh R. Quain, "TV Everywhere? We're Already There," foxnews.com, November 23, 2010.
59 Boddy, *New Media and Popular Imagination*, 70.
60 Dawson, "TV Repair," 264.
61 Ibid., 297.
62 Lynn Spigel, *Welcome to the Dreamhouse: Popular Media and Postwar Suburbs* (Durham, NC: Duke University Press, 2001), 60–103.
63 Amanda D. Lotz, *The Television Will Be Revolutionized* (New York: New York University Press, 2007), 68–69, notes as well that devices such as BlackBerry PDAs on which users might watch television programs seem like solutions to the problem of work/family balance, selling the idea that one can satisfy the demands of both simultaneously.
64 Max Dawson, "Failure to Communicate: Promoting Mobile Television in the United States," unpublished ms.
65 Don Clark, "Qualcomm CEO Comes Clean about Mobile TV Miscues," Digits blog (*Wall Street Journal*), December 1, 2010, http://blogs.wsj.com/digits/2010/12/01/qualcomm-ceo-comes-clean-about-mobile-tv-miscues/.
66 Glen Dickson, "Special Report: Mobile DTV Heats UP," *Broadcasting and Cable*, July 13, 2009; Eric A. Taub, "Local TV for Devices on the Move," *New York Times*, February 14, 2010.
67 Max Dawson, "Little Players, Big Shows: Format, Narration, and Style on Television's New Smaller Screens," *Convergence* 13, no. 3 (August 2007): 231–250, 233.
68 Michael Humphrey, "Names You Need to Know in 2011: Paul Scanlan of MobiTV," Michael Humphrey Techno-Tainers blog, *Forbes* magazine website, December 10, 2010, http://blogs.forbes.com/michaelhumphrey/2010/12/10/names-you-need-to-know-in-2011-paul-scanlan-of-mobitv/.
69 Dawson, "Failure to Communicate."
70 Ibid.
71 Brian Stelter, "The Myth of Fast-Forwarding Past the Ads," *New York Times*, December 20, 2010.
72 William Uricchio, "Television's Next Generation: Technology/Interface Culture/Flow," in *Television After TV*, ed. Lynn Spigel and Jan Olsson, 167.
73 Boddy, *New Media and Popular Imagination*, 100.

8 Television Scholarship and/as Legitimation

1 John Fiske, lectures presented at MIT: Comparative Media Studies program, 1995.
2 DiMaggio,"Cultural Boundaries and Structural Change, 21–57; Shyon Baumann, "Intellectualization and Art World Development: Film in the United States," *American Sociological Review* 66 (June 2001): 404–426.
3 Michael Z. Newman, *Zigzigger: On the Audiovisual and Beyond*, zigzigger.blogspot.com; Michael Z. Newman, http://twitter.com/#!/mznewman; Elana Levine, *Dr. Television*, drtelevision.blogspot.com; Elana Levine, http://twitter.com/#!/ehl.
4 "College," *30 Rock*, NBC, November 18, 2010.
5 Don Delillo, *White Noise* (New York: Penguin, 1984); Richard Russo, *Straight Man* (New York: Vintage, 1997).
6 See, for example, the character Slater referring to his "A" in *Gilligan's Island* for his History of Television course, "Guess Who's Coming to College," *Saved by the Bell: The College Years*, NBC, September 14, 1993.
7 Charlotte Brunsdon, "What is the 'Television' of Television Studies?" in *The Television Studies Book*, ed. Geraghty and Lusted, 95.
8 Ellen Messer-Davidow, David R. Shumway, and David J. Sylvan, "Introduction: Disciplinary Ways of Knowing," in *Knowledges: Historical and Critical Studies in Disciplinarity* (Charlottesville: University Press of Virginia, 1993), 2.

9   Dana B. Polan, *Scenes of Instruction: The Beginnings of the U.S. Study of Film* (Berkeley: University of California Press, 2007), 5.

10   Ibid.

11   William Boddy, "Loving a Nineteen-Inch Motorola: American Writing on Television," in *Regarding Television*, ed. E. Ann Kaplan, 5.

12   Lynn Spigel, "The Making of a TV Literate Elite," in *The Television Studies Book*, ed. Christine Geraghty and David Lusted, 68, notes that the first book of television criticism, *The Eighth Art*, was published in 1962, the same year as the founding of the journal *Television Quarterly* by the National Academy of Television Arts and Sciences.

13   Horace Newcomb, "The Development of Television Studies," in *The Companion to Television*, ed. Janet Wasko (Madden, MA: Blackwell Publishing, 2005), 19.

14   Richard Adler, "Understanding Television," in *Television as a Social Force: New Approaches to Criticism* (New York: Praeger, 1975), 42.

15   Richard Adler, ed., *Television as a Cultural Force* (New York: Praeger, 1975); Horace Newcomb, *TV: The Most Popular Art* (Garden City, NY: Anchor Press), 1974.

16   Hal Himmelstein, *On the Small Screen: New Approaches in Television and Video Criticism* (New York: Praeger, 1981), 87.

17   Tom Yee, Library of Congress, personal communication with Levine, January 3, 2011.

18   Horace Newcomb, Curriculum Vita, Grady College, University of Georgia, http://www.grady.uga.edu/CV/Newcomb_Vita09.pdf.

19   Peabody Awards, University of Georgia, http://www.peabody.uga.edu/overview_history/index.php.

20   "What is Console-ing Passions?" Console-ing Passions International Conference, http://www.cp.commarts.wisc.edu/home/index.htm. It would take until 2000 for the U.S. Library of Congress to create a subject heading for Feminist Television Criticism. Tom Yee, Library of Congress, personal communication with Levine, January 3, 2011.

21   Console-ing Passions Series, Duke University Press, http://www.dukeupress.edu/Catalog/ProductList.php?viewby=series&id=19. Jane Feuer, *Seeing Through the Eighties: Television and Reaganism* (Durham, NC: Duke University Press, 1995).

22   William Boddy comments on these scholarly practices in "In Focus: The Place of Television Studies," *Cinema Journal* 45, no. 1 (Fall 2005): 79–82. Hilmes writes of New York University's first graduate seminar in Television Studies being offered in 1978, when she was a Cinema Studies student there. Michele Hilmes, "The Bad Object: Television in the American Academy," *Cinema Journal* 45, no. 1 (Fall 2005): 112.

23   "Organizational History," Society for Cinema and Media Studies, http://www.cmstudies.org/?page=org_history.

24   Petro, "Mass Culture and the Feminine." The journal published its first article on television in 1985, William Boddy's "The Studios Move into Prime Time: Hollywood and the Television Industry in the 1950s," *Cinema Journal* 24, no. 4 (Summer 1985): 23–37. Editor Virginia Wright Wexman noted the significance of this in her "Editor's Introduction" to the issue. Wexman, 3.

25   Statistics compiled from SCS Job Lists, Fall 1999 and October 2000, SCMS Job List Archive, Society for Cinema and Media Studies. December 2010 data from Society of Cinema and Media Studies Job Opening search, http://cmstudies.site-ym.com/networking/opening_search.asp?.

26   Hilmes, "The Bad Object," 114.

27   Drake Bennett, "This Will Be on the Midterm. You Feel Me?" *Slate*, March 24, 2010, http://www.slate.com/id/2245788/.

28   Smart TV: Television as Art and Literature course website, http://smarttvclass.org/.

29   Brunsdon, "What is the 'Television' of Television Studies?" 96.

30   Hilmes, "The Bad Object," 115.

31   For examples of the latter, see *Flow*, edited by graduate students in the Department of Radio-TV-Film at the University of Texas at Austin, flowtv.org, *Antenna*, edited by media and cultural studies faculty and graduate students in the Department of Communication Arts at the University of Wisconsin-Madison, http://blog.commarts.wisc.edu/, and *In Media Res*, coordinated by faculty and graduate students in the Moving Image Studies program at Georgia State University, http://mediacommons.futureofthebook.org/imr/.

32   Thompson, *Television's Second Golden Age*. The book provides a careful dissection of the characteristics of the Quality drama trend of the 1980s and early 1990s. Although it focuses mostly on textual features and speaks quite admiringly of them, the book is rather self-conscious about the historicity of its claims. As Thompson writes, "I am not so much arguing that the quality dramas of the 1980s were inherently better than anything else that has been aired through the years, than I am suggesting that the shows were different." Thompson, 17.

33   Lavery and Thompson, 24.

34   Amelie Hastie, "The Epistemological Stakes of "Buffy the Vampire Slayer": Television Criticism and Marketing Demands," in *Undead TV: Essays on "Buffy the Vampire Slayer*," ed. Elana Levine and Lisa Parks (Durham, NC: Duke University Press, 2007), 90.

35   Paul Levinson, "Naked Bodies, Three Showings a Week, and No Commercials: *The Sopranos* as a Nuts-and-Bolts Triumph of Non-Network TV," in *This Thing of Ours*, ed. David Lavery, 29.

36   Ibid., 30.

37   Trisha Dunleavy, "Strategies of Innovation in 'High-End' TV Drama: The Contribution of Cable," *Flow*, March 6, 2009.

38   Brian G. Rose, "*The Wire*," *The Essential HBO Reader*, ed. Gary R. Edgerton and Jeffrey P. Jones, 82.

39   Jason Jacobs, "Issues of Judgement and Value in Television Studies," *International Journal of Cultural Studies* 4, no. 4 (December 2001): 432.

40   Craig Jacobsen, "How TV Met Narrative Sophistication," *Flow*, October 6, 2006.

41   Jason Mittell, "Narrative Complexity in Contemporary American Television," *The Velvet Light Trap* 58 (Fall 2006): 30.

42   Ibid.

43   Jason Mittell, "The Loss of Value (or the Value of *Lost*)," *Flow*, May 27, 2005.

44   Jason Mittell, "Television's New Golden Age," Middlebury College MiddCommunications, http://www.youtube.com/watch?v=bBePKf-IRCI.

45   Thompson, "Comedy Verité?," 63. Butler, *Television Style*, 19.

46   Caldwell, *Televisuality*.

47   Butler, *Television Style*, 216.

48   Lavery and Thompson, 19–20, 23.

49   Roberta Pearson, "*Lost* in Transition: From Post-Network to Post-Television," in *Quality TV: Contemporary American Television and Beyond*, ed. Janet McCabe and Kim Akass (London/New York: I.B. Tauris, 2007), 246.

50   Mittell, "Narrative Complexity . . .," 32.

51   Jason Mittell, "Scholar Jason Mittell on the Ties Between Daytime and Primetime Serials: Based on an Interview by Sam Ford," in *The Survival of Soap Opera: Transformations for a New Media Era*, ed. Sam Ford, Abigail De Kosnik, and C. Lee Harrington (Jackson: University Press of Mississippi, 2011), 138.

52   Henry Jenkins, "Historical Poetics," in *Approaches to Popular Film*, ed. Joanne Hollows and Mark Jancovich (Manchester: Manchester University Press, 1995), 111.

53   Greg M. Smith, *Beautiful TV: The Art and Argument of "Ally McBeal"* (Austin: University of Texas Press, 2007), 5.

54   Jenkins, "Historical Poetics," 112.

55 Smith, *Beautiful TV*, 7.
56 Mittell asserts that, "In reading interviews with, and talking to, primetime creators, I've never seen any reference to soap operas as a point of inspiration or influence." He takes this as evidence that there is no relationship between the two forms. "Scholar Jason Mittell . . .," 134.
57 Lotz, *The Television Will Be Revolutionized*, 217.
58 Marc Leverette, Brian L. Ott, and Cara Louise Buckley, eds., *It's Not TV: Watching HBO in the Post-Television Era* (New York: Routledge, 2008).
59 Gary Edgerton and Jeffrey P. Jones, eds., *The Essential HBO Reader* (Lexington: University Press of Kentucky, 2008).
60 Dana Polan, "Cable Watching: HBO, *The Sopranos*, and Discourses of Distinction," in *Cable Visions*, ed. Sarah Banet-Weiser, Cynthia Chris, and Anthony Freitas (New York: New York University Press, 2007), 272.
61 Jenkins, *Convergence Culture*, 18.
62 Henry Jenkins, "Afterword: The Future of Fandom," in *Fandom: Identities and Communities in a Mediated World*, ed. Jonathan Gray, Cornel Sandvoss, and C. Lee Harrington (New York: New York University Press, 2007), 362.
63 Gray, *Show Sold Separately*, 215.
64 Ibid., 21.
65 "About C3: Books," Convergence Culture Consortium website, http://www.convergenceculture.org/aboutc3/thebook.php.
66 Christopher Anderson, "Producing an Aristocracy of Culture in American Television," in *The Essential HBO Reader*, ed. Gary R. Edgerton and Jones, 29.
67 For example, see Avi Santo, "Para-Television and Discourses of Distinction," 19–45, as well as Polan, *The Sopranos*.
68 Joyrich, 32–33.
69 David Thorburn, "*The Sopranos*," in *The Essential HBO Reader*, 66–67.
70 In this respect, Thorburn's analysis escapes the critique Polan makes of much *Sopranos* scholarship, that "Few of the scholarly writings deal . . . with the television show as being in fact a television show." Polan, "Cable Watching," 268.
71 Kompare, "Publishing Flow: DVD Box Sets and the Reconception of Television"; Boddy, *New Media and Popular Imagination*; Polan, *The Sopranos*; Hills, *Fan Cultures*; Creeber, *Serial Television: Big Drama on the Small Screen*.
72 Klinger, *Beyond the Multiplex: Cinema, New Technologies and the Home*; Spigel, "Yesterday's Future, Tomorrow's Home," in *Welcome to the Dreamhouse*.

SELECT BIBLIOGRAPHY

Abbott, Stacey. "How *Lost* Found Its Audience: The Making of a Cult Blockbuster." In *Reading* "Lost," edited by Roberta Pearson, 9–26. London: I.B. Tauris, 2009.

Adler, Richard. "Understanding Television." In *Television as a Social Force: New Approaches to Criticism*, edited by Richard Adler, 1–16. New York: Praeger, 1975.

Adler, Richard, ed. *Television as a Cultural Force*. New York: Praeger, 1976.

Allen, Robert C. *Speaking of Soap Operas*. Chapel Hill: The University of North Carolina Press, 1985.

Alvey, Mark. "'Too Many Kids and Old Ladies': Quality Demographics and 1960s U.S. Television." In *Television: The Critical View*, 7th ed., edited by Horace Newcomb, 15–36. New York: Oxford University Press, 2007.

Anderson, Christopher. "Producing an Aristocracy of Culture in American Television." In *The Essential HBO Reader*, edited by Gary R. Edgerton and Jeffrey P. Jones, 23–41. Lexington: University Press of Kentucky, 2008.

Askwith, Ivan. "'Do You Even Know Where This Is Going? *Lost*'s Viewers and Narrative Premeditation." In *Reading* "Lost," edited by Roberta Pearson, 159–180. London: I.B. Tauris, 2009.

Baumann, Shyon. "Intellectualization and Art World Development: Film in the United States." *American Sociological Review* 66 (June 2001): 404–426.

Baumann, Shyon. *Hollywood Highbrow: From Entertainment to Art*. Princeton, NJ: Princeton University Press, 2007.

Becker, Howard S. *Art Worlds*. Berkeley: University of California Press, 1982.

Belton, John. *Widescreen Cinema*. Cambridge, MA: Harvard University Press, 1992.

Boddy, William. "Loving a Nineteen-Inch Motorola: American Writing on Television." In *Regarding Television*, edited by E. Ann Kaplan, 1–11. Los Angeles: The American Film Institute, 1983.

Boddy, William. "The Studios Move into Prime Time: Hollywood and the Television Industry in the 1950s." *Cinema Journal* 24, no. 4 (Summer 1985): 23–37.

Boddy, William. *Fifties Television: The Industry and Its Critics*. Urbana: University of Illinois Press, 1990.

Boddy, William. "Archaeologies of Electronic Vision and the Gendered Spectator." *Screen* 35, no. 2 (Summer 1994): 105–122.

Boddy, William. *New Media and Popular Imagination: Launching Radio, Television, and Digital Media in the United States*. Oxford: Oxford University Press, 2004.

Boddy, William. "In Focus: The Place of Television Studies." *Cinema Journal* 45, no. 1 (Fall 2005): 79–82.

Bodroghkozy, Aniko. *Groove Tube: Sixties Television and the Youth Rebellion*. Durham, NC: Duke University Press, 2001.

Bonner, Frances. *Ordinary Television: Analyzing Popular TV*. London: Sage, 2003.

Boorstin, Daniel J. *The Image: A Guide to Pseudo-Events in America*. New York: Athenaeum, 1961.

Bordwell, David. *The Way Hollywood Tells It: Story and Style in Modern Movies*. Berkeley: University of California Press, 2006.

Bourdieu, Pierre. *Distinction: A Social Critique of the Judgment of Taste*, trans. Richard Nice. Cambridge, MA: Harvard University Press, 1987.

Brantlinger, Patrick. *Bread and Circuses: Theories of Mass Culture as Social Decay*. Ithaca, NY: Cornell University Press, 1983.

Brinkley, Joel. *Defining Vision: The Battle for the Future of Television*. San Diego: Harcourt Brace, 1998.

Brunsdon, Charlotte. "*Crossroads*: Notes on Soap Opera." In *Regarding Television*, edited by E. Ann Kaplan, 76–83. Los Angeles: American Film Institute, 1983.

Brunsdon, Charlotte. "What is the 'Television' of Television Studies?" In *The Television Studies Book*, edited by Christine Geraghty and David Lusted, 95–113. London: Arnold, 1998.

Bryson, Bethany. "'Anything But Heavy Metal': Symbolic Exclusion and Musical Dislikes," *American Sociological Review* 61, no. 5 (October 1996): 884–889.

Butler, Jeremy. *Television Style*. New York: Routledge, 2010.

Caldwell, John Thornton. *Televisuality: Style, Crisis and Authority in American Television*. New Brunswick, NJ: Rutgers University Press, 1995.

Cantor, Muriel G. and Joel M. Cantor. *Prime-Time Television: Content and Control*, 2nd ed. Newbury Park, CA: Sage, 1992.

Carson, Tom. "Hip to the Squares." *American Film* 15 (September 1990): 16.

Chamberlain, Daniel. "Scripted Spaces: Television Interfaces and the Non-Places of Asynchronous Entertainment." In *Television as Digital Media*, edited by James Bennett and Niki Strange, 230–254. Durham, NC: Duke University Press, 2011.

Christopherson, Richard W. "From Folk Art to Fine Art: A Transformation in the Meaning of Photographic Work." *Urban Life and Culture* 3, no. 2 (July 1974): 123–157.

Corrigan, Timothy. *A Cinema Without Walls: Movies and Culture After Vietnam*. New Brunswick, NJ: Rutgers University Press, 1991.

Cox, Jim. *The Daytime Serials of Television, 1946–1960*. Jefferson, NC: McFarland & Company, 2006.

Creeber, Glen. "'TV Ruined the Movies': Television, Tarantino, and the Intimate World of *The Sopranos*." In *This Thing of Ours: Investigating "The Sopranos*,*"* edited by David Lavery, 124–134. New York: Columbia University Press, 2002.

Creeber, Glen. *Serial Television: Big Drama on the Small Screen*. London: BFI, 2004.

Curtin, Michael. *Redeeming the Wasteland: Television Documentary and Cold War Politics*. New Brunswick, NJ: Rutgers University Press, 1995.

Czitrom, Daniel J. *Media and the American Mind: From Morse to McLuhan*. Raleigh: University of North Carolina Press, 1982.

Dawson, Max. "Little Players, Big Shows: Format, Narration, and Style on Television's New Smaller Screens." *Convergence* 13, no. 3 (August 2007): 231–250.

Dawson, Max. "TV Repair: New Media 'Solutions' to Old Media Problems." Ph.D. diss., Northwestern University, 2008.

DiMaggio, Paul. "Cultural Boundaries and Structural Change: The Extension of the High Culture Model to Theater, Opera, and the Dance, 1900–1940." In *Cultivating Differences: Symbolic Boundaries and the Making of Inequality*, edited by Michèle Lamond and Marcel Fournier, 21–57. Chicago: University of Chicago Press, 1992.

Dolan, Mark. "The Peaks and Valleys of Serial Creativity: What Happened to/on *Twin Peaks*." In *Full of Secrets: Critical Approaches to "Twin Peaks*," edited by David Lavery, 30–50. Detroit: Wayne State University Press, 1995.

Donatelli, Cindy and Sharon Alward. "'I Dread You'? Married to the Mob in *The Godfather*, *Goodfellas*, and *The Sopranos*." In *This Thing of Ours: Investigating "The Sopranos*," edited by David Lavery, 60–71. New York: Columbia University Press, 2002.

Dunleavy, Trisha. "Strategies of Innovation in 'High-End' TV Drama: The Contribution of Cable." *Flow*, March 6, 2009.

Dupagne, Michel. "Exploring the Characteristics of Potential High-Definition Television Adopters." *Journal of Media Economics* 12, no. 1 (1999): 35–50.

Edgerton, Gary R. and Jeffrey P. Jones, eds. *The Essential HBO Reader*. Lexington: University Press of Kentucky, 2008.

Feuer, Jane. "MTM Enterprises: An Overview." In *MTM: Quality Television*, edited by Jane Feuer, Paul Kerr, and Tise Vahimagi, 1–31. London: British Film Institute, 1984.

Feuer, Jane. "The MTM Style," in *MTM: Quality Television*, edited by Jane Feuer, Paul Kerr, and Tise Vahimagi, 32–60. London: BFI, 1984.

Feuer, Jane. *Seeing Through the Eighties: Television and Reaganism*. Durham, NC: Duke University Press, 1995.

Feuer, Jane. "The Lack of Influence of *Thirtysomething*." In *The Contemporary Television Series*, edited by Michael Hammond and Lucy Mazdon, 27–36. Edinburgh: Edinburgh University Press, 2005.

Feuer, Jane, Paul Kerr and Tise Vahimagi, eds. *MTM: Quality Television*. London: BFI, 1984.

Fiske, John. *Television Culture*. London: Routledge, 1987.

Flynn, Bernadette. "Geography of the Digital Hearth." *Information, Communication and Society*, 6, no. 4 (2003): 551–576.

Foucault, Michel. "The Discourse on Language." In *The Archaeology of Knowledge*, 215–238. New York: Pantheon Books, 1971.

Foucault, Michel. "Two Lectures." In *Power/Knowledge*, edited by Colin Gordon, 78–108. New York: Pantheon Books, 1980.

Geraghty, Christine. "Exhausted and Exhausting: Television Studies and British Soap Opera." *Critical Studies in Television* 5, no. 1 (Spring 2010): 82–96.

Gitlin, Todd. *Inside Prime Time*. New York: Pantheon Books, 1983.

Goldsen, Rose K. *The Show and Tell Machine: How Television Works and Works You Over*. New York: Dial, 1975.

Gomery, Douglas. *Shared Pleasures: A History of Movie Presentation in the United States*. Madison: University of Wisconsin Press, 1992.

Gray, Jonathan. *Show Sold Separately: Promos, Spoilers, and Other Media Paratexts*. New York: New York University Press, 2010.

Groening, Stephen. "From 'A Box in the Theater of the World' to 'The World as Your Living Room': Cellular Phones, Television and Mobile Privatization." *New Media and Society* 12, no. 8 (2010): 1331–1347.

Gwenllian-Jones, Sara and Roberta Pearson. "Introduction." In *Cult Television*, edited by Sara Gwenllian-Jones and Roberta Pearson, ix–xx. Minneapolis: University of Minnesota Press, 2004.

Hastie, Amelie. "The Epistemological Stakes of *Buffy the Vampire Slayer*: Television Criticism and Marketing Demands." In *Undead TV: Essays on "Buffy the Vampire Slayer,"* edited by Elana Levine and Lisa Parks, 74–95. Durham, NC: Duke University Press, 2007.

Hayward, Jennifer. *Consuming Pleasures: Active Audiences and Serial Fictions from Dickens to Soap Opera*. Lexington: University Press of Kentucky, 1997.

Hibbett, Ryan. "What is Indie Rock?" *Popular Music and Society* 28, no. 1 (February 2005): 55–77.

Hills, Matt. *Fan Cultures*. London: Routledge, 2002.

Hills, Matt. "Defining Cult TV: Texts, Inter-texts and Fan Audiences." In *The Television Studies Book*, edited by Robert C. Allen and Annette Hill, 509–523. New York: Routledge, 2004.

Hills, Matt. "*Dawson's Creek*: 'Quality Teen TV' and 'Mainstream Cult'?" In *Teen TV: Genre, Consumption and Identity*, edited by Glyn Davis and Kay Dickinson, 54–67. London: BFI, 2004.

Hills, Matt. "From the Box in the Corner to the Box Set on the Shelf: TVIII and the Cultural/Textual Valorizations of DVD." *New Review of Film and Television Studies* 5, no. 1 (2007): 41–60.

Hilmes, Michele. *Radio Voices: American Broadcasting, 1922–1952*. Minneapolis: University of Minnesota Press, 1997.

Hilmes, Michele. "The Bad Object: Television in the American Academy." *Cinema Journal* 45, no. 1 (Fall 2005): 111–116.

Hilmes, Michele. "Desired and Feared: Women's Voices in Radio History." In *Television, History and American Culture: Feminist Critical Essays*, edited by Mary Beth Haralovich and Lauren Rabinovitz, 17–35. Durham: Duke University Press, 1999.

Hilmes, Michele. *Only Connect: A Cultural History of Broadcasting in the United States*. Belmont, CA: Thompson/Wadsworth, 2007.

Himmelstein, Hal. *On the Small Screen: New Approaches in Television and Video Criticism*. New York: Praeger, 1981.

Hollows, Joanne. "The Masculinity of Cult." In *Defining Cult Movies: The Cultural Politics of Oppositional Taste*, edited by Mark Jancovich, Antonio Lázaro Reboll, Julian Stringer, and Andy Willis, 35–53. Manchester: Manchester University Press, 2003.

Jacobs, David. "Confessions of a Story Editor." In *TV Book*, edited by Judy Fireman, 57–60. New York: Workman, 1977.

Jacobs, Jason. "Issues of Judgement and Value in Television Studies." *International Journal of Cultural Studies* 4, no. 4 (December 2001): 427–447.

Jacobsen, Craig. "How TV Met Narrative Sophistication." *Flow*, October 6, 2006.

Jancovich, Mark and Nathan Hunt. "The Mainstream, Distinction, and Cult TV." In *Cult Television*, edited by Sara Gwenllian-Jones and Roberta Pearson, 27–44. Minneapolis: University of Minnesota Press, 2004.

Jenkins, Henry. *Textual Poachers: Television Fans and Participatory Culture.* New York: Routledge, 1992.

Jenkins, Henry. "Historical Poetics." In *Approaches to Popular Film*, edited by Joanne Hollows and Mark Jancovich, 99–122. Manchester: Manchester University Press, 1995.

Jenkins, Henry. "'Do You Enjoy Making the Rest of Us Feel Stupid?' alt.tv.twinpeaks, the Trickster Author, and Viewer Mastery." In *Full of Secrets: Critical Approaches to "Twin Peaks,"* edited by David Lavery, 51–69. Detroit: Wayne State University Press, 1995.

Jenkins, Henry. "'Infinite Diversity in Infinite Combinations': Genre and Authorship in *Star Trek.*" In *Science Fiction Audiences: Watching* "Doctor Who" *and* "Star Trek," edited by John Tulloch and Henry Jenkins, 173–194. New York: Routledge, 1995.

Jenkins, Henry. *Convergence Culture: Where Old and New Media Collide.* New York: New York University Press, 2006.

Jenkins, Henry. "Afterword: The Future of Fandom." In *Fandom: Identities and Communities in a Mediated World*, edited by Jonathan Gray, Cornel Sandvoss, and C. Lee Harrington. New York: New York University Press, 2007.

Johnson, Catherine. "Quality/Cult Television: *The X-Files* and Television History." In *The Contemporary Television Series*, edited by Michael Hammond and Lucy Mazdon, 57–71. Edinburgh: Edinburgh University Press, 2005.

Johnson, Derek. "Inviting Audiences in: The Spatial Reorganization of Production and Consumption in 'TVIII.'" *New Review of Film and Television Studies* 5, no. 1 (April 2007): 61–80.

Johnson, Steven. *Everything Bad Is Good for You: How Today's Popular Culture Is Actually Making Us Smarter.* New York: Riverhead, 2005.

Joyrich, Lynne. *Re-viewing Reception: Television, Gender, and Postmodern Culture.* Bloomington: Indiana University Press, 1996.

Kendrick, James. "What is the Criterion? The Criterion Collection as an Archive of Film as Culture." *Journal of Film and Video* 53, no. 2/3 (Summer/Fall 2001): 124–139.

Kendrick, James. "Aspect Ratios and Joe Six-Packs: Home Theater Enthusiasts' Battle to Legitimize the DVD Experience." *The Velvet Light Trap* 56 (Fall 2005): 58–70.

Klinger, Barbara. *Beyond the Multiplex: Cinema, New Technologies and the Home.* Berkeley: University of California Press, 2006.

Klinger, Barbara. "Becoming Cult: *The Big Lebowski*, Replay Culture and Male Fans." *Screen* 51 (2010): 1–20.

Kompare, Derek. "Publishing Flow: DVD Box Sets and the Reconception of Television." *Television and New Media* 7, no. 4 (November 2006): 335–360.

Kompare, Derek. "What Is a Showrunner?: Considering Post-Network Television Authorship." Paper presented at Console-ing Passions International Conference on Television, Audio, Video, New Media and Feminism, Santa Barbara, California, April 25, 2008.

Kompare, Derek. "Reruns 2.0: Revising Repetition for Multiplatform Television Distribution." *Journal of Popular Film and Television* (2010): 79–83.

Kompare, Derek. "More 'Moments of Television': Online Cult Television Authorship." In *Flow TV: Television in the Age of Media Convergence*, edited by Michael Kackman, Marnie Binfield, Matthew Thomas Payne, Allison Perlman, and Bryan Sebock, 95–113. New York: Routledge, 2011.

Lavery, David. "*Buffy the Vampire Slayer.*" In *Fifty Key Television Programmes*, edited by Glen Creeber, 31–35. London: Arnold, 2004.

Lavery, David and Robert J. Thompson. "David Chase, *The Sopranos*, and Television Creativity." In *This Thing of Ours: Investigating* "The Sopranos," edited by David Lavery, 18–25. New York: Columbia University Press, 2002.

Lentz, Kirsten Marthe. "Quality Versus Relevance: Feminism, Race, and the Politics of the Sign in 1970s Television." *Camera Obscura* 15, no. 1 (2000): 45–93.

Leverette, Marc, Brian L. Ott, and Cara Louise Buckley, eds. *It's Not TV: Watching HBO in the Post-Television Era.* New York: Routledge, 2008.

Levine, Elana. *Wallowing in Sex: The New Sexual Culture of 1970s American Television.* Durham, NC: Duke University Press, 2007.

Levine, Elana. "Distinguishing Television: The Changing Meanings of Television Liveness." *Media, Culture and Society* 30, no. 3 (2008): 393–409.

Levine, Lawrence W. *Highbrow/Lowbrow: The Emergence of Cultural Hierarchy in America.* Cambridge, MA: Harvard University Press, 1988.

Levinson, Paul. "Naked Bodies, Three Showings a Week, and No Commercials: *The Sopranos* as a Nuts-and-Bolts Triumph of Non-Network TV." In *This Thing of Ours*, edited by David Lavery, 26–31. New York: Columbia University Press, 2002.

Lopes, Paul. *The Rise of a Jazz Art World.* Cambridge: Cambridge University Press, 2002.

Lotz, Amanda D. *The Television Will Be Revolutionized.* New York: New York University Press, 2007.

Mander, Jerry. *Four Arguments for the Elimination of Television.* New York: William Morrow and Co., 1978.

Mann, Denise. "It's Not TV, It's Brand Management TV: The Collective Author(s) of the *Lost* Franchise." In *Production Studies: Cultural Studies of Media Industries*, edited by Vicki Mayer, Miranda J. Banks, and John Thornton Caldwell, 99–114. New York: Routledge, 2009.

Marc, David and Robert J. Thompson. *Prime Time, Prime Movers: From* "I Love Lucy" *to* "L.A. Law"—*America's Greatest TV Shows and the People Who Created Them.* Syracuse: Syracuse University Press, 1995.

Marchand, Roland. *Advertising the American Dream: Making Way for Modernity, 1920–1940.* Berkeley: University of California Press, 1985.

McCabe, Janet and Kim Akass. "It's Not TV, It's HBO's Original Programming: Producing Quality TV." In *It's Not TV: Watching HBO in the Post-Television Era*, edited by Marc Leverette, Brian L. Ott, and Cara Louis Buckley, 83–94. New York: Routledge, 2008.

McCarthy, Anna. *Ambient Television: Visual Culture and Public Space.* Durham, NC: Duke University Press, 2001.

McCracken, Alison. "'Say Goodnight, Mrs. Ron': Ronald D. Moore and the Gender Politics of the *Battlestar Galactica* Podcast." Paper presented at Console-ing Passions International Conference on Television, Audio, Video, New Media and Feminism, Santa Barbara, California, April 25, 2008.

McLuhan, Eric and Frank Zingrone, eds. *Essential McLuhan.* New York: Basic Books, 1995.

McNutt, Myles. "Tweets of Anarchy: showrunners on Twitter." *Antenna*, September 17, 2010.

Melnick, Ross. "Station R-O-X-Y: Roxy and the Radio." *Film History* 17 (2005): 217–233.

Messer-Davidow, Ellen, David R. Shumway, and David J. Sylvan. *Knowledges: Historical and Critical Studies in Disciplinarity.* Charlottesville, VA: University Press of Virginia, 1993.

Miller, Mark Crispin. *Boxed in: The Culture of TV.* Chicago: Northwestern University Press, 1988.

Mills, Brett. "Comedy Verite: Contemporary Sitcom Form." *Screen* 45, no. 1 (Spring 2004): 63–78.

Mills, Brett. *Television Sitcom*. London: BFI, 2005.

Mittell, Jason. "The Cultural Power of an Anti-Television Metaphor: Questioning the 'Plug-In Drug' and a TV-Free America." *Television and New Media* 1, no. 2 (May 2000): 215–238.

Mittell, Jason. *Genre and Television: From Cop Shows to Cartoons in American Culture*. New York: Routledge, 2004.

Mittell, Jason. "The Loss of Value (or the Value of *Lost*)." *Flow*, May 27, 2005.

Mittell, Jason. "Narrative Complexity in Contemporary American Television." *The Velvet Light Trap* 58 (Fall 2006): 29–40.

Mittell, Jason. "*Lost* in a Great Story: Evaluation in Narrative Television (and Television Studies)." In *Reading* "Lost," edited by Roberta Pearson, 119–138. London: I.B. Tauris, 2009.

Mittell, Jason. "Scholar Jason Mittell on the Ties Between Daytime and Primetime Serials: Based on an Interview by Sam Ford." In *The Survival of Soap Opera: Transformations for a New Media Era*, edited by Sam Ford, Abigail De Kosnik, and C. Lee Harrington, 133–139. Jackson: University Press of Mississippi, 2011.

Modleski, Tania. *Loving with a Vengeance: Mass-Produced Fantasies for Women*, 2nd ed. New York: Routledge, 2008.

Morris, Bruce B. *Prime Time Network Serials*. Jefferson NC: McFarland & Co., 1997.

Moseley, Rachel. "The Teen Series." In *The Television Genre Book*, edited by Glen Creeber, 41–43. London: BFI, 2001.

Muntean, Nick and Anne Helen Peterson. "Celebrity Twitter: Strategies of Intrusion and Disclosure in the Age of Technoculture," *MC Journal* 12, no. 5 (December 2009), http://journal.media-culture.org.au/index.php/mcjournal/article/viewArticle/194.

Murphy, Caryn. "Selling the Continuing Story of *Peyton Place*." Paper presented at Console-ing Passions International Conference on Television, Audio, Video, New Media and Feminism, Eugene, Oregon, April 24, 2010.

Ndalianis, Angela. "Television and the Neo-Baroque." In *The Contemporary Television Series*, edited by Michael Hammond and Lucy Mazdon, 83–101. Edinburgh: Edinburgh University Press, 2005.

Negroponte, Nicholas. *Being Digital*. New York: Vintage, 1995.

Nelson, Robin. *TV Drama in Transition: Forms, Values and Cultural Change*. New York: St. Martin's Press, 1997.

Newcomb, Horace. *TV: The Most Popular Art*. New York: Anchor, 1974.

Newcomb, Horace M. "*Magnum*: The Champagne of TV?" *Channels of Communications* 5:1 (1985): 23–26.

Newcomb, Horace. "The Development of Television Studies." In *The Companion to Television*, edited by Janet Wasko, 15–28. Madden, MA: Blackwell Publishing, 2005.

Newcomb, Horace. "'This Is Not *Al Dente*': *The Sopranos* and the New Meaning of 'Television.'" In *Television: The Critical View*, 7th ed., edited by Horace Newcomb, 561–578. New York: Oxford University Press, 2007.

Newman, Michael Z. "From Beats to Arcs: Toward a Poetics of Television Narrative." *The Velvet Light Trap* 58 (Fall 2006): 16–28.

Newman, Michael Z. "TV Binge." *Flow*, January 23, 2009.

Newman, Michael Z. *Indie: An American Film Culture*. New York: Columbia University Press, 2011.

Pearson, Roberta. "The Writer/Producer in American Television." In *The Contemporary Television Series*, edited by Michael Hammond and Lucy Mazdon, 11–26. Edinburgh: Edinburgh University Press, 2005.

Pearson, Roberta. "*Lost* in Transition: From Post-Network to Post-Television." In *Quality TV: Contemporary American Television and Beyond*, edited by Janet McCabe and Kim Akass, 239–256. New York: I.B. Tauris, 2007.

Peterson, Richard A. "Understanding Audience Segmentation: From Elite and Mass to Omnivore and Univore." *Poetics* 21 (1992): 243–258.

Peterson, Richard A. and Roger M. Kern. "Changing Highbrow Taste: From Snob to Omnivore." *American Sociological Review* 61, no. 5 (October 1996): 900–907.

Petro, Patrice. "Mass Culture and the Feminine: The 'Place' of Television in Film Studies." *Cinema Journal* 25, no. 3 (Spring 1986): 5–21.

Polan, Dana. "Cable watching: HBO, *The Sopranos*, and Discourses of Distinction." In *Cable Visions*, edited by Sarah Banet-Weiser, Cynthia Chris, and Anthony Freitas, 261–283. New York: New York University Press, 2007.

Polan, Dana B. *Scenes of Instruction: The Beginnings of the U.S. Study of Film*. Berkeley: University of California Press, 2007.

Polan, Dana. *The Sopranos*. Durham, NC: Duke University Press, 2009.

Postman, Neil. *Amusing Ourselves to Death*. New York: Penguin, 1985.

Putnam, Robert. *Bowling Alone: The Collapse and Revival of American Community*. New York: Simon and Schuster, 2000.

Rapping, Elayne. *The Movie of the Week: Private Stories, Public Events*. Minneapolis: University of Minnesota Press, 1992.

Reeves, Jimmie L., Marc C. Rodgers, and Michael Epstein. "Rewriting Popularity: The Cult *Files*." In *"Deny All Knowledge": Reading "The X-Files,"* edited by David Lavery, Angela Hague, and Marla Cartwright, 22–35. Syracuse, NY: Syracuse University Press, 1996.

Rogers, Mark C., Michael Epstein, and Jimmie L. Reeves. "*The Sopranos* as HBO Brand Equity: The Art of Commerce in the Age of Digital Reproduction." In *This Thing of Ours: Investigating* "The Sopranos," edited by David Lavery, 42–57. New York: Columbia University Press, 2002.

Rose, Brian G. "*The Wire*." In *The Essential HBO Reader*, edited by Gary R. Edgerton and Jeffrey P. Jones, 82–91. Lexington: University Press of Kentucky, 2008.

Ross, Sharon Marie and Louisa Ellen Stein. "Introduction: Watching Teen TV." In *Teen Television: Essays on Programming and Fandom*, edited by Sharon Marie Ross and Louisa Ellen Stein, 3–26. Jefferson, NC: McFarland & Co., 2008.

Santo, Avi. "Para-television and Discourses of Distinction: The Culture of Production at HBO." In *It's Not TV: Watching HBO in the Post-Television Era*, edited by Marc Leverette, Brian L. Ott, and Cara Louis Buckley, 19–45. New York: Routledge, 2008.

Sarris, Andrew. *The American Cinema: Directors and Directions, 1929–1968*. New York: Da Capo, 1968.

Sarris, Andrew. "Notes on the Auteur Theory in 1962." In *Film Theory and Criticism: Introductory Readings*, 6th ed., edited by Gerald Mast, Marshall Cohen, and Leo Braudy, 561–564. New York: Oxford University Press, 2004.

Schauer, Bradley. "The Criterion Collection in the New Home Video Market: An Interview with Susan Arosteguy." *The Velvet Light Trap* 56 (Fall 2005): 32–35.

Schubin, Mark. "Searching for the Perfect Aspect Ratio." *SMPTE Journal* (August 1996): 460–478.

Scodari, Christine. "Possession, Attraction, and the Thrill of the Chase: Gendered Myth-Making in Film and Television Comedy of the Sexes." *Critical Studies in Mass Communication* 12 (1995): 23–39.

Scodari, Christine and Jenna L. Felder. "Creating a Pocket Universe: 'Shippers,' Fan Fiction, and *The X-Files* Online." *Communication Studies* 51, no. 3 (2000): 238–257.

Sconce, Jeffery. "What If? Charting Television's New Textual Boundaries." In *Television After TV: Essays on a Medium in Transition*, edited by Lynn Spigel and Jan Olssen, 93–112. Durham, NC: Duke University Press, 2004.

Seabrook, John. *Nobrow: The Culture of Marketing, the Marketing of Culture.* New York: Vintage, 2001.

Sewell, Philip W. "From Discourse to Discord: Quality and Dramedy at the End of the Classic Network System," *Television & New Media* 11, no. 4 (2010): 235–259.

Sklar, Robert. *Movie-Made America: A Cultural History of American Movies*, rev. ed. New York: Vintage, 1994.

Smith, Greg M. *Beautiful TV: The Art and Argument of "Ally McBeal."* Austin: University of Texas Press, 2007.

Smith, Jacob. "The Frenzy of the Audible: Pleasure, Authenticity and Recorded Laughter." *Television and New Media* 6, no. 1 (February 2005): 23–47.

Spigel, Lynn. *Make Room for TV: Television and the Family Ideal in Postwar America.* Chicago: University of Chicago Press, 1992.

Spigel, Lynn. "The Making of a TV Literate Elite." In *The Television Studies Book*, edited by Christine Geraghty and David Lusted, 63–85. London: Arnold, 1998.

Spigel, Lynn. *Welcome to the Dreamhouse: Popular Media and Postwar Suburbs.* Durham, NC: Duke University Press, 2001.

Spigel, Lynn. *TV by Design: Modern Art and the Rise of Network Television.* Chicago: University of Chicago Press, 2008.

Taylor, Greg. *Artists in the Audience: Cults, Camp and American Film Criticism.* Princeton, NJ: Princeton University Press, 1999.

Thompson, Ethan. "Comedy Verité? The Observational Documentary Meets the Televisual Sitcom." *The Velvet Light Trap* 60 (Fall 2007): 63–72.

Thompson, Robert J. *Television's Second Golden Age: From "Hill Street Blues" to "ER."* Syracuse: Syracuse University Press, 1997.

Thorburn, David. "*The Sopranos.*" In *The Essential HBO Reader*, edited by Gary R. Edgerton and Jeffrey P. Jones, 61–70. Lexington: University Press of Kentucky, 2008.

Trow, George W.S. *Within the Context of No Context.* New York: Atlantic Monthly Press, 1997.

Uricchio, William. "Television's Next Generation: Technology/Interface Culture/Flow." In *Television After TV: Essays on a Medium in Transition*, edited by Lynn Spigel and Jan Olsson, 163–182. Durham, NC: Duke University Press, 2004.

Vancour, Shawn. "Popularizing the Classics: Radio's Role in the American Music Appreciation Movement, 1922–34." *Media, Culture and Society* 31, no. 2 (2009): 289–307.

Wajcman, Judy. *Feminism Confronts Technology.* Cambridge: Polity Press, 1991.

Wallace, David Foster. *A Supposedly Fun Thing I'll Never Do Again.* Boston: Little Brown, 1997.

Wang, Jennifer Hyland. "Convenient Fictions: The Construction of the Daytime Broadcast Audience, 1927–1960." Ph.D. diss., University of Wisconsin-Madison, 2006.

Wexman, Virginia Wright. "Editor's Introduction." *Cinema Journal* 24, no. 4 (Summer 1985): 3.

Wild, David. *The Showrunners: A Season Inside the Billion-Dollar, Death-Defying, Madcap World of Television's Real Stars.* New York: HarperCollins, 1999.

Williams, Raymond. *Television: Technology and Cultural Form.* London: Routledge, 1974.

Winn, Marie. *The Plug-In Drug*, rev. ed. New York: Viking, 1985.

INDEX

Initial articles in titles (A, An, The) are ignored in sorting. Names beginning with 'Mc' are sorted as Mac. Figures are indicated by f, and endnotes by n following the page number.